STEVE EMANUEL'S
BOOTCAMP FOR THE MBE:
CRIMINAL LAW AND PROCEDURE

EMANUEL BAR REVIEW ADVISORS

Steven L. Emanuel
Founder and Editor-in-Chief
Emanuel Bar Review

Joel Wm. Friedman
Jack M. Gordon Professor of Procedural Law and Jurisdiction and
　Director of Tulane ITESM Ph.D. Program
Tulane University Law School

James J. Rigos
Owner and Editor-in-Chief
Rigos Professional Education Programs

emanuel® BAR REVIEW

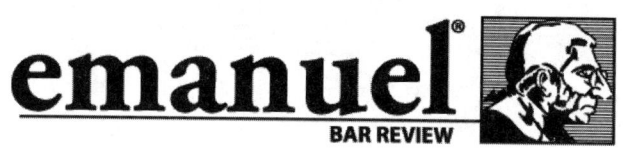

STEVE EMANUEL'S
Bootcamp for the MBE

CRIMINAL LAW AND PROCEDURE

STEVEN L. EMANUEL

Founder & Editor-in-Chief,
Emanuel Bar Review
Member, NY, CT, MD and VA bars

www.aspenlaw.com

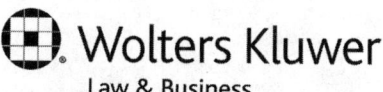

Wolters Kluwer Law & Business | Aspen Publishers

Emanuel Bar Review is a division of Aspen Publishers, a Wolters Kluwer company.

© 2010 Aspen Publishers. All Rights Reserved.
http://lawschool.aspenpublishers.com

Certain publicly disclosed questions and answers from past MBE examinations have been included herein with the permission of the NCBE, the copyright owner. These questions and answers are the only actual MBE questions and answers included in Aspen Publisher's materials. Permission to use the NCBE's questions does not constitute an endorsement by NCBE or otherwise signify that NCBE has reviewed or approved any aspect of these materials or the company or individuals who distribute these materials.

Some questions that have been included herein come from the following NCBE publications:
"Multistate Bar Examination Questions 1992," Copyright © 1992, National Conference of Bar Examiners. All Rights Reserved.
"Sample MBE," Copyright © 1995 by the National Conference of Bar Examiners. All Rights Reserved.
"Sample MBE II," Copyright © 1997 by the National Conference of Bar Examiners. All Rights Reserved.
"Sample MBE III," Copyright © 2002 by the National Conference of Bar Examiners. All Rights Reserved.
"MBE-OPE 1," Copyright © 2006 by the National Conference of Bar Examiners. All Rights Reserved.
"MBE-OPE 2," Copyright © 2009 by the National Conference of Bar Examiners. All Rights Reserved.

No part of this publication may be reproduced or transmitted in any form or by any means, electronic or mechanical, including photocopy, recording, or any information storage and retrieval system, without permission in writing from the publisher. Requests for permission to make copies of any part of this publication should be mailed to:

> Aspen Publishers
> Attn: Permissions Department
> 76 Ninth Avenue, 7th Floor
> New York, NY 10011-5201

For information about Emanuel Bar Review, contact:

> email: info@emanuelbarprep.com
> phone: 1-888-MBE-PREP
> fax: 781-207-5815
> website: www.emanuelbarprep.com

Printed in the United States of America.

1 2 3 4 5 6 7 8 9 0

ISBN 978-0-7355-9734-1

TABLE OF CONTENTS

Preface... vii

Criminal Law Outline

   Table of Contents to Outline.. 3

   Outline... 7

Criminal Procedure Outline

   Table of Contents to Outline... 81

   Outline.. 85

Criminal Law and Procedure MBE-Style Questions

   Questions... 141

   Answers 155

PREFACE

Dear *Bootcamp* enrollee:

This book consists mainly of a short outline on substantive Criminal Law and the other on Criminal Procedure. I hope that you'll read the outline before you watch the online substantive lecture that's part of Steve Emanuel's Bootcamp for the MBE. If you can't read the outline before watching the online lecture, read it by way of review afterwards.

The outline section of this book does not contain any MBE-format questions — that's what we'll be doing in the 2-volume "*Emanuel's Essentials*" set of multi-choice questions and answers in context, which is part of your materials.

I have written the outline in an attempt to cover virtually all the substantive rules of law that the MBE examiners test in their Criminal Law and Procedure questions, and to highlight the traps they set. I've tried to omit any topic or rule of law that doesn't seem to pop up on the MBE, no matter how important that topic may have been in your law school Criminal Law and Procedure course.

The last part of the book consists of the 33 questions on Criminal Law and Procedure extracted from our 200-Question Self-Assessment Test, together with our model answers to those questions. I hope that you will first take the Self-Assessment Test on a stand-alone basis, and that you will only consult the Criminal Law and Procedure questions in this book as a means of reviewing after you've taken the Self Assessment Test.

Good luck, and see you online soon!

Steve Emanuel
Larchmont, NY
April 2010

CRIMINAL LAW OUTLINE

TABLE OF CONTENTS
CRIMINAL LAW OUTLINE

Chapter 1
ACTUS REUS AND *MENS REA*

I.	GENERAL	7
II.	*ACTUS REUS*	7
III.	*MENS REA*	10
IV.	CONCURRENCE	14

Chapter 2
CAUSATION

I.	INTRODUCTION	15
II.	CAUSE IN FACT	15
III.	PROXIMATE CAUSE GENERALLY	15
IV.	PROXIMATE CAUSE — UNINTENDED VICTIMS	17
V.	PROXIMATE CAUSE — UNINTENDED MANNER OF HARM	18

Chapter 3
RESPONSIBILITY

I.	THE INSANITY DEFENSE	20
II.	INTOXICATION	21

Chapter 4
JUSTIFICATION AND EXCUSE

I.	GENERAL PRINCIPLES	23
II.	DURESS	23
III.	SELF-DEFENSE	23
IV.	ENTRAPMENT	28

Chapter 5
ATTEMPT

I.	ATTEMPT — INTRODUCTION	28
II.	MENTAL STATE	28
III.	THE ACT — ATTEMPT VS. "MERE PREPARATION"	30
IV.	IMPOSSIBILITY	31
V.	RENUNCIATION	33

Chapter 6
CONSPIRACY

I.	INTRODUCTION	33
II.	THE AGREEMENT	33
III.	*MENS REA*	34
IV.	THE CONSPIRATORIAL OBJECTIVE	36
V.	SCOPE: MULTIPLE PARTIES	38
VI.	DURATION OF THE CONSPIRACY	38
VII.	PLURALITY	39
VIII.	PUNISHMENT	42

Chapter 7
ACCOMPLICE LIABILITY AND SOLICITATION

I.	PARTIES TO CRIME	42
II.	ACCOMPLICES — THE ACT REQUIREMENT	42
III.	ACCOMPLICES — MENTAL STATE	44
IV.	ACCOMPLICES — ADDITIONAL CRIMES BY PRINCIPAL	46
V.	GUILT OF THE PRINCIPAL	47
VI.	WITHDRAWAL BY THE ACCOMPLICE	49
VII.	POST-CRIME ASSISTANCE	50

VIII.	SOLICITATION	50

Chapter 8
HOMICIDE AND OTHER CRIMES AGAINST THE PERSON

I.	HOMICIDE — INTRODUCTION	50
II.	MURDER — GENERALLY	51
III.	FELONY-MURDER	54
IV.	DEATH PENALTY AS PUNISHMENT FOR MURDER	57
V.	MANSLAUGHTER — VOLUNTARY	58
VI.	MANSLAUGHTER — INVOLUNTARY	60
VII.	ASSAULT AND BATTERY	63
VIII.	RAPE	64
IX.	KIDNAPPING	65

Chapter 9
THEFT CRIMES

I.	INTRODUCTION	66
II.	LARCENY	67
III.	EMBEZZLEMENT	70
IV.	FALSE PRETENSES	72
V.	BURGLARY	72
VI.	ROBBERY	74
VII.	ARSON	77

CRIMINAL LAW OUTLINE

This Outline attempts to cover only topics that have been repeatedly tested on actual MBE exams.

References to "LaFave" are to Wayne LaFave, *Principles of Criminal Law* (Thomson / West, 2003). References to "LaFave Criminal Law" are to Wayne LaFave, *Criminal Law* Hornbook (3d Ed., West, 2000). References to "M.P.C." are to the *Model Penal Code*.

On the MBE substantive criminal law questions, you should apply common-law principles unless instructed otherwise in the particular question (which doesn't happen very often). When this outline refers to the "common-law definition" of a crime, it is usually referring to the definition of the crime as worked out by English and American judges in decisions, mostly from before 1900.

CHAPTER 1
ACTUS REUS AND *MENS REA*

I. GENERAL

  A. **Four elements:** All crimes have several basic common elements: (1) a *voluntary act* ("*actus reus*"); (2) a *culpable intent* ("*mens rea*"); (3) "*concurrence*" between the *mens rea* and the *actus reus*; and (4) *causation* of harm.

II. *ACTUS REUS*

  A. **Significance of concept:** The defendant must have committed a *voluntary act*, or "*actus reus*." Look for an *actus reus* problem anytime you have one of the following situations on the MBE:

   [1] D has *not a committed a physical act*, but has "guilty" *thoughts*, *words*, states of *possession* or *status*;

   [2] D does an *involuntary act*; and

   [3] D has an *omission*, or failure to act.

  B. **Thoughts, words, possession and status:** *Mere thoughts* are never punishable as crimes.

   Example: D writes in his diary, "I intend to kill V." This statement alone is not enough to constitute any crime, even attempted murder.

  1. **Possession as criminal act:** However, mere *possession* of an object may sometimes constitute the necessary criminal act.

   Example: Possession of narcotics frequently constitutes a crime in itself.

   a. **Knowledge:** When mere possession is made a crime, the act of "possession" is almost always construed so as to include only *conscious* possession.

   Example: If the prosecution fails to prove that D knew he had narcotics on his person, there can be no conviction.

  C. **Act must be voluntary:** An act cannot satisfy the *actus reus* requirement unless it is *voluntary*.

1. **Reflex or convulsion:** An act consisting of a *reflex* or *convulsion* does not give rise to criminal liability.

   Example: D, while walking down the street, is stricken by epileptic convulsions. His arm jerks back, and he strikes X in the face. The striking of X is not a voluntary act, so D cannot be held criminally liable. But if D had known beforehand that he was subject to such seizures, and unreasonably put himself in a position where he was likely to harm others — for instance, by driving a car — this initial act might subject him to criminal liability.

2. **Unconsciousness:** An act performed during a state of *"unconsciousness"* does not meet the *actus reus* requirement. But D will be found to have acted "unconsciously" only in rare situations.

   Example: If D can show that at the time of the crime he was on "automatic pilot," and was completely unconscious of what he was doing, his act will be involuntary. (But the mere fact that D has *amnesia* concerning the period of the crime will *not* be a defense.)

D. **Omissions:** The *actus reus* requirement means that in most situations, there is *no criminal liability* for an *omission* to act (as distinguished from an affirmative act).

   Example: D sees V, a stranger, drowning in front of him. D could easily rescue V. D will normally not be criminally liable for failing to attempt to rescue V, because there is no general liability for omissions as distinguished from affirmative acts.

   1. **Mere presence not enough:** Therefore, the mere fact that D was *present* at the moment a crime was committed by someone else (call her X) will not cause D to have liability for failing to *intervene* to stop the crime, or failing to *aid the victim* after the crime was committed. (If D encouraged X, D would likely have accomplice liability; see *infra*, p. 42. But here, we're talking about a mere failure to intervene to stop the crime.)

      Example: Two rival gangs, the Reds and the Blues, had long been enemies. One day, A and B (members of the Reds gang) encountered C and D (members of the Blues gang) in the town square. This meeting happened without any planning or prior discussion by any of the four, and none of those four had ever discussed committing acts of violence against any rival. After some mildly angry words between A and C, but no threats of violence by anyone, A said quietly to B, "I'm gonna shut C up forever. Just watch this." A took out a switchblade and stepped toward C. B realized that A would likely knife C in an attempt to kill him. B secretly desired that A kill C, but said nothing to A either encouraging or discouraging A from carrying out the knifing. A stabbed C, and B watched while C bled to death.

      B is not guilty of murder (or any other common-law crime). A person will not be liable for a crime unless he took an affirmative act, or else omitted to perform a legally-required duty. B took no affirmative act that was causally connected to C's death, and merely happened to be present at what turned out to be a crime scene. Nor did he fail to perform any legally-required duty. Therefore, he fell within the general common-law rule that an omission to act cannot normally be a crime.

   2. **No duty to warn:** Similarly, the fact that D knew of a danger to V, and for no good reason *failed to warn V*, won't subject D to criminal liability.

      Example: D knows that his wife W is planning the next day to shoot to death their next-door neighbor V, whom W hates. D does not warn V of the danger, though he could easily do so. W carries out the shooting exactly as planned. D is not guilty of any crime on these facts — D committed no voluntary act that was causally related to V's death.

   3. **Existence of legal duty to act:** But there are some "special situations" where courts deem D to have a *legal duty to act*. Where this occurs, D's omission may be punished under a statute that

speaks in terms of positive acts. These "special duty to act" scenarios are tested surprisingly often on the MBE.

    a. Special relationship: Where D and V have a *special relationship* — most notably a *close blood relationship* — D will be criminally liable for a failure to act.

    Example: Child, a three-year old, becomes ill with a staph infection. The infection could easily be cured if treated promptly. Mom and Dad, Child's parents, believe that organized medicine is corrupt, and that prayer will be enough to cure Child. They therefore do not seek medical assistance. Child dies, and Mom and Dad are charged with involuntary manslaughter.

    Mom and Dad can be convicted (assuming that the fault inherent in their failure to summon help met the gross negligence or recklessness required in the jurisdiction for manslaughter; see *infra*, p. 60). Although Mom and Dad took no affirmative action that contributed to Child's death, and although failure to act will ordinarily not trigger criminal liability, a parent has a legal duty to take reasonable actions to protect a child's health.

        i. Permitting child abuse: Some courts have applied this theory to hold one parent liable for child abuse for *failing to intervene* to stop affirmative abuse by the other parent.

    b. Contract or statute: Similarly, a legal duty may arise out of a *contract* or a *statute*.

        i. Contract: Thus D might contract with someone under which D agrees to render some duty of care to third persons. Such a contractual duty will probably give rise to an obligation by D — enforced by the criminal law — to act affirmatively to provide the promised care.

        Example: Lifeguard is hired by City to guard a beach. Lifeguard intentionally fails to save Victim from drowning, even though he could easily do so. Lifeguard will probably be criminally liable despite the fact that his conduct was an omission rather than an act; his contract with City imposed a duty to take affirmative action.

        ii. Statute: Similarly, a *statute* may impose on D, because of D's special relationship or job, an obligation to provide some type of care or warning.

        Example: A city requires by ordinance that any licensed pediatrician promptly report to child-welfare authorities any injuries to a child that would cause a reasonable person in the pediatrician's position to suspect child abuse. Doc sees that Child, a patient, has bruises that would cause a reasonable person (and caused Doc) to suspect child abuse. Doc does not make the required report. A week later, Dad, Child's father (who was the source of the bruises seen by Doc) batters Child to death.

        Doc can be held criminally liable for proximately causing Child's death. (For instance, Doc could be convicted of involuntary manslaughter if Doc's failure to report rose to the level of recklessness.) By virtue of the statute, and Doc's special doctor-patient relationship with Child, Doc's failure to act (failure to give the required report) will be treated as being the equivalent of action.

    c. D caused danger: If the *danger was caused* (even *innocently*) by *D himself*, D generally has an affirmative duty to then take reasonable steps to avoid the type of harm stemming from that risk.

    Example 1: D non-negligently digs a hole in the sidewalk in front of his house, acting legally under a building permit. D sees V about to step into the hole, but says nothing. V falls in and dies. D can be held criminally liable for manslaughter, because he created the condition — even though he did so innocently — and thus had an affirmative duty to protect those he knew to be in danger.

Example 2: Wife is angry at Husband for having an affair with Wife's best friend. At dinner one night, Wife accidentally drops a knife that lands on Husband's thigh, making a small gash. Because Husband is a hemophiliac (as Wife knows), Husband bleeds a lot, and quickly goes into shock and unconsciousness. Wife does not call 911 (which she could have easily done), and Husband bleeds to death. Had Wife called promptly, Husband would have been saved. Wife declined to call because she decided (with an intent formed only after the knife-dropping accident) that she would be better off with Husband dead.

Wife is guilty of murder. Once Wife, however innocently and non-negligently, brought about the condition of peril to Husband (the cut), she had the obligation to use reasonable efforts to help him avoid further harm (e.g., by calling 911). Since her failure to call was coupled with a simultaneous desire by her that he die, she met the actus reus, mental-state and concurrence requirements for murder.

III. *MENS REA*

A. **Meaning:** The term *"mens rea"* symbolizes the requirement that there be a *"culpable state of mind."*

   1. **Not necessarily state of mind:** Most crimes require a true *"mens rea,"* that is, a state of mind that is truly guilty. But other crimes are defined to require merely "negligence" or "recklessness," which is not really a state of mind at all. Nonetheless, the term *"mens rea"* is sometimes used for these crimes as well: thus one can say that "for manslaughter, the *mens rea* is recklessness." There are also a few crimes defined so as to require no *mens rea* at all, the so called "strict liability" crimes.

B. **"Knowingly":** On the MBE, you may be given the text of a criminal statute that includes the requirement that D *"knowingly"* take an act or produce a result.

   1. **Knowledge of attendant circumstances:** Where a statute specifies that D must act "knowingly," and the statute then specifies various *attendant circumstances* which the definition of the crime makes important, usually the requirement of knowledge is held applicable to *all these attendant circumstances*. In other words, D doesn't "knowingly" violate a provision if he doesn't "know" all the facts that would have to be true for the situation to be covered by the provision.

      Example: A statute makes it an offense to "knowingly violate a regulation of" the state Tobacco Regulation Commission. A regulation of that Commission prohibits the sale of tobacco products to a person below the age of 22 unless the buyer presents official identification showing him or her to be over 18. D is charged with violating the statute by selling tobacco to X, an undercover operative aged 21, without demanding identification. If the jury believes that D honestly (even if stupidly) believed that X was over 21, the jury must acquit, because D did not "knowingly" violate the regulation. That is, the "knowing" requirement will be construed to require proof that D knew that the regulation applied to the situation at hand. This in turn required that D be shown to have known that the buyer was under 22.

   2. **Unreasonableness doesn't negate:** Where a statute requires knowledge of some fact, the prosecution will lose unless it convinces the jury that D knew that fact. And that doesn't change merely because it was *unreasonable* for D not to know the fact — if the jury really believes that D didn't know, her unreasonableness in not knowing is irrelevant (though the unreasonableness may cause the jury to *infer* that D really knew).

      Example: A statute makes it a crime to "possess goods that defendant knows to be stolen." D buys a genuine Rolex gold watch, with a used-market value of $10,000, for $500 from a street vendor. D is charged with violating the stolen-goods statute, on the theory that the $500 price was so far below the lowest-plausible price for a real Rolex that D must have known the watch was stolen. D testifies that she believed that the Rolex was counterfeit, not stolen. If the jury believes D's testimony, it must acquit her, no matter how unreasonable it concludes that D's belief was.

3. **"Practically certain" standard for unintended effects:** If D does not intend or desire to produce a certain result, he will still be guilty of "knowingly" causing that result if he knew that the result was *"practically certain"* to occur from his conduct. But the fact that he recognized a *high probability or risk* that the result would occur is *not* enough — he has to know that the bad result is virtually certain to occur. M.P.C. §2.02(2)(b)(ii); LaFave, §3.5, p. 232.

   Example: A statute makes it a crime to "knowingly damage another person's commercial property." D attempts to steal a car parked at the top of a hill by hot-wiring the ignition. After D starts the car, it begins to roll down the hill, and D discovers the brakes don't work. D therefore jumps out of the car, which continues 200 feet down the hill, where it plows into the front window of V's store. D is charged with knowingly damaging V's commercial property. May he properly be convicted?

   No. The statute requires that D "knowingly damage" the property in question. Even actual recognition by D of a *high risk* of damage won't be enough — assuming that D didn't actually desire the damage, D will be guilty only if he can be shown to have known that it was "practically certain" that the damage would occur. Here, at the time of the last voluntary act by D (jumping out of the car), the distance to the bottom of the hill was great enough that a jury can't reasonably infer that D knew that damage to the store was practically certain to occur. And, since there's no indication that he desired the damage to occur, he won't be deemed to have "knowingly" caused it.

4. **D need not know of illegality:** On the other hand, a statute that forbids "knowingly" doing X does *not* require the prosecution to prove that D knew *that doing X was illegal.* LaFave, §3.5(b), p. 234. In other words, the use of the word "knowingly" does not change the traditional rule that "ignorance of the law is no excuse," i.e., that ignorance of the fact that the law forbids a particular type of conduct is no defense. (For more about the "ignorance of the law" problem, see *infra*, p. 13.)

   Example: Same basic facts as the Example on p. 10: A statute makes it an offense to "knowingly violate a regulation of" the state Tobacco Regulation Commission. A regulation of that Commission prohibits the sale of any "tobacco product" to a person below the age of 22 unless the buyer presents official identification showing him or her to be over 18. The regulation classifies snuff as a tobacco product. D is charged with violating the statute by selling snuff to X, an undercover operative aged 21, without demanding identification.

   It will not be a defense that D did not know of the regulation's existence, or the details of what conduct it forbade. In other words, to "knowingly violate" the regulation, D must be shown to have known the facts making the regulation applicable in the matter at hand (i.e., that the buyer was under 22), but *not* to have known that the regulation existed, or that it classified snuff as a regulated "tobacco product."

C. **"Recklessly":** A person acts *"recklessly"* if he *"consciously disregards a substantial and unjustifiable risk...."* M.P.C. §2.02(2). The idea is that D has behaved in a way that represents a *gross deviation* from the conduct of a law-abiding person.

Example: In most states (and on the MBE), the crime of involuntary manslaughter requires the prosecution to show that D behaved recklessly with respect to the risk of death or serious bodily injury. It's not enough that D behaved negligently with respect to such risks. (See *infra*, p. 60.)

D. Strict liability: Some offenses are *"strict liability."* That is, no culpable mental state at all must be shown — it is enough that D performed the act in question, regardless of his mental state. Strict liability offenses are sometimes labelled *"public welfare offenses."*

Examples of statutes likely to be strict-liability offenses: Sale of liquor to minors; sale of adulterated food or beverages; littering; hunting without a license.

1. **Constitutionality:** Generally there is no constitutional problem with punishing a defendant without regard to his mental state.

2. **Factors:** On the MBE, you will sometimes be called upon to determine whether a given statute is or is not probably a strict liability statute. The examiners will just describe in general terms what the statute punishes, and you'll have to surmise whether the legislature likely intended strict liability. Here are some *factors* that would make a court more likely to conclude that the legislature intended strict liability:

    [1] the violation is in the nature of *neglect* or *inaction*, rather than positive aggression;

    [2] the statute has a *regulatory* flavor;

    [3] there is no necessary direct injury to person or property, but simply a *danger* of such, and it is this danger that the statute seeks to curtail;

    [4] the *penalty* prescribed is *small*;

    [5] conviction does no grave damage to the defendant's *reputation*; and

    [6] it was relatively easy for the defendant to *find out the true facts* before she acted, making it not unfair to punish her without regard to fault.

    [Cf. *Morisette v. U.S.* (1952); Lafave, §3.8, pp. 258-260.]

3. **Statutory rape:** Most *statutory rape* provisions also impose strict liability, at least with respect to D's knowledge of V's *age*. In other words, D can't defend on the grounds, "I didn't know she was underage" or even "I made a reasonable mistake, because a reasonable person in my situation wouldn't have suspected she was underage."

E. Vicarious liability: Statutes sometimes impose upon one person liability for the *act of another*; this is commonly called *"vicarious liability."* In essence, the requirement of an act (*actus reus*) has been dispensed with, not the requirement of the wrongful intent.

Example: Statutes frequently make an *automobile owner* liable for certain acts committed by those to whom he lends his car, even without a showing of culpable mental state on the part of the owner.

1. **Constitutionality:** Generally, the imposition of vicarious liability does *not* violate D's due process rights.

    a. **D has no control over offender:** However, if D did not have any *ability to control* the person who performed the actual *actus reus*, his conviction is probably unconstitutional. So, for instance, if D's car is stolen without D's negligence, and the thief kills someone, it would probably be a violation of D's due process rights to make him vicariously criminally liable.

F. Mistake: Defendants raise the defense of *mistake* when they have been mistaken either about the facts or the law. Do not think of "mistake" as being a separate "doctrine." Instead, look at the effect of the particular mistake on D's *mental state*, and examine whether he was thereby prevented from having the mental state required for the crime.

> **Example:** Assume that the requisite mental intent for larceny is the intent to take property which one knows or believes to belong to another. D takes V's umbrella from a restaurant, thinking that it is his own. D's factual mistake — his belief about who owns the umbrella — is a defense to the theft charge, because it negates the requisite mental state (intent to take the property which one knows or believes belongs to another).

1. **Crimes of "general intent":** D's mistake is *least likely* to assist him where the crime is what is sometimes called a *"general intent"* crime (i.e., one for which the most general kind of culpable intent will suffice).

   > **Example:** Murder is often thought of as a "general intent" crime in the sense that it will be enough that D either intends to kill, intends to commit grievous bodily injury, is recklessly indifferent to the value of human life or intends to commit any of certain non-homicide felonies. Suppose D shoots a gun at V, intending to hit V in the arm and thus create a painful but not serious flesh wound. D mistakenly believes that V is in ordinary health, when in fact he is a hemophiliac. D's mistake will not help him, because even had the facts been as D supposed them to be, D would have had a requisite mental state, the intent to commit grievous bodily injury.

2. **Mistake need not be "reasonable":** For purposes of the MBE, assume that *even an unreasonable mistake* will block conviction if the mistake prevented D from *having the requisite intent or knowledge*.

   > **Example:** D checks his attache case at a restaurant, then gets drunk. D then sees V leave the restaurant carrying an attache case that D believes is D's. D wrestles the attache case away from V, takes it home, then (when sober) realizes that the case really was V's all along. Assume that D's mistake was an unreasonable one, and was due to D's being drunk.
   >
   > For MBE purposes, D is not guilty of larceny. Although his mistake about the ownership of the case was unreasonable, that mistake prevented D from having the requisite intent for larceny (intent to take the property of another).

3. **Mistake of law:** It is especially hard for D to prevail with a defense based on *"mistake of law."*

   a. **Generally no defense:** As a general rule, *"mistake of law is no defense."* More precisely, this means that *the fact that D mistakenly believes that no statute makes his conduct a crime does not furnish a defense* to most crimes. This principle is captured in the old saying, *"Ignorance of the law is no defense,"* which is essentially a *true* statement.

      i. **How crime is defined:** The core situation covered by the "mistake of law is no defense" rule is the situation in which D is *mistaken about how a particular crime is defined.*

         > **Example:** D, who is retarded, does not realize that unconsented-to intercourse is a crime. D has unconsented-to intercourse with V. D's ignorance that unconsented-to intercourse is a crime will not be a defense; so long as D intended the act of intercourse while knowing that V did not consent, he is guilty.

      ii. **Reasonable mistake:** In this core "D mistakenly believes that no statute makes his conduct a crime" situation, even a *reasonable mistake* about the meaning of the statute will usually *not* protect D. In other words, so long as the crime is not itself defined in a way that makes D's guilty knowledge a prerequisite, there is usually no "reasonable mistake" exception to the core "mistake of law is no defense" rule.

b. Bigamy: One scenario often tested on the MBE involves *bigamy* — if D is mistaken (even reasonably) in his belief that the bigamy statute does not cover his own factual situation, this will not offer him a defense.

> **Example:** D goes through a marriage ceremony with B while still legally married to A. He defends on the grounds that three years ago, A moved to Mexico, where she is cohabiting with another man, and that D's lawyer told him that under these facts D would be considered no longer married, and may thus remarry. Even if the trier of fact believes everything that D is asserting, and even if D's mistake is considered "reasonable," D can still be convicted of bigamy — D has made a mistake about whether the bigamy statute applies to his particular fact pattern, and a mistake about how a crime is defined does not supply a defense.

IV. CONCURRENCE

A. Concurrence between mind and act: There must be *"concurrence"* between the *mental state* and the *criminal act* (the "actus reus").

    1. Same time: This requirement is not met if, *at the time of the act*, the required mental state does not exist.

> **Example:** Common-law larceny is defined as the taking of another's property with intent to deprive him of it. D takes V's umbrella from a restaurant, thinking that it is his own. Five minutes later, he realizes that it belongs to V, and decides to keep it. D has not committed larceny, because at the time he committed the act (the taking), he did not have the requisite mental intent (the intent to deprive another of his property). The fact that D later acquired the requisite intent is irrelevant.

    2. Concurrence with act, not with later result: On the other hand, the concurrence principle requires merely that there be temporal concurrence between the mens rea and the actus reus, *not* concurrence between mens rea and the *bad result* (in the case of a crime defined in terms of bad result).

        a. Change of mind: This means that if D does an act with an intent to achieve a *certain result*, the fact that he later *changes his mind* and doesn't desire that result will not nullify the crime, if the result occurs due to his act and the crime is defined in terms of intentionally causing that result.

        b. Bombs and poison: On the MBE, look for this timing issue whenever D puts in motion some *device* (such as *bomb or poison*) that *doesn't take effect until later* — as long as D intended to bring about a death at the moment she engaged the device, and death resulted from the device, the fact that D later changed her mind and tried to stop the death won't prevent her from being guilty of murder.

> **Example:** D puts a bomb in V's car, which is set to blow up when the car is started. D later changes his mind, but can't warn V in time. V starts the car, and is blown to bits. The requisite concurrence between act and intent existed (since the act was the placing of the bomb, which D did with intent to kill). The fact that there was no concurrence between mental state and result (V's death) is irrelevant, and D is guilty of intent-to-kill murder.

    3. Omission to act: Cases involving D's *omission to act* can also pose a concurrence issue, but on the MBE the concurrence requirement will generally be *satisfied* in an omission case. Where D has failed to act in circumstances imposing a duty on her to act, the concurrence-of-timing requirement is met as long as D had the required mental state at *any single moment when D had a duty to act* and failed to act.

Example: Recall the example on p. 10, in which Wife accidentally drops a knife that cuts the thigh of Husband, a hemophiliac who then bleeds to death while Wife doesn't summon assistance. As long as there was at least one moment in which Wife (1) actively desired Husband's death and (2) simultaneously had the obligation to render Husband assistance but didn't, the required concurrence between mental state (intent to bring about death) and actus reus (here, failure to act while having a duty to act) is satisfied.

4. **Mental state must cause act:** Another aspect of the concurrence requirement is that the mental state must *cause* the act.

    Example: D intends to kill V. While driving to the store to buy a gun to carry out his intent, D accidentally runs over V and kills him. D is not guilty of murder, even though the intent to kill V existed at the time the act (driving the car over V) took place. This is because D's intent to kill did not "cause" the act (driving the car over V).

CHAPTER 2
CAUSATION

I. INTRODUCTION

A. **Two aspects of causation:** "Causation" in criminal law relates to the link between the *act* and the *harmful result*. The prosecution must show that the defendant's *actus reus* "caused" the harmful result, in *two different senses*: (1) that the act was the *"cause in fact"* of the harm; and (2) that the act was the *"proximate"* cause (or the "legal" cause) of the harm.

II. CAUSE IN FACT

A. **Two ways:** There are two ways in which an act can be the "cause in fact" of harm: (1) by being the *"but for"* cause of the harm; and (2) by being a *"substantial factor"* in creating the harm. These categories overlap, but not completely. On the MBE, you should mainly have to worry about "but for" causation, which is what we'll focus on here.

B. **The "but for" rule:** An act will be the "cause in fact" of the harm if it is the *"but for"* cause of that harm. To put the idea negatively, if the result *would have happened anyway*, even had the act not occurred, the act is *not a cause in fact* of that result.

    Example: D shoots at V, but only grazes him, leaving V with a slightly bleeding flesh wound. X, who has always wanted to kill V, finds V (in the same place V would have been in had D not shot at V), and shoots V through the heart, killing him instantly. D's act is not a "cause in fact" of V's death, under the "but for" test — since V would have died, in just the manner and at the same time he did, even if D had not shot him, D's act was not the "but for" cause of V's death. Unless D's act is found to have been a "substantial factor" in V's death (the other test for causation in fact), which it probably would not, D's act is not the "cause in fact" of V's death, and D therefore cannot be punished for that death.

III. PROXIMATE CAUSE GENERALLY

A. **Definition of "proximate cause":** It is not enough that D's act was a "cause in fact" of the harm. The prosecution must also show that the act and harm are sufficiently closely related that the act is a *"proximate"* or "legal" cause of that harm. This is a *policy* question: *Is the connection between the act and the harm so stretched that it is unfair to hold D liable for that harm?*

1. **No precise definition:** There is no precise or mechanical definition of proximate cause — each case gets decided on its own facts.

2. **Model Penal Code formulation:** But a good general definition to keep in mind is the Model Penal Code's: D's act will be the proximate cause of the harmful result if the result is "not too remote or accidental in its occurrence to have a [just] bearing on the actor's liability or on the gravity of his offense." M.P.C. §2.03(2)(b).

3. **Multiple proximate causes possible:** A single bad effect (e.g., a death) can have *multiple proximate causes,* as well as multiple causes in fact. So D will not be permitted to argue that because some other act or event was "a" or "the" proximate cause of particular harm, D's conduct was automatically not the proximate cause. The presence of other contributing causes may help the trier of fact to conclude that D's act was too far removed from the harm to be viewed a proximate cause, but this is a matter of degree, not a mathematical theorem — there is simply no rule that one effect cannot have multiple proximate causes, as MBE wrong choices will sometimes suggest.

B. **Year-and-a-day rule in homicide:** One common-law rule that expresses the proximate-cause idea is the *"year and a day"* rule in homicide cases: D cannot be convicted if the victim did not die until a year and a day following D's act. Many states continue to impose this rule, and MBE questions sometimes turn on it.

1. **MBE Tip:** On the MBE, the examiners will generally not directly refer to the year-and-a-day rule. They'll simply give you a problem in which D takes a voluntary act, and V dies more than a year later in a way that is arguably caused by that act. Typically, the correct answer will be that D was not (or at least her best defense is that she was not) the proximate cause of V's death.

    Example: See the example on p. 19, in which D posts a blog entry accusing V of various wrongdoing, and V commits suicide (leaving a note blaming D) more than one year later. In an MBE question involving this scenario, the correct answer might be something like "D's best argument is that she was not the proximate cause of V's death." The year-and-a-day rule would be relevant, but not spelled out in the correct choice.

C. **Types of problems raised:** Look for two main types of proximate cause problems: (1) situations where the type of harm intended occurred, and occurred in roughly the manner intended, but the *victim was not the intended one*; and (2) cases where the general type of harm intended did occur and occurred to the intended victim, but occurred in an *unintended manner*.

1. **Reckless and negligent crimes:** Proximate cause issues are most common in cases where the *mens rea* for the crime is intent. But similar problems also arise where the mental state is recklessness or negligence.

    a. **Misdemeanor-manslaughter rule:** Proximate cause issues can also arise in situations that seem to involve the *misdemeanor-manslaughter rule* (*infra*, p. 62). Under that doctrine, the commission of a misdemeanor can establish criminal negligence, which when combined with the fact of V's death establishes the elements of involuntary manslaughter. If what makes D's act a misdemeanor is not causally related to the bringing about of V's death, then the proximate cause requirement will not be satisfied, and D will be acquitted.

        i. **Licensing requirements:** This can happen on the MBE in the case of a *licensing* requirement: If the jurisdiction requires a license to pursue some activity, but D would be entitled to the license as a matter of right, his conducting of the activity without a license, coupled with a harm (e.g., a death) stemming from the activity, won't trigger the misdemeanor-manslaughter rule because the failure to get a license is not deemed to be the proximate cause of the harm.

Example: After D's driver's license expires, D fails to renew it, and continues driving. Driving without a currently-valid license is a misdemeanor in the jurisdiction. While D is driving non-negligently, D's car collides with V, a pedestrian, when V darts out from between two parked cars. V dies. D is not guilty of misdemeanor-manslaughter because his misdemeanor of driving without a currently-valid license was not the proximate cause of the accident.

D. **Failure to intervene:** Proximate cause issues can also arise where *D fails to act*, under circumstances imposing on her a duty to act. Remember that although the general rule is that failure to act will not give rise to criminal liability (*supra*, p. 8), there are important exceptions (pp. 8-10). If one of these exceptions applies, and D fails to take affirmative action to protect V, D's failure to act is quite likely to be the cause-in-fact and proximate cause of the harm to V. For this to be so, all that is required is that:

[1] had D acted, the harm *would, beyond a reasonable doubt, have been avoided* (satisfying cause-in-fact), and

[2] the causal chain between D's failure to do the required act and the harm is *not too tenuous* (satisfying proximate cause).

1. **MBE Tip:** Generally speaking on the MBE, where D fails to fulfill a duty to act and a death or other harm occurs that wouldn't have occurred had D fulfilled the duty, D will be deemed a proximate cause of the death. In other words, in an omission-to-act case, be skeptical of a choice that says D is not guilty because his omission was not the proximate cause of death.

   Example: Because of the special parent-child relationship, a parent who knows that his child is seriously ill has a duty to make reasonable efforts to procure medical care. Dad fails to procure medical care for Kid, who has a dangerous infection — Dad believes that prayer alone is all that is ever required. If Kid dies from the infection, and wouldn't have died with prompt medical treatment, a court would likely conclude that Dad's failure to procure aid was the proximate cause of Kid's death — here, the failure is clearly the but-for cause, and there's nothing in the chain of causation (e.g., no bizarre intervening events) that would lead a court to the conclusion that the causal link between failure-to-get-aid and death was too tenuous for criminal liability.

IV. PROXIMATE CAUSE — UNINTENDED VICTIMS

A. **Transferred intent:** It will not generally be a defense that the actual victim of D's act was *not the intended victim*. Instead, courts apply the doctrine of *"transferred intent,"* under which D's intent is "transferred" from the actual to the intended victim.

   Example: D, intending to kill X, shoots at X. Because of D's bad aim, D hits and kills V instead. D is guilty of the murder of V, because his intent is said to be "transferred" from X to V.

B. **Mistaken ID:** The fact that D is mistaken about the victim's *identity* will not be a defense.

   Example: D shoots at V, mistakenly thinking that V is really X, D's enemy. D will be guilty of the murder of V, just as if he had been shooting at the person who was actually X, and had mistakenly hit V. The crime of murder requires an intent to kill, but does not require a correct belief as to the victim's identity.

C. **Crimes of recklessness or negligence:** The "unforeseen victim" problem also arises in crimes where the mental state is *recklessness* or *negligence*, rather than intent. But in these situations, a *tighter link* between D's act and V's injury is probably required than where the crime is intentional.

1. **Must be reckless to V, not to someone else:** Therefore, if the crime is one for which the or a required mental state is *recklessness,* and V is not one of the persons the risk of danger to whom made D's conduct reckless, probably D won't be guilty of recklessly harming V. LaFave, §3.12(e), p. 304. This means that involuntary manslaughter (*infra*, p. 60) probably can't be committed against V if D's only recklessness was vis-á-vis the risk to someone other than V.

   Example: D is hunting in the woods with a rifle, accompanied by his friend F. D has no reason to believe that any other humans are around. D fires at a bush, recklessly failing to verify that F is not within rifle range. The bullet narrowly misses F. But it strikes V, a hiker whose presence D had no reason to anticipate, and kills V.

   D is probably not guilty of involuntary manslaughter ("IM"). IM requires at least gross negligence (see *infra*, p. 61). Furthermore, D's conduct must probably be grossly negligent as to the ultimate victim (in this case V); it's not enough that it was grossly negligent as to someone else.

V. PROXIMATE CAUSE — UNINTENDED MANNER OF HARM

A. **Generally:** If D's intended victim is harmed, but the harm occurs in an *unexpected manner* (though it is the same general type of harm intended), the unexpected manner of harm may or may not be enough to absolve D. In general, D will not be liable where the harm occurs through a *completely bizarre, unforeseeable chain of events*.

   Example: D gets into a street fight with V, and tries to seriously injure him. As a result of the fight, V is knocked unconscious, recovers a few minutes later, drives away, and is hit by the 8:02 train at a crossing. D's act is certainly a "but for" cause of the harm to V, since had V not been knocked out, he would have continued on his way and crossed earlier than 8:02. And the general type of harm to V — severe bodily injury — is the same as that intended by D. Yet all courts would agree that the chain of events here was so unforeseeable from D's perspective that he should not be held liable for V's death.

B. **Direct causation:** We say that D's act was a *"direct"* cause of V's harm if the harm followed D's act without the presence of any clearly-defined act or event by an outside person or thing. In direct causation situations, D is rarely able to convince the court that the chain of events was so bizarre that D should be absolved.

   1. **Pre-existing weakness:** If V has a *pre-existing condition*, unknown to D, that makes him much more *susceptible to injury or death* than a normal person would be, D *"takes his victim as he finds him."* Thus D may not argue that his own act was not the proximate cause of the unusually severe result.

      Example: D beats V up, with intent to kill him. V runs away before many blows have fallen, and a person in ordinary health would not have been severely hurt by the blows that did fall. Unknown to D, however, V is a hemophiliac, who bleeds to death from one slight wound. D is guilty of murder, even though from D's viewpoint V's death from the slight wounds was unforeseeable.

      Note: When you are looking at a proximate cause problem, don't forget to also apply the rules of concurrence and to insist on the *correct mental state*. For instance, suppose D in the above example had only been trying to commit a minor battery on V, instead of trying to kill him. If V died as a result of his hemophilia, D would not be liable for common-law intent-to-kill murder, because he did not have the requisite mental state, the intent to kill. (But he would probably be liable for *manslaughter* under the misdemeanor- manslaughter rule.)

2. **Fright or stress:** Where V's death results even *without physical impact*, as the result of a *fright* or *stress* caused by D, D's conduct can nonetheless be a proximate cause of the death.

   Example: During a holdup by D, V, a storekeeper, has a fatal heart attack from the stress. In most courts, V's death will be held to be the proximate result of D's act of robbery; coupled with the felony-murder doctrine, this will be enough for D to be guilty of murder, even if there was no way he could have known of V's heart condition. [*People v. Stamp*]

C. **Intervening acts:** D's odds of escaping liability are better where an *"intervening act"* or intervening *event* contributes to the result than where D has "directly" caused the harmful result.

   1. **Intervening acts by third persons:** Sometimes, the intervening act is by a *third person*.

      a. **Medical treatment:** The most common third-person intervening act is *medical treatment* performed by a doctor or nurse upon V, where this treatment is necessitated by injuries inflicted by D. Here, the treatment will only supersede if the treatment is *"abnormal."*

         i. **Negligent treatment:** The fact that the treatment is *negligently performed* will *not*, by itself, usually be enough to make it so "abnormal" that it is a superseding event. But if the treatment is performed in a *reckless* or *grossly negligent* manner, the treatment *will* usually be found to be "abnormal" and thus superseding.

      b. **Failure to act never supersedes:** A third party's *failure to act* will almost *never* be a superseding cause.

         Example: D shoots V. There is a doctor, X, standing by who could, with 100% certainty, prevent V from dying. X refuses to render assistance because he hates V and wants V to die. D will still be the proximate cause of death — a third party's failure to act will virtually never supersede.

   2. **Act by V:** Sometimes the *victim herself* will take an action that is possibly a superseding intervening cause. Acts by victims are generally taken in direct response to D's act, so they will not be superseding unless they are "abnormal" (not merely "unforeseeable").

      a. **Victim refuses medical aid:** If the victim refuses to receive *medical assistance* which might prevent the severe harm imposed by D, the victim's refusal usually will *not* be superseding.

         Example: D stabs V repeatedly. V refuses a blood transfusion because she is a Jehovah's Witness. *Held*, V's refusal to allow the transfusion is not a superseding cause. [*Regina v. Blaue*]

      b. **Manslaughter where V commits suicide:** Where V's intervening act is to *commit suicide*, that act may well be considered superseding. This is especially likely if the crime charged is one for which recklessness rather than intent will suffice, such as involuntary manslaughter — the less culpable D's mental state, the more likely the trier of fact is to give D relief by holding that V's suicide was not proximately caused by D's act.

         Example: D, a high school student, posts an Internet blog entry accusing V, another senior, of cheating on a school math exam and lying on a college application to State U. V, humiliated, loses weight, becomes clinically depressed, and fails to get into State U (for reasons unrelated to D's blog entry). 13 months after the blog post V commits suicide, leaving a note blaming her decision on D's conduct. If D is prosecuted for involuntary manslaughter, D has a good argument that her conduct was not the proximate cause of V's death, because other factors — including V's own voluntary act of suicide, the relatively long passage of time and the rejection from State U — should be viewed as superseding. It's not clear that D will succeed with this argument, but it's certainly a plausible one.

CHAPTER 3
RESPONSIBILITY

I. THE INSANITY DEFENSE

A. General purpose: If D can show he was *insane* at the time he committed a criminal act, he may be entitled to the verdict "not guilty by reason of insanity."

B. Tests for insanity: The principal tests for whether D was insane — each used in some jurisdictions — are the *M'Naghten* and *irresistible-impulse* tests. We consider each in turn.

1. *M'Naghten* "right from wrong" rule: At least half the states apply the so-called *M'Naghten* rule. M'Naghten is a fairly tough standard for D to meet. D must show two things:

   a. **Mental disease or defect:** That he suffered a *mental disease* causing a *defect* in his reasoning powers; and

   b. **Result:** That as a result, either: (1) he did not understand the *"nature and quality"* of his act; or (2) he did not know that his act was *wrong*.

   Example 1: D strangles V, his wife, believing that he is squeezing a lemon. Even under the relatively strict *M'Naghten* test, D would probably be ruled insane, on the grounds that he did not understand the "nature and quality" of his act.

   Example 2: D is attracted to bright objects, and therefore shoplifts jewelry constantly, though intellectually he knows that this is morally wrong and also illegal. D is not insane under the *M'Naghten* test, because he understood the nature and quality of his act, and knew that his act was wrong. The fact that he may have acted under an "irresistible impulse" is irrelevant under the *M'Naghten* rule.

   i. **Meaning of "wrong":** Even under *M'Naghten* (a relatively strict, i.e., narrow, definition of insanity), D can be acquitted if he did not know that his conduct was "wrong." Courts are split about whether D can be acquitted if he knew that his act was a legal crime, but believed that it was morally justified. Therefore, on the MBE if D takes an act that he thinks is morally justified but knows is legally prohibited, the correct answer is likely to be that D has at least a chance of succeeding with a *M'Naghten* defense because he "didn't know his act was wrong."

   Example: D, due to hallucinations caused by his schizophrenia, believes that his next-door neighbor V is a terrorist who plans, in 3 months, to bomb the local courthouse. D therefore decides to shoot V to death. D knows that the killing will be regarded as a crime (he thinks that the authorities won't prosecute V because they're collaborating with him), but D believes that he is acting in the way God and George Washington would want him to act.

   D has a plausible insanity defense under *M'Naghten*, since, even though he knows his act is legally forbidden, he believes that it is morally justified.

   ii. **D's unreasonable belief he's being attacked:** D can likely satisfy the "didn't know his conduct was wrong" prong of *M'Naghten* if he incorrectly (and with gross unreasonableness) *believes he is being attacked*. This "unreasonable self-defense" scenario is common on the MBE, so any time it occurs consider the possibility of an insanity acquittal.

   Example: As the result of chronic hallucinations deriving from D's alcoholism, D believes that V, a fellow passenger on the bus where D is riding, is about to pull a gun and shoot D. D pulls a knife and stabs V to death to defend himself. D has a respectable chance of an insanity acquittal even in a jurisdiction applying the *M'Naghten* standard: (1) he has a mental disease affecting his reasoning powers (the alcoholism and ensuing hallucinations); and (2) that disease has caused him to believe that stabbing V is not morally wrong.

2. **"Irresistible impulse" test:** Many states, including about half of those states that follow *M'Naghten*, have added a *second standard* by which D can establish his insanity: that D was *unable to control his conduct*. This is sometimes loosely called the *"irresistible impulse"* defense.

   Example: On the facts of Example 2 above, D would be acquitted, because although he understood that it was wrong to shoplift shiny things, he was unable to control his conduct.

II. INTOXICATION

A. **Voluntary intoxication:** *Voluntary self-induced intoxication* does *not "excuse"* criminal conduct, in general.

   Example: D decides to rob a bank. Normally, he would be too timid to do so. However, he takes several drinks to increase his courage, and goes out and does the robbery. The fact that D was legally intoxicated when he committed the robbery will be completely irrelevant.

   1. **Effect on mental state:** Although voluntary intoxication is not an "excuse," it may *prevent D from having the required mental state*. If so, D will not be guilty.

      a. **MBE tactic:** Therefore, on the MBE you will have to examine the *particular crime(s)* charged, and decide whether D's intoxication might negate any element of the crime. There is no general rule that will help you much with this — you simply have to know the mental-state requirements of each crime, and then figure out whether D's drunkenness does or does not negate that mental state.

   2. **Recklessness-based crimes:** The most important single fact to remember about intoxication is that in most courts, intoxication *will not negate the element of recklessness*. In other words, if a particular element of a crime can be satisfied by a mental state of recklessness, D's intoxication will be irrelevant.

      a. **Involuntary manslaughter:** Therefore, in the case of either *voluntary* or *involuntary* manslaughter — each of which can be committed by a reckless state — D's voluntary intoxication is very unlikely to negate D's recklessness.

   3. **Murder:** Similarly, for garden-variety *murder*, D's intoxication will rarely negate an element, because murder is a crime that can be supported by a variety of mental states, and some of these are unlikely to be negated by intoxication. Thus if D's drunkenness did not prevent him from: (1) acting with reckless indifference to the possibility of V's death ("depraved heart" murder; see *infra*, p. 52); or (2) desiring to cause V serious bodily injury, the fact that the drunkenness prevented D from desiring V's death won't negate his guilt of murder. (But the MBE examiners may tell you that some specific degree of murder, such as first-degree murder, has some narrower intent requirement, in which case intoxication may negate that intent; see *infra*, p. 22.)

      Example: D has enough drinks to raise his blood-alcohol level to twice the legal limit. He then drives his car through Times Square at rush hour, knowing that his coordination is badly impaired. He runs over V, killing him. A trier of fact could quite plausibly conclude that D has displayed reckless indifference to the value of human life, notwithstanding his lack of intent to kill. If so, D's voluntary intoxication would not prevent his guilt of the reckless-indifference form of murder.

    a. **Attendant circumstances:** On the MBE, you will often see a question in which intoxication causes D to be confused about the *"attendant circumstances,"* but will not prevent D from intending to kill what D knows is a person. Such an intoxication-induced mistake about the surrounding circumstances will typically *not negative* any element of the crime.

        i. **D falsely believes he's being attacked:** For instance, D's intoxication may cause him to believe that he's being *attacked* when he's not. D's intoxication will not help him in this situation, because an unreasonable belief in the need for self-defense does not negate any element of any common-law crime. (See *infra*, p. 27.)

        Example: D is walking down the street, very drunk. V, a police officer, approaches him. D unreasonably, because of hallucinations brought on by his intoxication, believes that V is about to try to kill him with a knife. Therefore, D shoots V to death to prevent being killed himself.

        D can be convicted of murder. D's intoxication will not negate the mental state required for murder. D had an intent to kill the person who was approaching him, and the fact that he was wrong about the need for self-defense won't change that. (Indeed, because self-intoxication is viewed as being reckless, D's mistaken belief in the need for self-defense won't even qualify him for the lesser charge of voluntary manslaughter on an "imperfect self-defense" theory; see *infra*, p. 60.)

4. **Negatives mental state:** On the other hand, there are many crimes defined in such a way that self-induced intoxication *may prevent D from having the requisite mental state*.

    Example: Suppose that in a particular jurisdiction, first degree murder is defined so that D must be shown to have had the intent to kill, and it is not enough for him to recklessly disregard the risk of death. At a time when D has no intent to do anyone harm, he gets drunk in a bar. He then shoots his pistol towards V, intending only to frighten V as a joke. Had D been sober, he would have realized that V would be hit and possibly killed. D will be acquitted of first-degree murder, because his drunken state prevented him from having the required intent, namely an intent to kill.

    a. **Negatives "deliberation":** Where a crime is defined so as to require *"deliberation,"* D's intoxication may cause him not to meet that element. For instance, if D's drunkenness causes him to fly off the handle and kill V in a rage, the likely outcome is that D did not act "deliberately." That's true even if "deliberation" is defined so as to exist as long as D engages in "cool reflection, no matter how briefly."

    Example: The jurisdiction defines first-degree murder as a killing of another, after "deliberation." "Deliberation" is defined as "cool reflection for any period of time, no matter how brief." D, riding the bar car of a commuter train, gets drunk. The passenger next to him, V, needles D about D's favorite presidential candidate, and D becomes more and more angry. After one further remark, D becomes instantly enraged, and reflexively reaches into his pocket, pulls a knife, and stabs V to death. D cannot be convicted of first-degree murder, because his intoxication prevented him from engaging in "cool reflection" for even a brief period.

CHAPTER 4
JUSTIFICATION AND EXCUSE

I. GENERAL PRINCIPLES

A. **Justification and excuse generally:** The twin doctrines of *"justification"* and *"excuse"* allow D to escape conviction even if the prosecution proves all elements of the case. There is no important distinction between those defenses referred to as "justification" and those referred to as "excuses." The three main justification doctrines tested on the MBE are *duress, self-defense* and *entrapment*.

II. DURESS

A. **General nature:** D is said to have committed a crime under *"duress"* if he performed the crime because of a *threat of*, or *use of, force* by a third person sufficiently strong that D's will was *overborne*. The term applies to force placed upon D's *mind*, not his body.

> **Example:** X forces D to rob Y, by threatening D with immediate death if he does not. D will be able to raise the defense of duress.

B. **Elements:** D must establish the following elements for duress:

1. **Threat:** A *threat* by a third person,

2. **Fear:** Which produces a *reasonable fear* in D,

3. **Imminent danger:** That he will suffer *immediate* or *imminent*,

4. **Bodily harm:** *Death* or *serious bodily injury*.

C. **Model Penal Code test:** Under the M.P.C., the defense is available where the threat to D was sufficiently great that "a person of *reasonable firmness* in [D's] situation would have been *unable to resist*." M.P.C. §2.09(1).

D. **Not available for homicide:** In most states (and on the MBE), the defense of duress is *not available* if D is charged with *homicide*, i.e., the intentional killing of another.

> **Example:** D is a member of a gang run by X. X and the other gang members tell D that if D does not kill V, an innocent witness to one of the group's crimes, they will kill D immediately. D reasonably and honestly believes this threat. D kills V. D will not be permitted to assert the defense of duress on these facts, because he is charged with the intentional killing of another. (The result probably would not change even if D had originally been coerced into joining the gang.)

III. SELF-DEFENSE

A. **Self-defense generally:** There is a general right to *defend oneself* against the use of *unlawful force*. When successfully asserted, the defense is a complete one, leading to acquittal.

B. **Requirements:** The following requirements must generally be met:

1. **Resist unlawful force:** D must have been resisting the *present or imminent use* of *unlawful force*;

2. **Force must not be excessive:** The degree of force used by D must not have been *more than was reasonably necessary* to defend against the threatened harm;

3. **Deadly force:** The force used by D may not have been *deadly* (i.e., intended or likely to cause death or serious bodily injury) unless the danger being resisted was also deadly force;

4. **Aggressor:** D must not have been the *aggressor*, unless: (1) he was a *non-deadly aggressor* confronted with the unexpected use of deadly force; or (2) he *withdrew* after his initial aggression, and the other party continued to attack; and

5. **Retreat:** (In some states) D must not have been in a position from which he could *retreat* with complete safety, unless: (1) the attack took place in D's dwelling; or (2) D used only non-deadly force.

C. **Requirement of "unlawful force":** Self-defense applies only where D is resisting force that is *unlawful*.

1. **Other party commits tort or crime:** Generally, this means that the other party must be committing a *crime or tort*.

D. **Degree of force:** D may not use more force than is *reasonably necessary* to protect himself.

1. **Use of non-deadly force:** D may use *non-deadly force* to resist virtually any kind of unlawful force (assuming that the level of non-deadly force D uses is not more than is necessary to meet the threat).

    a. **No need to retreat:** D may use non-deadly force without *retreating* even if retreat could be safely done.

    b. **Prevention of theft:** D may use non-deadly force to resist the other person's attempted theft of *property*.

2. **Deadly force:** D may defend himself with *deadly force* only if the attack threatens D with *serious bodily harm*.

    a. **Kidnapping and rape:** Most courts expand the concept of "serious bodily harm" to cover *kidnapping* and forcible *rape* — so if V threatens D with kidnapping or forcible rape, V may use deadly force to resist if lesser force would not suffice.

    b. **Can't use deadly force to prevent non-serious harm:** On the other hand, some attacks clearly *don't pose the risk of serious bodily harm*, so D *may not use deadly force in response.* Thus MBE questions sometimes involve a *"slap"* by V — a slap normally does not pose the risk of present serious bodily harm (or foreshadow serious bodily harm in the imminent future), so D may not respond with deadly force.

        Example: D and V, drinking in a bar, get into a verbal argument about politics. D insults V's mother. V slaps D. D whips out a knife and stabs V in the stomach. V bleeds to death. D is charged with murder of the intent-to-do-serious-bodily-harm variety (see *infra*, p. 52).

        D does not have the defense of self-defense. V's slap did not pose the risk of serious bodily harm, and there was nothing to indicate that the slap was a prelude to the danger of worse harm from V. Therefore, D's use of the knife was the use of deadly force in response to non-deadly force, and was not privileged. (It's likely that D can get the murder charge reduced to voluntary manslaughter, under an "imperfect self-defense" theory; see *infra*, p. 60.)

3. **No more force than reasonably necessary:** Whether D uses deadly or non-deadly force, D *may not use more force than seems reasonably necessary in the circumstances.* Thus even if V uses deadly force against D, D may not use deadly force in return if the use of non-deadly force would seem sufficient to one in D's position:

    Example: V takes out a knife and approaches D menacingly, with an intent to kill D. D is a martial arts specialist, and knows that he could easily take the knife away from D. Instead, D takes out his own knife and stabs V in the stomach, intending to put him in the hospital to teach him a lesson. V bleeds to death.

D cannot claim self-defense — he used more force than a person in his position would conclude was reasonably necessary to deal with the threat.

- **a. Effect of mistake:** As with other sorts of mistakes, if D is reasonably mistaken in the belief that he is threatened with serious bodily harm, he will not lose the right to reply with deadly force. See *infra*, p. 26.

E. Aggressor may not claim self-defense: If D is the *initial aggressor* — that is, one who strikes the first blow or otherwise precipitates the conflict — he may ordinarily *not claim self-defense*.

Example: D starts a fight in a bar with V, by brandishing a knife at V. V, using his own knife, tries to cut D's knife-wielding hand. D hits V in the face with his other hand, injuring him. D cannot claim self-defense, because he precipitated the conflict by brandishing the knife.

1. **"Aggressor" is narrowly defined:** D will be considered an aggressor only if D *initiated the use of force*. You'll see various scenarios on the MBE where a choice suggests that D loses the right of self-defense because she was an aggressor, but where D really wasn't an aggressor. Here are some scenarios in which D is not an aggressor:

   a. **Trespass:** The mere fact that D *trespassed* will generally not be enough to make D an aggressor, and D will therefore be permitted to use force to repel an attack by the owner.

   Example: D trespasses onto rangeland owned by V, on which D is planning to walk his dog. V shouts at D, "You filthy trespasser," and without giving D a chance to leave starts striking at D with a cane. D blocks the cane and twists it, breaking V's wrist. D is prosecuted for battery, and claims self-defense. The prosecution claims that D, by trespassing, was the aggressor and thus lost the right to use force in his self-defense.

   The prosecution is wrong. The fact that D was a trespasser was not by itself enough to make D an aggressor — nothing that D did, initially, posed a risk of bodily harm to V, which is what is required before a person will be an aggressor. Therefore, D had the right to defend himself with reasonable force when V began to strike him.

   b. **Larceny:** The mere fact that D was committing *larceny*, in a way that did not pose a danger of physical harm to anyone, typically won't make D an aggressor.

   Example: D, shopping at Store, picks up a small item and puts it in her pocket, intending to shoplift it. V, a store detective, sees D do this, grabs D, and starts to put a dangerous choke-hold on her. D kicks V hard in the shin, causing V to fall and break his leg. D is prosecuted for assault, and claims self-defense.

   The fact that D committed larceny did not make D the aggressor. Therefore, D was entitled to use self-defense against V's unlawful use of force (the chokehold).

   c. **Verbal provocation:** Similarly, the fact that D acts in a *verbally provocative way* towards V (while not threatening physical harm) won't make D an aggressor.

   Example: D and V get into a verbal altercation in a bar, while each is a bit tipsy. D shouts at V, "You are a drunk and a thief, and you're too yellow-bellied to even try to stop me from saying it." V, enraged, starting hitting D in the face. D, a far better fist-fighter, hits back, breaking V's jaw.

   D was not the aggressor, because verbal taunts not amounting to threats of imminent harm won't be considered aggression for self-defense purposes. Therefore, D had the right to use reasonable force in self-defense once V attacked him.

F. Retreat: Some states (but not a majority) require that if D could *safely retreat*, he must do so *rather than use deadly force*.

   1. No retreat before non-deadly force: *No states* require retreat before the use of *non-deadly force*. Therefore, on the MBE, if the fact pattern shows that D is not using deadly force, you can be confident that D could not possibly have a duty to retreat.

   Example: D, a woman, is walking down the street near her home when V approaches her and acts in a manner that reasonably causes D to believe that V is likely to sexually assault her. D is a fast runner, is wearing sneakers, and knows for nearly certain that she could outrun V and get safely to her home. Instead, D reaches into her purse, pulls out a can of Mace, and sprays V in the face, causing V significant pain and some eye damage.

   D cannot be prosecuted for battery on the grounds that she didn't retreat — the Mace was non-deadly force, and in all states D had the right to use that force to protect herself from attack rather than retreating.

   2. Retreat only required where it can be safely done: The retreat rule, in states requiring it, only applies where D could retreat with *complete safety* to himself and others. Also, if D reasonably but mistakenly believes that retreat cannot be safely done, he will be protected.

   3. Retreat in D's dwelling: Those states requiring retreat do not generally require it where the attack takes place in *D's dwelling*.

   a. MBE Tip: So on the MBE, if the attack takes place in *D's dwelling* (which is not also V's dwelling), you can be *confident that retreat is not required*, without worrying whether the jurisdiction is one that sometimes requires retreat as an alternative to deadly force.

   Example: D invites V to D's house, and the two parties get into a dispute. V attacks D with a knife. D could easily go into a bedroom which can be locked from the inside; while there, he could readily call the police. Instead, D grabs a knife — the only reasonably available means of combatting V, given D's inferior martial arts skills — and seriously wounds V. Even in states imposing a general duty of retreat, D is exempt from the duty here, since the attack is taking place in his own dwelling.

   4. Only matters if D has right to use deadly force: Even in states sometimes requiring retreat, that duty can make a difference only if D would *otherwise have the right to use deadly force* in self-defense. Therefore, if V does not threaten to impose serious bodily harm on D (or on a third person), any duty to retreat could not be relevant.

   Example: Recall the fight Example on p. 24, in which D responds to V's slap by stabbing V in the stomach. Although D cannot successfully assert self-defense, the reason is not that D failed to retreat. Even in a jurisdiction requiring retreat, D's failure to retreat before using deadly force only makes a difference to the outcome if D would have had the right to use deadly force apart from the retreat issue, and here, D had no right to use deadly force (since he wasn't threatened with serious bodily harm).

G. Effect of mistake: The effect of a *mistake* by D concerning the need for self-defense will depend largely on whether the mistake is *"reasonable."* Observe that there are various kinds of mistakes that D might make concerning the need for self-defense: (1) a mistaken belief that he is about to be attacked; (2) a mistaken belief that the force used against him is unlawful; (3) a mistaken belief that only deadly force will suffice to repel the threat; or (4) a mistaken belief that retreat could not be accomplished safely.

   1. Reasonable: As long as D's mistaken belief as to any of these points is *reasonable*, all courts will allow him to claim self-defense.

Example: While D is walking down the street one evening, V says, "Your money or your life," and points what appears to be a gun at D. In fact, the "gun" is merely V's finger poking through V's jacket. A reasonable person in D's position would be likely to believe that there was a real gun. D also reasonably believes that V may shoot D even if D gives up the property, because this has happened in the neighborhood on several recent occasions. D pulls his own gun and shoots V to death. Later evidence shows that V, a career mugger, would never have dreamt of actually doing physical harm to a victim. Because D's mistakes (about the existence of a gun, and about whether it would be used against him) were "reasonable," D is entitled to claim self-defense despite the mistakes.

2. **Unreasonable mistake:** But if D's mistake is *unreasonable*, most states hold that he *loses* the right to claim self-defense.

   a. **Intoxication:** If the cause of D's unreasonable mistake as to the need for self-defense is his *intoxication*, all courts agree that the intoxication does not excuse the mistake, and D will not be entitled to a claim of self-defense. (But the intoxication and resulting mistake about the need for self-defense may entitle D to a reduction of the charge from murder to voluntary manslaughter; see *infra*, p. 60.)

      Example: D gets drunk in a bar. He mistakenly believes that V is about to shoot him. He instead draws first, and shoots V to death. Had D been sober, he would have realized that V was not about to attack him. All courts agree that because D's mistake was caused by his intoxication, he loses the claim of self-defense.

H. **"Imperfect" self-defense:** D may be entitled to a claim of *"imperfect"* self-defense, sufficient to reduce his crime from murder to *voluntary manslaughter*, if D killed in self-defense but failed to satisfy one of the requirements for acquittal by reason of self-defense. See *infra*, p. 60.

   1. **Unreasonable mistake:** Thus if D makes an *unreasonable mistake* as to the need for force in self-defense, or as to the unlawfulness of the other party's first use of force, most states will reduce what would otherwise be murder to voluntary manslaughter.

      Example: D gets into a verbal dispute with V while both are drinking at a bar. At one point in the dispute V reaches into his pocket. D, because he is slightly intoxicated, genuinely but unreasonably believes that V is reaching for a knife with which to stab D. D therefore stabs V first, reluctantly concluding that D must kill V before V can kill D. (Assume that if D's belief that V was reaching for a knife had been reasonable, the way in which D used his own knife would have been a reasonable response.) V bleeds to death. D is prosecuted for murder.

      D will be entitled to have murder reduced to voluntary manslaughter, because D honestly (though unreasonably) believed that he needed to use deadly force in self-defense.

   2. **Initial aggressor:** Similarly, if D was the *initial aggressor*, and thus lost the right to claim true self-defense, he can still use imperfect self-defense to get his crime reduced to manslaughter.

      Example: X insults D. D pulls a knife and advances towards X. X pulls a gun and is about to shoot D. With his spare hand, D pulls a gun and shoots X to death. Because D was the aggressor — and he was the first to use physical violence rather than mere words — he does not have a "full" claim of self-defense. However, he met all the requirements for use of deadly force except that he not have been the aggressor, so he'll probably be entitled to have the charge reduced from murder to voluntary manslaughter.

I. **Burden of proof:** Nearly all states make a claim of self-defense an *affirmative defense*, i.e., one which must be raised, in the first instance, by D. Many states also place the *burden of persuasion* on D, requiring him to prove by a *preponderance of the evidence* that all the requirements for the defense are met. It is constitutional for a state to put this burden of persuasion upon the defendant. [*Martin v. Ohio* (1987)]

IV. ENTRAPMENT

A. **Entrapment generally:** The defense of *entrapment* exists where a *law enforcement official*, or someone cooperating with him, has *induced* D to commit the crime.

B. **"Predisposition" test:** The majority test, and the one used in the federal system, is that entrapment exists where: (1) the government *originates* the crime and *induces* its commission; and (2) D is an *innocent person*, i.e., one who is *not predisposed* to committing this sort of crime. This is the so-called *"predisposition"* test. This is the test you should apply on the MBE.

> **Example:** X, an undercover narcotics operative, offers to sell V heroin for V's own use. If the offer originated entirely with X, and V had never used or sought heroin, V would have a good chance at an entrapment defense, on the theory that he was an "innocent" person who was not predisposed to committing this sort of crime. But if the evidence showed that V had frequently purchased heroin from other sources, then V would not be entrapped under the "predisposition" test, even if the transaction between X and V was entirely at X's instigation.

CHAPTER 5

ATTEMPT

I. ATTEMPT — INTRODUCTION

A. **Attempt generally:** All states, in general, punish certain unsuccessful *attempts* to commit crimes.

B. **Two requirements:** For most attempt statutes, there are two principal requirements, corresponding to the *mens rea* and the *actus reus*:

1. **Mental state:** First, D must have had at least a *mental state* which would have been enough to satisfy the *mens rea* requirement of the substantive crime itself. In fact, generally D must *intend* to *commit all acts* needed for commission of the *underlying crime*.

2. **Act requirement:** Second, D must be shown to have committed some *affirmative act* in furtherance of his plan of criminality.

II. MENTAL STATE

A. **Intent usually required:** Generally, D will be liable for an attempt only if he *intended* to do all acts which, if they had been carried out, would have resulted in the commission of that crime.

1. **Narrower than for completed crime:** The requirement of intent means that the mental state that will make D guilty of an attempt to commit crime X may well be *narrower* than the range of mental states that will suffice for completed crime X.

    a. **Murder:** This is especially true of *murder*. There are several mental states for murder, and they don't all require intent to kill — for instance, intent to commit *serious bodily harm* will suffice (*infra*, p. 52) and *reckless indifference* to the value of human life ("depraved heart") will also suffice (*infra*, p. 52). If D acts with either of these intents, and death does not result, D *won't* be guilty of attempted murder even though he would have been guilty of completed murder if death had resulted.

Example: D attacks V with a knife, intending only to seriously injure him, not kill him. V is badly cut and is hospitalized, but recovers. D is not guilty of attempted murder — that requires an intent to kill, which D didn't have. (And the fact that D would have been guilty of murder if V had died from the attack is irrelevant.)

2. **Effect of intoxication:** The principle that attempt crimes require the intent to do an act that would constitute the underlying crime means that *intoxication* may be *relevant evidence* tending to show that D did not intend to commit the underlying crime, and thus relevant to D's defense against attempt liability. And that's true even if the intoxication would be irrelevant to D's liability for the completed underlying crime. This is especially likely to be true in an *attempted murder* prosecution.

    Example: D gets drunk at a bar, and becomes convinced that V, another patron, has insulted D. (Assume that a sober man in D's position would not have had that belief.) D stabs V in the abdomen with a knife, and badly wounds V. D intended only to "put V in the hospital," and did not believe or hope that V would die. A reasonable person in D's position, if sober, would have realized that there was a very great chance that V would die from the type of abdominal wound that D tried to inflict and succeeded in inflicting. V in fact recovers.

    D is not guilty of attempted murder. That's because D did not intend to kill V, merely to injure him badly. If V had died, D would have been guilty of the intent-to-commit-serious-bodily-harm version of murder, and his intoxication would not furnish a defense. (See *supra*, p. 21.) But since the intoxication has helped prevent D from having an intent to kill, it helps him avoid attempted-murder liability.

3. **Crimes defined by recklessness or negligence:** Ordinarily, there can be no attempt to commit a crime defined in terms of *recklessness* or *negligence*.

    a. **Bringing about certain result:** This is clearly true as to crimes defined in terms of recklessly or negligently bringing about a *certain result* — there can be no attempt liability for these crimes.

        Example: D gets into his car knowing that it has bad brakes, but recklessly decides to take a chance. D almost runs into V because he can't stop in time, but V dives out of the way. D will not be guilty of attempted involuntary manslaughter, because crimes defined in terms of recklessly or negligently bringing about a certain result cannot give rise to attempt liability.

4. **Strict-liability crimes:** Where a crime is defined as bringing about a certain result regardless of the defendant's mental state — i.e., the crime is a *strict-liability crime* — the prevailing view is that D won't be guilty of attempting that crime unless he *attempted to bring about the forbidden result*. Lafave, §6.2(c)(3), pp. 543-44.

    Example 1: Statutory rape is defined in the jurisdiction as "having sexual intercourse with a person not one's spouse, where the person is under the age of 17." Assume that the case law of the jurisdiction imposes liability even where D honestly and reasonably, but incorrectly, believes that the other person is 17 or older. D believes that V, whom he has recently met, is 19 (that's how old she looks), but she is in fact 16. The two go out to dinner on a date, and then go back to D's apartment. There, D repeatedly tries to persuade V to have sexual intercourse with him. V agrees, and allows D to partly undress her, then changes her mind, gets dressed again, and leaves.

    D will not be convicted of attempted statutory rape. While he might have been convicted of actual statutory rape if he had had sex with V, he won't be convicted of attempt, under the prevailing view, unless he intended to have sex with a person he believed was under the age of 17. Since he actually believed V was 17, he did not have the requisite intent. (And that's true even if his mistaken belief was unreasonable, as long as it was genuine.)

Example 2: A federal statute makes it a crime to "sell an adulterated pharmaceutical." The statute has been interpreted to be a strict liability crime — that is, defendant will be guilty if she sells an adulterated drug, even if she didn't know it was adulterated. A federal inspector inspects an aspirin-packaging plant owned and operated by D, and discovers that some samples that were manufactured abroad and that have been packaged by D's plant and not yet shipped or sold to customers, contain dangerous contaminants. D did not know of the contamination (but was negligent in not suspecting that contamination might be occurring).

D will not be convicted of attempted violation of the adulteration statute — even though the substantive crime does not require an intent to sell a contaminated drug, under the prevailing view liability for attempted violation of the statute will be construed to require such an intent.

5. **Completion of crime no bar:** Suppose D actually *commits* crime X — does this fact prevent D from being instead convicted of attempt to commit X? The modern view is *"no"* — D can't be convicted of *both* attempt and the completed crime, but no legal rule prevents her from being convicted of just attempt.

III. THE ACT — ATTEMPT VS. "MERE PREPARATION"

A. **The problem:** All courts agree that D cannot be convicted of attempt merely for thinking evil thoughts, or plotting in his mind to commit a crime. Instead, D must commit some real-world act. Courts vary in their precise definition of the required act. Typical formulations are that D must have committed some act *"in furtherance"* of the criminal purpose, or *"towards the completion of"* that purpose, or representing a *"substantial step"* towards completion.

   a. **Illustrations:** Here are some illustrations of conduct that would *suffice* for attempt in virtually all jurisdictions:

   i. *Lying in wait,* searching for or *following* the contemplated victim of the crime.

   ii. *Enticing* or seeking to entice the contemplated victim to *go to the* place contemplated for its commission.

   iii. *Reconnoitering* the place contemplated for commission of the crime.

   Example: D is caught while hiding in the bushes observing V's residence, while V is away from home. This "casing the joint" will probably suffice.

   iv. Unlawful *entry* of a structure, vehicle or enclosure where the crime is to be committed.

   v. *Possession of materials* to be employed in the commission of the crime, if the materials are *specially designed* for such unlawful use or can serve no lawful purpose of D under the circumstances.

   Example: D is stopped on the street at night and is found to be in possession of lock-picking tools. Probably he can be convicted of attempted burglary.

   b. **Vague plans:** On the other hand, if D and another person merely make *vague plans* about committing crime X, without agreeing on the details, this probably *won't* suffice for attempt to commit X.

   Example: H desires the death of his wife W. H happens to meet an acquaintance on the street, X. H asks X whether X would consider killing W for money. X says that for the right price, he would. They agree to meet again in a week to discuss details. Unbeknownst to H, X is a police informant, who reports the conversation to the police. Two hours later (before H has done anything further), the police arrest H.

H has not attempted to kill W — the mere propositioning of X, and the agreement to meet again later to discuss details, are not sufficiently substantial steps to meet any state's requirement of an act in furtherance of the criminal plan.

IV. IMPOSSIBILITY

A. **Nature of "impossibility" defense:** The *"impossibility"* defense is raised where D has done everything in his power to accomplish the result he desires, but, due to external circumstances, no substantive crime has been committed. The basic "factual impossibility" defense is always *unsuccessful* today. But the "true legal" impossibility defense, discussed *infra*, p. 32, is a valid defense.

B. **Factual impossibility:** A claim of *factual impossibility* arises out of D's mistake concerning an issue of fact. D in effect says, "I made a mistake of fact. Had the facts been as I believed them to be, there would have been a crime. But under the true facts, my attempt to commit a crime could not possibly have succeeded."

   1. **Not accepted:** The defense of factual impossibility is *rejected* by all modern courts. That is, impossibility is *no defense* in those cases where, *had the facts been as D believed them to be, there would have been a crime*. Thus D is guilty of an attempt (and his "factual impossibility" defense will fail) in all of the following examples:

      Example 1: D points her gun at A, and pulls the trigger. The gun does not fire because, unbeknownst to D, it is not loaded.

      Example 2: D intends to rape X, but is unable to do so because he is impotent.

      Example 3: D is a "con man" who tries to get X to entrust money to him, which D intends to steal. Unbeknownst to D, X is a plainclothes police officer who is not fooled.

      Example 4: D attempts to poison X with a substance D believes is arsenic, but which is in fact harmless.

      a. **Combined with accomplice liability:** On the MBE, a factual-impossibility issue will often be *combined with an accomplice issue* — the principal tries to carry out a criminal act but fails to do so because of factual impossibility, and the issue is whether the *accomplice* is liable for attempt. Typically, the answer will be *yes*, because factual impossibility doesn't work any better for the accomplice than it does for the principal.

      Example: Wife hates Husband, and hires Hitman to murder Husband in a way that cannot be traced to her. While Wife is out of town, Hitman waits for Husband in the parking garage adjacent to Husband's place of business. As Husband approaches his car, he falls and hits his head on the pavement. Hitman, thinking Husband is merely unconscious, fires two shots into Husband's head. The shots would have been fatal if Husband was still alive. However, an autopsy shows that Husband died immediately of head trauma from the impact of his fall, before Hitman fired the shots. May Wife be convicted of attempted murder?

      Yes. To get the answer, you need to combine analysis of factual impossibility and accomplice liability. Because factual impossibility is not a defense, the fact that Husband was dead before Hitman fired does not supply Hitman a defense against attempted murder charges. Then, under the principles of accomplice liability, since Wife aided or encouraged Hitman to kill Husband (by hiring him), she became liable for any crime he committed at her urging, as long as she had the requisite intent for that crime. Since Wife intended the killing, she had the requisite intent for attempted murder. And factual impossibility is not a valid defense for her any more than it is for Hitman.

C. "True legal" impossibility: A different sort of defense arises where D is mistaken about *how an offense is defined*. That is, D engages in conduct which he believes is forbidden by a statute, but D has misunderstood the meaning of the statute. Let's refer to this as the *"true legal impossibility"* scenario.

1. **Result is acquittal:** In this "true legal impossibility" scenario, D will be *acquitted* — the defense of "true legal" impossibility is a successful one. You can recognize the situation giving rise to the "true legal" impossibility defense by looking for situations where, *even had the facts been as D supposed them to be*, no crime would have been committed. Or, you can think of the situation as being covered by the following rule: "A person can't be liable for attempt by intending to commit an act that she thinks is defined as a crime but that isn't defined as a crime." And that's true whether the person succeeds in committing the act or not.

    Example: D is questioned by X, a police officer, during a criminal investigation. D lies, while believing that lying to the police constitutes perjury. D cannot be convicted of attempted perjury, because the act he was performing (and in fact the act he thought he was performing) is simply not a violation of the perjury statute.

    Note: The defense of "true legal impossibility" is the flip side of the rule that "mistake of law is no excuse." Just as D cannot defend on the grounds that he did not know that his acts were prohibited, so D will be acquitted even of attempt where he commits an act that he thinks is forbidden but that is not forbidden.

2. **Burglary on the MBE:** On the MBE, one way "true legal" impossibility is often tested is in the context of *burglary*: D breaks into a structure for the purpose of performing, once inside, an act *X* that D thinks is defined as a crime, but that is not in fact defined as a crime. D is not guilty of burglary, because burglary requires "an intent to commit a felony therein" (see *infra*, p. 74), and because D does not have the intent to commit an act that is in fact a felony, D does not have an intent to commit a felony. (Nor is D guilty of an attempt to commit the underlying felony.)

    Example: D breaks into his friend F's house, with the sole intent of reclaiming an iPod that D previously lent to F and that F has refused to return. D believes that taking back the iPod from F's house would be larceny if D were caught, but in fact it would not be (since D would be acting under a claim of right; see *infra*, p. 69). D is caught immediately after entering the house, and charged with burglary.

    Although D may be guilty of breaking-and-entering, he is not guilty of burglary or attempted burglary — the act he was planning to commit inside the house was not defined as a felony, so D did not "intend to commit a felony" inside the house. Similarly, D is not guilty of attempted larceny, since even had D taken the iPod this would not have been completed larceny — D would successfully be able to raise the defense of "true legal" impossibility.

3. **Arson on the MBE:** On the MBE, *arson* gives the examiners a good opportunity to test true legal impossibility.

    Example: D attempts to burn down his house for insurance proceeds, but the fire doesn't ignite. D believes that intentionally burning one's house constitutes arson, but he's wrong (only the intentional burning of a structure of "another" qualifies at common law; see *infra*, p. 78.) D has not committed attempted arson. He has tried to commit act X (burning his own house), and even if he had succeeded in committing act X he would not have committed arson, so he can't be guilty of attempted arson.

V. RENUNCIATION

A. Defense generally accepted: Where D is charged with an attempted crime, most courts accept the defense of *renunciation*. To establish this defense, D must show that he *voluntarily abandoned* his attempt before completion of the substantive crime.

> **Example:** D decides to shoot V when V comes out of V's house. D carries a loaded gun, and waits in the bushes outside V's house. Five minutes before he expects V to come out, D decides that he doesn't really want to kill V at all. D returns home, and is arrested and charged with attempted murder. All courts would acquit D in this circumstance, because he voluntarily abandoned his plan before completing it (even though the abandonment came after D took sufficient overt acts that he could have been arrested for an attempt right before the renunciation).

B. Voluntariness: All courts accepting the defense of abandonment require that the abandonment be *"voluntary."*

   1. Threat of imminent apprehension: Thus if D, at the last moment, learns facts causing him to believe that he will be *caught* if he goes through with his plan, the abandonment will generally not be deemed voluntary.

> **Example:** On the facts of the above example, just before V is scheduled to come out of his house, D spots a police officer on the sidewalk near D. D's abandonment has been motivated by the fear of imminent apprehension, so his abandonment will not be deemed voluntary, and D can be convicted of attempted murder.

      a. Abandoned robbery: On the MBE, an abandonment that is involuntary (and that therefore doesn't save D from attempt liability) is especially likely in a *robbery* context: D enters a premises, demands money, and then abandons the plan and flees because something happens to make D fear getting caught (e.g., a customer enters). This is attempted robbery, because D's abandonment is due to fear of getting caught, rather than being voluntary.

CHAPTER 6

CONSPIRACY

I. INTRODUCTION

A. Definition of "conspiracy": The common-law crime of *conspiracy* is defined as *an agreement between two or more persons to do either an unlawful act or a lawful act by unlawful means.* At common law, the prosecution must show the following:

1. **Agreement:** An *agreement* between two or more persons;
2. **Objective:** To carry out an act which is either *unlawful* or which is lawful but to be accomplished by *unlawful means*; and
3. *Mens rea:* A *culpable intent* on the part of the defendant.

II. THE AGREEMENT

A. "Meeting of the minds" not required: The essence of a conspiracy is an *agreement* for the joint pursuit of unlawful ends. However, no true "meeting of the minds" is necessary — all that is needed is that the parties communicate to each other in some way their intention to pursue a joint objective.

B. Parties don't agree to commit object crime: Although there must be an agreement, it is not necessary that each conspirator agree to commit the *substantive object crime(s)*. A particular defendant can be a conspirator even though he agreed to help only in the *planning stages*.

> **Example:** D1, D2 and D3 work together to commit a bank robbery. D3's only participation is to agree to obtain the getaway car, not to participate in the bank robbery itself. D3 is still guilty of conspiracy to commit bank robbery.

C. Feigned agreement: MBE examiners like to test the effect of a *feigned agreement* by one party (e.g., an undercover cop) to go through with the conspiracy. In brief, under the common-law view, if only one party really intends to go through with the conspiracy, that party cannot be convicted, because of the "plurality" requirement. But under the modern "unilateral" or "Model Penal Code" view, the sole "true" conspirator can be convicted. The topic is discussed more fully *infra*, p. 39.

III. MENS REA

A. Intent to commit object crime: Normally, the conspirators must be shown to have agreed to commit a crime. It is then universally held that each of the conspirators must be shown to have had *at least the mental state required for the object crime*.

> **Example:** A and B are caught trying to break into a dwelling at night. The prosecution shows only that A and B agreed to attempt to break and enter the dwelling, and does not show anything about what A and B intended to do once they were inside. A and B cannot be convicted of conspiracy to commit burglary, because there has been no showing that they had the intent necessary for the substantive crime of burglary, i.e., it has not been shown that they had the intent to commit any felony once they got inside.

1. Must have intent to achieve objective: Also, where the substantive crime is defined in terms of causing a *harmful result,* for conspiracy to commit that crime the conspirators must be shown to have *intended to bring about that result*. This is true even though the intent is not necessary for conviction of the substantive crime.

> **Example:** A and B plan to blow up a building by exploding a bomb. They know there are people in the building who are highly likely to be killed, but they have no desire to kill anyone. If the bomb goes off and kills X, A and B are guilty of murder even though they did not intend to kill X (because one form of murder is the "depraved heart" or "reckless indifference to the value of human life" kind). But A and B are *not* guilty of conspiracy to murder X, because they did not have an affirmative intent to bring about anyone's death.

2. Crime of recklessness or negligence: If an underlying crime can be committed by a *reckless* state of mind, the fact that two people acted recklessly together is *not* enough to make them guilty of conspiracy to commit that crime.

> **Example:** D1 and D2 agree that they will steal clothing from a department store by shouting "fire," waiting for everyone to leave, and then helping themselves. (The two don't desire to hurt anyone or think anyone will be hurt — they just want to empty out the store.) The two go the store, shout "Fire," and wait. In the ensuing stampede, V is knocked down and injured. D1 and D2 are charged with battery and conspiracy to commit battery. Assume that the jurisdiction is one in which battery can be committed by a reckless disregard of the possibility that another will be subjected to a harmful bodily contact, and assume further that D1 and D2's conduct of shouting "Fire" amounted to a reckless disregard of the possibility that shoppers might be trampled.
>
> Even though D1 and D2 have committed battery (since they acted recklessly with respect to the risk of trampling), they cannot be convicted of conspiracy to commit battery. That's

because, when a crime X is defined in part by reference to a particular harmful result, conspiracy to commit crime X requires an intent to bring about that harm. So only if D1 and D2 intended to bring about a harmful bodily contact could they be guilty of conspiracy to commit battery.

3. **Attendant circumstances:** But where the substantive crime contains some elements relating to the *attendant circumstances* surrounding the crime, and strict liability applies to those attendant circumstances, then two people *can* be convicted of conspiracy even though they had no knowledge or intent regarding the surrounding circumstances.

    a. **Federal jurisdiction:** Elements relating to *federal jurisdiction* illustrate this problem. Even if the Ds are shown not to have been aware that the elements of federal jurisdiction were present, they can still be held liable for conspiracy to commit the underlying federal crime.

    Example: It is a federal crime to assault a federal officer engaged in the performance of his duties. Assume that case law on this crime holds that the defendant need not be shown to have been aware that his victim was a federal officer. D1 and D2 orally agree to attack V, thinking he is a rival drug dealer. In fact, V is a federal officer. D1 and D2 can be convicted of conspiracy to assault a federal officer, because V's status as such was merely an attendant circumstance, as to which intent need not be shown for conspiracy. [*U.S. v. Feola* (1975)]

B. **Supplying of goods and services:** D must be shown to have *intended* to further a criminal objective. It is not generally enough that D merely *knew* that his acts might tend to enable others to pursue criminal ends. The issue arises most often where D is charged with conspiracy because he *supplied goods or services* to others who committed or planned to commit a substantive crime.

    1. **Mere knowledge not sufficient:** Thus it is *not* enough for the prosecution to show that D supplied goods or services with *knowledge* that his supplies might enable others to pursue a criminal objective. Instead, the supplier must be shown to have *desired* to further the criminal objective. On the other hand, this desire or intent can be shown by *circumstantial* evidence.

        a. **"Stake in venture":** For instance, the supplier's desire to further the criminal objective can be shown circumstantially by the fact that the supplier in some sense acquired a *"stake in the venture."*

        Example: D and S agree that if S supplies D with equipment to make an illegal still, D will pay S 10% of the profits S makes from his illegal liquor operations. S will be held to have had such a stake in the venture that the jury may infer that he desired to bring about the illegal act of operating his still.

        b. **Inflated charges:** The fact that the supplier is charging his criminal purchasers an *inflated price* compared with the cost of the items if sold for legal purposes is evidence of intent.

        c. **Serious crime:** The more *serious* the crime, the more likely it is that the supplier's participation will be found to be part of the conspiracy.

    2. **Agreement to buy stolen goods:** Conversely, an MBE fact pattern may involve D's agreement to buy goods that he *knows are or will be stolen*. At least where D does not intend to bring about the theft — merely to take advantage of the stolen goods by buying them — D *won't* be guilty of *conspiracy to steal* them.

        Example: D1 and D2 call D3 and say, "Would you like a brand new 'hot' Sony LCD TV, MSRP $3,000, for just $299?" D3 says, "Sure, bring it right over." D3 knows that the TV, when he gets it, will be stolen goods. D1 and D2 steal the TV from a warehouse later that night, bring it to D3, and sell it to him for the promised $299.

D3 is not guilty of conspiracy to steal the TV. That's because he did not help plan the theft or assist in carrying it out. The fact that he knowingly agreed to buy what he knew was stolen goods is not enough, because conspiracy to commit act X requires an intent to help bring about act X, not mere knowledge that others have committed or will commit act X. (Also, the "bring it right over" remark suggests that D3 thought the goods had already been stolen, making it even more unlikely that he would be found to have conspired to steal goods that he thought had already been stolen.)

IV. THE CONSPIRATORIAL OBJECTIVE

A. **The "overt act" requirement:** At common law, the crime of conspiracy is *complete as soon as the agreement has been made*. So at common law, *no "overt act" is required* for there to be a conspiracy.

   1. **Act of one attributable to all:** Even in states that have changed the common-law rule by requiring an overt act, it is *not* necessary that *each D* charged with the conspiracy be shown to have committed an overt act. Instead, if the overt act requirement applies, the overt act of a *single person* will be *attributable to all*.

      a. **MBE Tip:** The MBE examiners like to test you on this point — they try to mousetrap you into thinking that if a particular D did not do any overt act, she can't be liable for conspiracy. This isn't true. At common law (which is what's tested on the MBE unless the particular question tells you otherwise), no overt act is required at all.

         i. **Alibi for underlying crime irrelevant:** This means that a defendant who has a perfect *alibi* (e.g., he's in jail or out of the country) when some overt act in furtherance of the conspiracy occurs, *won't benefit* — once D agrees to the conspiratorial objective with some other person, liability is complete.

         Example: On Friday, D1 and D2 agree to rob the First National Bank of Ames the following Tuesday. D1 gets arrested on Saturday, and remains in jail. On Tuesday, D2 robs the bank himself. D1 (and D2) can be convicted of conspiracy to rob the Bank — the fact that only D2 committed any overt act in furtherance of the conspiracy is irrelevant. (Indeed, at common law the conspiracy was complete the second D1 and D2 reached their agreement, so that no overt act by *either* was required.)

B. **Impossibility:** The same rules concerning *"impossibility"* apply in conspiracy as in attempt. For instance, the defense of *"factual impossibility"* is always rejected.

   Example: D1 and D2 agree to pick the pocket of a certain victim. The pocket turns out to be empty. The Ds are liable for conspiracy to commit larceny.

C. **Substantive liability for crimes of other conspirators:** The most frequently-tested aspect of conspiracy law relates to a member's liability for the *substantive crimes* committed by other members of the conspiracy. This subject is complicated, and requires close analysis.

   1. **Aiding and abetting:** Normally, each conspirator *"aids and abets"* the others in furtherance of the aims of the conspiracy. Where this is the case, a D who has aided and abetted one of the others in accomplishing a particular substantive crime will be liable for that substantive crime — this is not a result having anything to do with conspiracy law, but is instead merely a product of the general rules about accomplice liability (discussed *infra*, pp. 42-50).

      Example: A and B agree to a scheme whereby A will steal a car, pick B up in it, and wait outside the First National Bank while B goes in and robs the teller. A steals the car, picks up B, and delivers B to the bank. Before B can even rob the teller, A is arrested out on the street. B robs the teller anyway. A is clearly liable for the substantive crime of bank robbery, because he has "aided and abetted" B in carrying out this crime. It is also true that A and B are guilty of conspiracy to commit bank robbery, but this fact is not necessary to a finding that A is liable for B's substantive crime — aiding and abetting is all that is required for A to be liable for bank robbery, given that B has actually committed the bank robbery as principal.

2. **Substantive liability without "aiding and abetting":** The more difficult question arises where A and B conspire to commit crime X, and B commits *additional crimes* "in furtherance" of the conspiracy, but without the direct assistance of A. Does A, by his *mere membership* in the conspiracy, become liable for these additional crimes by B in furtherance of the conspiracy?

   a. **Traditional view:** The common-law view — which is what you will normally be tested on in the MBE — is that each member of a conspiracy, by virtue of her *membership alone*, is liable for *reasonably foreseeable crimes* committed by the others in *"furtherance"* of the conspiracy.

      Example: Same basic fact pattern as prior example. Now, however, assume that A knows that B is carrying a gun into the bank, and A also knows that B would rather shoot anyone attempting to stop him than go to prison. However, A has done nothing to help B get the gun, and has not encouraged B to use the gun. While A waits in the car, B goes into the bank and shoots V, a guard, who is trying to capture B. V is seriously wounded. Under the common-law view, if B is liable for assault with a deadly weapon, A will be liable also, merely because (1) he was a member of a conspiracy, and (2) the assault was (from A's perspective) a reasonably-foreseeable one, committed by another member in furtherance of the aims of the conspiracy (robbery with successful escape).

      i. **Crime that was not reasonably foreseeable to other D:** The MBE examiners might give you a scenario in which the "additional crime" is reasonably foreseeable to the accomplice. But the examiners may instead give you a scenario in which A is *not* liable for B's substantive crime, on the grounds that B's crime was either *not reasonably foreseeable* to A, or was not done in furtherance of the conspiracy.

      Example: Able and Baker, brothers, run an illegal "numbers" operation, in which customers come to the brothers' storefront and pay cash to bet on a number. The brothers have never used violence, or been threatened with violence by anyone else. Nor have they ever discussed between themselves whether or when to use violence in pursuit of the operation. One day V, an undercover officer, visits the storefront when only Able is present, picks a number, pays for it, and then arrests Able for illegal gambling. Able, enraged and determined not to be arrested, pulls out a pistol (which Baker did not even know Able owned) and fires at V, wounding him in the arm. While V is lying on the ground, Baker shows up. Baker is arrested by another officer, and does not resist. Able and Baker are charged with the battery of V.

      Even under the common-law view, Baker is not guilty of battery. It's of course true that Able is guilty of battery. It's also true that Baker is guilty of conspiracy to run a gambling operation. But given the lack of any history or planning of violence by the brothers, and Baker's lack of knowledge that Able even possessed a pistol, it was not reasonably foreseeable to Baker that Able would commit a shooting or other battery if arrested. Therefore, even if Baker's firing of the pistol is deemed to have been an act taken in "furtherance of the aims" of the brothers' conspiracy, Baker won't be guilty of the substantive crime of battery. (If Baker had aided and abetted Able's act of shooting — even if this had happened long before the actual shooting [e.g., "If any cop ever tries to arrest us, we'll shoot our way out, right, Able?"]— this *would* be enough to make Baker liable for the battery carried out by Able.)

V. SCOPE: MULTIPLE PARTIES

A. **Party who comes late or leaves early:** Special problems arise as to a conspirator who *enters* the conspiracy *after* it has begun, or *leaves it before* it is finished.

   1. **Party comes late:** One who enters a conspiracy that has *already committed substantive acts* will be a conspirator as to those acts only if he is told about them and *accepts them* as part of the general scheme in which he is participating.

      Example: D is a fence who buys from A and B, two jewelry thieves. D is clearly conspiring to receive stolen property. But he will normally *not* be a conspirator to the original crime of theft, unless he somehow involved himself in that venture, as by making the request for particular items in advance.

   2. **Party who leaves early:** One who *leaves* a conspiracy before it is finished is liable for acts that occur later only if those acts are *fairly within the confines of the conspiracy as it existed* at the time D was still present.

      Example: D agrees to help A and B rob a bank; D is to procure the transportation, and to deliver it to A. D steals a car and delivers it to A, then leaves the conspiracy. D is guilty of conspiring to rob the bank even though he does nothing further, since the bank robbery is part of the original agreement. But if A and B, totally unbeknownst to D, decided after D left the conspiracy that they wished to use the car to rob a grocery store, D would not be guilty of conspiracy to rob the grocery store.

VI. DURATION OF THE CONSPIRACY

A. **Why it matters:** You may have to determine the *ending point* of a conspiracy. Here are some issues on which the ending point may make a difference:

   1. **Who has joined:** A person can be held to have *joined* the conspiracy only if it still existed at the time he got involved in it;

   2. **Statute of limitations:** The *statute of limitations* on conspiracy does not start to run until the conspiracy has *ended*; and

   3. **Statements by co-defendants:** Declarations of co-conspirators may be admissible against each other, despite the hearsay rule, but only if those declarations were made in furtherance of the conspiracy while it was still in progress.

B. **Abandonment:** A conspiracy will come to an end if it is *abandoned* by the participants.

   1. **Abandoned by all:** If *all* the parties abandon the plan, this will be enough to end the conspiracy (and thus, for instance, to start the statute of limitations running).

      a. **No defense to conspiracy charge:** But abandonment does *not* serve as a defense to the *conspiracy charge itself*. Under the common-law approach, the conspiracy is *complete as soon as the agreement is made*. Therefore, abandonment is irrelevant.

      Example: A and B, while in their prison cell, decide to rob the first national bank the Tuesday after they are released. Before they are even released, they decide not to go through with the plan. However, X, to whom they previously confided their plans, turns them in to the authorities. A and B are liable for conspiracy to commit bank robbery, even though they abandoned the plan — their crime of conspiracy was complete as soon as they made their agreement, and their subsequent abandonment did not, at common law, change the result.

2. **Withdrawal by individual conspirator:** A similar rule applies to the *withdrawal* by an *individual conspirator*.

   a. **Procedural issues:** Thus for *procedural* purposes, D's withdrawal ends the conspiracy as to him. So long as D has made an *affirmative act* bringing home the fact of his withdrawal to his confederates, the conspiracy is over as to him, for purposes of: (1) running of the statute of limitations; (2) inadmissibility of declarations by other conspirators after he left; or (3) non-liability for the substantive crimes committed by the others after his departure. (Instead of notifying each of the other conspirators, the person withdrawing can instead notify the police.)

   b. **As defense to conspiracy charge:** But if D tries to show withdrawal as a *substantive defense* against the conspiracy charge itself, he will fail: the common-law rule is that *no act of withdrawal*, even thwarting the conspiracy by turning others in to the police, will be a defense. This comes from the principle that the crime is *complete* once the agreement has been made.

VII. PLURALITY

A. **Significance of the plurality requirement:** At common law, a conspiracy necessarily involves *two or more* persons who are agreeing to the criminal plan. This is called the *"plurality"* requirement. Since on the MBE you should assume that common-law conspiracy rules apply unless you're told otherwise, the plurality requirement may lead to the acquittal of a person who seems to meet all the requirements for conspiracy.

   1. **Feigned agreement:** An important application of the plurality requirement arises where one of the parties to a "conspiracy" is merely *feigning* his agreement. The problem typically arises where one of the parties is secretly an *undercover agent*.

      a. **Common-law view says plurality requirement not satisfied:** Under the common-law approach, if only one party really means to agree, and the other(s) is/are merely feigning agreement, the plurality requirement is *not met*, so the "real" conspirator cannot be convicted.

         Example: *A* and *B* agree that they will rob a bank. *B* is secretly an undercover agent, and never has any intention of committing the robbery. In fact, *B* makes sure that the FBI is present at the bank, and *A* is arrested when he and *B* show up. Under the common-law application of the plurality requirement, *A* cannot be convicted of conspiracy to commit bank robbery, because there was no second person who met all the requirements (including true agreement) for conspiracy.

   2. **Modern view allows conspiracy finding:** But the modern (and Model Penal Code) view *reverses* the common-law approach. Under the modern/M.P.C. view, regardless of one party's lack of subjective intent to carry out the object crime, *the other party may nonetheless be convicted of conspiracy*. This is the so-called *"unilateral"* approach to conspiracy — a given individual is liable for conspiracy if he "agrees with another person or persons," whether or not the other person is really part of the plan. See, e.g., M.P.C., §5.03, Comm. 2(b). Thus under the unilateral view, *A* in the above example has clearly agreed to rob the bank (even though *B* has not truly agreed), and *A* can therefore be prosecuted for conspiracy.

   3. **MBE Tip:** On the MBE, the examiners will typically tell you *either* (a) that the jurisdiction follows the common-law view (in which case the sole "real" conspirator cannot be convicted)

or (b) that the jurisdiction follows what the examiners call either the "unilateral" view or the "Model Penal Code" view (in which case the sole real conspirator *can* be convicted). Once you identify which approach the examiners are telling you to use in the feigned-agreement situation, getting the right answer should be easy.

B. Statutory purpose not to punish one party: The court will not convict a party of conspiracy where it finds that the legislature *intended not to punish* such a party for the *substantive* crime. Typically, this situation arises where the legislature that defined the substantive crime recognized that two parties were necessarily involved, but chose to punish only one of those parties as being the "more guilty" one. As the idea is usually put, a member of a *"protected class"* — one whom the legislature intended to protect by criminalizing particular conduct — can't be convicted of conspiracy to commit that underlying conduct either.

   1. Statutory rape: The classic illustration is *statutory rape*. All courts agree that where an underage person has sex with an adult, the *underaged person cannot be charged* with conspiracy to commit statutory rape — since the whole purpose of the statutory rape provision is to protect underage persons, allowing a conspiracy conviction of the protected person would defeat the purpose of the statute.

C. Inconsistent disposition: On the MBE, the plurality requirement is most likely to be relevant where one or more members of the alleged conspiracy either cannot legally be convicted, or end up being acquitted. Either of these scenarios this may well prevent the conviction of the others. For now, let's assume that there are only *two* purported members, *A* and *B*.

   1. Acquittal: Where *A* and *B* are tried in the *same proceeding*, and *A* is acquitted, all courts agree that *B must also be acquitted.*

   2. One is member of protected class: Now, assume that *A* is a *member of a "protected class,"* whom the legislature has decided cannot be convicted of the underlying crime. Under the *common-law* conspiracy rules this fact means that *B* (assumed to be the sole other possible conspirator) *cannot be convicted either*. This result comes from the following reasoning: (1) because *A* is a member of the protected class, *A* can't be convicted of conspiracy to commit the underlying crime either; (2) that facts leaves *B* as the only possible conspirator (remember we're assuming that only *A* and *B* made the agreement); and (3) the common-law plurality requirement means that *B* may not be convicted of conspiracy either.

      a. Statutory rape: The classic illustration of this "protected class" consequence is *statutory rape*. As we saw above, the minor can't be convicted of conspiracy to commit statutory rape; therefore, at common law the adult can't be convicted of conspiracy to commit statutory rape either (assuming that only one adult and the minor are involved).

      Example: Barbara is 22 and Adam is 15. The jurisdiction makes it statutory rape for a person over the age of 21 to have sexual intercourse with a person under the age of 16. Barbara and Adam agree to have sex, and then do so. Barbara is charged with conspiracy to violate the statutory rape provision. Assume that all relevant common-law doctrines apply.

      Barbara cannot be convicted of conspiracy at common law. First, statutory rape provisions are designed to protect the minor. Therefore, in all states the minor who has sex with an adult cannot be prosecuted for either statutory rape (of himself) or conspiracy to commit statutory rape. Since the only possible conspirators here are Barbara and Adam, and since Adam cannot be prosecuted or convicted of conspiracy, that would leave Barbara as the only conspirator who could be convicted. But the common-law plurality requirement says that a single person cannot be guilty of conspiracy — there must either be (legally speaking) two or more conspirators, or no conspirators. Therefore here there are no conspirators.

b. Modern / Model Penal Code "unilateral" view: But under the modern/Model Penal Code *"unilateral"* view of conspiracy (see *supra*, p. 39), the fact that all but one conspirator are members of a protected class, or have some sort of *personal defense,* won't bar the conviction of the one conspirator who doesn't have such a defense. So in the above example, in a court following the unilateral view Barbara *could* be convicted of conspiracy. Another illustration is the "personal defense" scenario shown in the following example.

Example: D1 is a foreign diplomat. D2 is an American citizen. The two agree that they will burglarize a bank together. Before they can carry out the plan, the police get wind of it, and arrest them both. At the start of their joint trial for conspiracy to commit burglary, D1 moves to dismiss the case against him on the grounds that he has diplomatic immunity. The court agrees, and dismisses the case. If the jurisdiction follows the Model Penal Code view of all relevant issues, does the dismissal of the case against D1 bar the court from convicting D2?

No. The Model Penal Code follows the modern "unilateral" view of conspiracy, whereby even if all defendants except one either don't satisfy the elements of conspiracy or have some personal defense, the sole remaining defendant can still be convicted. So the fact that D1 cannot and will not be convicted due to diplomatic immunity will not shield D2, the sole remaining alleged conspirator, from conviction for conspiracy.

D. Wharton's Rule: Under the common-law *Wharton's Rule*, where a substantive offense is defined so as to necessarily require more than one person, a prosecution for the substantive offense must be brought, rather than a conspiracy prosecution. The classic examples are *adultery*, *incest*, *bigamy* and *dueling* crimes.

Example: Howard and Wanda are husband and wife. Marsha is a single woman. Howard and Marsha agree to meet later one night at a specified motel, to have sex. They are arrested before the rendezvous can take place. Since the crime of adultery is defined so as to require at least two people, Howard and Marsha cannot be convicted of conspiracy to commit adultery, under the common-law Wharton's Rule.

1. **More persons than necessary:** A key *exception* to Wharton's Rule is that there is no bar to a conspiracy conviction where there were *more participants* than were logically necessary to complete the crime.

   Example: Same facts as above example. Now, however, assume that Steve, Howard's friend, has urged him to have sex with Marsha, and has reserved the hotel room for them. Despite Wharton's Rule, Howard, Marsha and Steve can all be prosecuted for conspiracy, because there were more persons involved than merely the two necessary direct parties to the substantive crime of adultery.

2. **Defined to require multiple culpable persons:** Another thing to remember about Wharton's Rule is that the Rule applies only where if the law defining the substantive crime *requires the culpable participation of two or more people.* LaFave, §6.5(g)(4), p. 611.

   Example: Reconsider the statutory rape example on p. 40, in which an adult (Barbara) and a minor (Adam) agree to have sex and then have sex. Because statutory rape does not require guilty participation of more than one person, Wharton's Rule does not apply. Therefore, the Rule doesn't bar Barbara from being convicted of conspiracy to commit statutory rape. (On the other hand, the *plurality* requirement *does* bar Barbara from being convicted, at least at common law; that's the whole point of the Example on p. 40.)

VIII. PUNISHMENT

A. **Cumulative sentencing allowed:** Most states allow a *cumulative sentence*, i.e., conviction for *both conspiracy and the underlying crime.* LaFave, §6.5(h), p. 612. Therefore, that's the rule you should apply on the MBE.

> **Example:** D1 and D2 agree to rob a 7/11 at gunpoint the next Friday night. They meet as scheduled, and commit the robbery. They are arrested shortly thereafter. The two may be charged with the separate crimes of robbery and conspiracy to commit robbery. Each may be convicted of both counts, and given consecutive sentences.

CHAPTER 7
ACCOMPLICE LIABILITY AND SOLICITATION

I. PARTIES TO CRIME

A. **Modern nomenclature:** Modern courts and statutes dispense with common-law designations like "principal in the first degree," "accessory before the fact," "accessory after the fact," etc. Instead, modern courts and statutes usually refer only to two different types of criminal actors: "accomplices" and "principals." These are the only terms you're likely to see on the MBE.

1. **Accomplice:** An *"accomplice"* is one who *assists* or *encourages* the carrying out of a crime, but does not commit the *actus reus*.

2. **Principal:** A *"principal,"* by contrast, is one who *commits* the *actus reus* (with or without the assistance of an accomplice).

   > **Example:** As part of a bank robbery plan, A steals a car, and drives B to the First National Bank. A remains in the car acting as lookout. B goes inside and demands money, which he receives and leaves the bank with. A drives the getaway car. Since B carried out the physical act of robbery, he is a "principal" to bank robbery. Since A merely assisted B, but did not carry out the physical act of bank robbery, he is an "accomplice" to bank robbery.

3. **Accomplice is guilty:** The most important rule to remember in dealing with accomplices is that generally, the accomplice is *guilty of the substantive crime* he assisted or encouraged, if the principal carried out that crime.

4. **Significance of distinction:** Relatively little turns today on the distinction between "accomplice" and "principal." The main significance of the distinction is that, generally, the accomplice may not be convicted unless the prosecution *also proves that the principal is guilty* of the substantive crime in question (see *infra*, p. 47).

II. ACCOMPLICES — THE ACT REQUIREMENT

A. **Liability for aiding and abetting:** The key principle of accomplice liability is that one who *aids, abets, encourages* or *assists* another to perform a crime, will himself be *liable for that crime*.

   > **Example 1:** Same facts as the above bank-robbery example. A is guilty of bank robbery, even though he did not himself use any violence, or even set foot inside the bank or touch the money. It's enough that A aided or encouraged the robbery by driving B to the location and being a lookout.

Example 2: A and B have a common enemy, V. A and B, in conversation, realize that they would both like V dead. A encourages B to kill V, and supplies B with a rifle with which to do the deed. B kills V with the rifle. A is guilty of murder — he assisted and encouraged another to commit murder, so he is himself guilty of murder.

1. **Words alone may be enough:** *Words*, by themselves, will often be enough to constitute the requisite link between accomplice and principal — if the words constituted *encouragement* and *approval* of the crime, and thereby assisted commission of the crime, then the speaker is liable even if he did not take any physical acts.

    a. **Fight scenario:** On the MBE, you'll often see it be the case that "words alone" are sufficient for accomplice liability in a group *fight* scenario. If *A* encourages *B* to commit acts constituting, say, battery or murder, and *B* commits those acts, that's enough to make *A* an accomplice, and thus to make *A* substantively liable for *B*'s completed crime of battery or murder.

        Example: Joe and Jerry are members of the Jets gang, and Steve and Sue are members of the rival Sharks gang. One day, all four happen to gather on the town square without any pre-arrangement. Steve shouts an insult at Jerry. Jerry shouts back, but does not take any other immediate action. Joe whispers in Jerry's ear, "Kill that [expletive deleted]!" Jerry pulls out a knife he happens to be carrying, and stabs Steve to death. (Assume that Jerry's conduct constitutes murder rather than voluntary manslaughter.) Joe takes no other action, nor makes any other comment, during the entire episode.

        Joe is an accomplice to the killing by Jerry, and is therefore guilty of murder. This is so because Joe rendered assistance or encouragement to Jerry (he "aided and abetted" him) in Jerry's commission of the murder. The fact that Joe's involvement consisted of "words alone" doesn't lessen his accomplice liability.

2. **Presence at crime scene not required:** One can be an accomplice even *without* ever being *present* at the *crime scene*. That is, the requisite encouragement, assistance, etc., may all take place before the actual occasion on which the crime takes place.

    Example: On the facts of Example 2 above, A is not shielded from guilt of murder merely because he was 1,000 miles away when B fired the rifle at V.

3. **Presence not sufficient:** Conversely, *mere presence* at the scene of the crime is *not*, by itself, sufficient to render one an accomplice. The prosecution must also show that D was at the crime scene for the *purpose of approving and encouraging* commission of the offense.

    Example: On the facts of the above Joe/Jerry gang-fight example, Joe's mere presence at the scene of the fight, and his friendship with Jerry, wouldn't be enough to give Joe accomplice liability for the killing committed by Jerry. It is only Joe's encouragement of Jerry's act of killing that caused Joe to have accomplice liability.

    a. **Presence as evidence:** But D's presence at the crime scene can, of course, be convincing circumstantial *evidence* that D encouraged or assisted the crime.

        Example: If the prosecution shows that A's presence at the crime was so that he could serve as a "look out" while B carried out the physical acts, A is obviously an accomplice and is thus guilty of the substantive crime.

4. **Failure to intervene:** Normally, the mere fact that D *failed to intervene* to prevent the crime will *not* make him an accomplice, even if the intervention could have been readily done.

    Example: Once more on the facts of the above Joe/Jerry gang-fight Example: now, let's suppose that Joe remained silent throughout the encounter, including after Jerry pulled the knife. Assume further that Joe (1) knew that Jerry would likely stab Steve; (2) desired that Jerry stab Steve; and (3) failed to hold Jerry back or dissuade him from attacking Steve, even though Joe knew that he could safely and effectively do that. Nothing in these facts would give Joe accomplice liability for Jerry's act of killing — active encouragement or assistance, not mere failure-to-intervene (even if accompanied by the requisite mental state for the underlying crime) is what is required for accomplice liability.

- a. **Duty to intervene:** There are a few situations, however, where D has an *affirmative legal duty* to intervene. If he fails to exercise this duty, he may be an accomplice.

    Example: Under general legal principles, both parents have an affirmative duty to safeguard the welfare of their child. Mother severely beats Child while Father remains silently by. Father is probably an accomplice to battery or child abuse, because he had an affirmative duty to protect Child and failed to carry out that duty.

5. **"Crime for hire" scenario:** Accomplice liability will figure in *"crime for hire"* scenarios on the MBE. Thus where D1 conceives of a crime, and hires an intermediary, D2, to carry out the crime, D1 is an "accomplice" even though she is the moving force and originator of the crime. If the crime is carried out by D2, D1 will of course be substantively liable for the crime just as D2 will be.

    Example: Wife desires to have her husband, Hubby, die so that Wife can collect his life insurance. Wife advertises on the Internet for a hired killer. Ken answers the ad. Wife agrees to pay Ken $10,000 if Hubby is killed. Ken shoots Hubby to death. Wife is an "accomplice" to the murder. By virtue of that accomplice status, Wife is guilty of murder.

III. ACCOMPLICES — MENTAL STATE

- A. **General rule:** For D to have accomplice liability for a crime, the prosecution must generally show the following about D's *mental state*: (1) that D *intentionally aided or encouraged* the other to commit the criminal act; and (2) that D had the mental state *necessary for the crime* actually committed by the other.

    1. **Must have purpose to further crime:** The first requirement listed above means that it is not enough that D intends acts which have the *effect* of inducing another person to commit a crime — D must have the *purpose* of helping bring that crime about.

        Example: D writes to X, "Your wife is sleeping with V." X, enraged, shoots V to death. D does not have the requisite mental state for accomplice liability for murder or manslaughter merely by virtue of intending to write the letter — the prosecution must also show that D intended to encourage X to kill V.

    2. **Must have *mens rea* for crime actually committed:** D must be shown to have the *mens rea* for the *underlying crime*. Thus if the person assisted commits a *different crime* from that intended by D, D may escape liability.

        Example: D believes that X will commit a burglary, and wants to help X do so. D procures a weapon for X, and drives X to the crime scene. Unbeknownst to D, X really intends all along to use the weapon to frighten V so that X can rape V; X carries out this scheme. D is not an accomplice to rape, because he did not have the *mens rea* — that is, he did not intend to cause unconsented-to sexual intercourse. The fact that D may have had the *mens rea* for burglary or robbery is irrelevant to the rape charge, though D might be held liable for attempted burglary or attempted robbery on these facts.

3. **Police undercover agents:** Where a *police undercover agent* helps bring about a crime by a suspect, the agent will usually have a valid defense based on his lack of the appropriate mental state.

4. **Mere knowledge not sufficient:** As with conspiracy (see *supra*, p. 35), it is *not* enough for accomplice liability that the prosecution is merely able to show that D *supplied goods or services* with *knowledge* that his supplies might enable others to pursue a criminal objective. Instead, the supplier must be shown to have *desired* to further the criminal objective. On the other hand, this desire or intent can be shown by *circumstantial* evidence, as with conspiracy.

   a. **"Stake in venture":** For instance, the supplier's desire to further the criminal objective can be shown circumstantially by the fact that the supplier acquired a *"stake in the venture"* (e.g., that the supplier was promised a bonus expressed as a percentage of the profit from the crime).

   b. **Inflated charges:** Similarly, the fact that the supplier charged his criminal purchasers an *inflated price* compared with the cost of the items if sold for legal purposes, is evidence of intent to further the criminal objective.

   c. **Serious crime:** The more *serious* the underlying crime (as known to the supplier), the more likely it is that the supplier's participation will be found to make him an accomplice to that crime.

      Example of (b) and (c): Jill visits a gun store owned by Dave, and explains to him that she needs a small pistol to use in an upcoming bank robbery. Dave answers, "You shouldn't blab about your criminal plans to someone like me. Now, I'll have to charge you a lot extra because of the risk you've put me under." He charges her five times the market price for the revolver. Jill then uses the gun in the bank robbery, by pointing it at V, a cashier. The gun accidentally goes off, killing V. Dave is charged with murder, in a state that applies felony-murder.

      Dave can be convicted. Although a supplier of a good or service normally will not become liable as an accomplice to a crime merely because he knows the customer intends to commit that crime with the supplied item, additional factors may change this outcome. The fact that the supplier charges a very inflated rate, and the fact that the proposed crime is (as the supplier knows) a very serious one, are both factors that dramatically increase the chance that the supplier will be found to be an accomplice. So here, the presence of both of these factors means that a court would likely find that Dave was an accomplice to Jill's announced bank robbery. In that event, Dave becomes substantively liable for the robbery, and for the felony-murder that was part of that robbery. (For more about the use of felony-murder to convict accomplices to the underlying felony, see *infra*, p. 56.)

B. **Assistance with crime of recklessness or negligence:** If the underlying crime is not one that requires intent, but merely *recklessness or negligence*, most courts hold D *liable* as an accomplice upon a mere showing that D was reckless or negligent concerning the risk that the principal would commit the crime.

   1. **"Depraved indifference" murder:** For instance, most courts are willing to impose accomplice liability on D where X commits a killing with *reckless indifference* to human life, and D (acting with the same reckless indifference) encourages X in the conduct leading to the death.

      a. **Drag races and gun battles:** Thus if D and X engage in joint activity of an extremely dangerous sort — such as a *drag race* on a city street, or a *gun battle* while bystanders are nearby — D may well be held liable as an accomplice to depraved-heart murder if X's act results in a bystander's death. That may be true even if D and X are opposing each other — even trying to kill each other — instead of being allied in a cooperative activity.

  b. Carrying dangerous weapons: Another scenario you may see on the MBE involving accomplice liability for depraved-indifference murder is where multiple Ds all *carry very dangerous weapons into a robbery* or other crime scene, and then a gunfight breaks out that leads to death. Even in a jurisdiction that does not apply the felony murder doctrine (*infra*, p. 54), D1's act of assisting D2 in carrying out the armed robbery may impose on D1 accomplice liability for the resulting depraved-indifference murder.

   Example: D1, D2 and D3 all agree to carry loaded fully-automatic machine guns for a robbery of the First National Bank. To terrify the tellers and customers and make sure that they don't summon the police, D1 shouts, "Nobody move," and then fires a sustained burst of bullets (about 20 in all) at the ceiling. A bullet ricochets off the marble that lines the ceiling, then strikes and kills a teller. D1, D2 and D3 are all charged with murder. The jurisdiction does not apply felony-murder.

   D2 and D3 can be convicted of murder on an accomplice-liability theory. D1 acted with depraved indifference to the value of human life by firing the weapon in circumstances where there was a large risk of just the sort of ricochet that occurred. D2 and D3 aided and abetted D1 in the commission of the underlying robbery, and in the carrying by all Ds of the loaded machine guns. Therefore, D2 and D3 (not just D1) probably had the requisite depraved-indifference mental state. Consequently, D2 and D3 are accomplices to the killing, making them substantively guilty of depraved-indifference murder.

IV. ACCOMPLICES — ADDITIONAL CRIMES BY PRINCIPAL

 A. "Natural and probable" results that are not intended: A frequently-tested scenario on the MBE involves a principal who commits not only the offense that the accomplice has assisted or encouraged, but *other offenses* as well. The accomplice will be liable for these additional crimes if and only if: (1) the additional offenses are the *"natural and probable"* consequences of the conduct that D did intend to assist (even though D did not intend these additional offenses); *and* (2) the principal committed the additional crimes *in furtherance of the original criminal objective* that D was trying to assist.

  Example: D1 and D2 agree to commit an armed robbery of a convenience store owned by V. D1 personally abhors violence. However, he knows that D2 is armed, and that D2 has been known to shoot in the course of prior robberies. D1 urges D2 not to shoot no matter what, but D2 refuses to make this promise. During the robbery, V attempts to trip an alarm, and D2 shoots her to death. A court would probably hold that D1 is liable for murder on an accomplice theory, since the shooting was a "natural and probable" consequence of armed robbery, and the shooting was carried out to further the original criminal objective of getting away with robbery.

  On the other hand, if D2 forcibly raped V instead of shooting her, and D1 had no reason to expect D2 to do this, D1 would not be liable for rape on an accomplice theory. This is because the rape was not the "natural and probable" consequence of the conduct encouraged by D1, nor was it committed in furtherance of the original objective of robbery.

  1. Unforeseeable: Thus if D can show that the additional offenses were *unlikely* or *unforeseeable*, D will not be liable for them.

   Example: This is why D1 would not be liable for rape on the above hypothetical.

  2. Felony-murder and misdemeanor-manslaughter rules: Wherever the additional offense is a *death*, the accomplice may end up being guilty not because of the "natural and probable consequences" rule, but because of the specialized *felony-murder* or *misdemeanor-manslaughter* rules.

a. Felony-murder: On the MBE, interaction between accomplice-liability and *felony-murder* is especially likely. Under the felony-murder rule (discussed *infra*, p. 54), if in the course of certain dangerous felonies the felon kills another, even *accidentally*, he is liable for murder. The examiners like to give you fact patterns in which an accessory helps a principal commit dangerous-felony X, and an unintended death directly results. *The accessory ends up being liable for murder*, on the theory that the accessory is *guilty of the dangerous felony* by operation of the accomplice-liability principles, and that guilt then makes the accessory directly guilty of felony-murder. This result occurs even if the jurisdiction does not make an accomplice automatically liable for "natural and probable" consequences of other crimes by the principal.

Example: D1 and D2 agree to commit an armed robbery together, with D2 carrying the only gun. D1 does not desire that anybody be shot. D2 points his gun at V and asks for money; the gun accidentally goes off, killing V. D1 is probably guilty of murder on these facts. However, this is not because V's death was a "natural and probable consequence" of armed robbery.

Instead, it is because under the felony-murder doctrine, even an accidental death that directly stems from the commission of a dangerous felony such as armed robbery will constitute murder. Since D1 was D2's accomplice in the armed robbery, D1 is liable for armed robbery. Since the killing occurred in the furtherance of the robbery *by D1* (even though he was not the shooter), and since D1 had the mental state required for felony-murder (intent to commit a dangerous felony), D1 is liable for murder without any use of the "natural and probable consequences" rule.

V. GUILT OF THE PRINCIPAL

A. Principal must be guilty: Most courts hold that the accomplice cannot be convicted unless the prosecution shows that the person being aided or encouraged — the principal — is *in fact guilty* of the underlying crime.

Example: Iago falsely tells Othello that Othello's wife Desdemona is having an affair; Iago hopes that Othello will kill her in a fit of jealousy. Othello does so, without further involvement by Iago. Note that Othello is guilty only of voluntary manslaughter (not murder), assuming that he acted in the heat of passion. Most courts would hold that Iago cannot be convicted of being an accomplice to murder, because Othello, the principal, is guilty only of the lesser offense. [Cf. *People v. McCoy* (2001)] (But for analysis of why Iago is guilty of murder as a *principal*, see *infra*, p. 48.)

1. MBE tip: The MBE examiners like to test you on this point — they give you a fact pattern in which A does lots of aiding and abetting of a crime to be carried out by B, but B never completes the underlying crime. Obviously A *can't have accomplice liability* in this situation, but the fact pattern can hide this result. So you have to look closely to verify that the principal really committed the underlying crime.

Example: Acc and Prin agree that Prin will break into a particular home at night to steal any portable electronic devices in it. Acc will drive Prin to the site, will serve as lookout, and will drive them both away afterward. Acc drives Prin to the site, and waits in the car while Prin goes around to the back. Prin has second thoughts, and never even attempts to break into the house. He then comes back to the car, and, lying, says, "I got inside, but they didn't have anything good so I left." As they drive away, both are arrested and charged with burglary.

Acc cannot be convicted of burglary based on an accomplice theory. That's because Prin is not guilty as a principal — he didn't commit the *actus reus*, breaking and entering with intent to commit a felony. Therefore, even though Acc gave assistance to the venture, and had the requisite mental state (desire that the burglary take place), Acc has no accomplice liability. (He is guilty of *conspiracy* to commit burglary, and *attempted* burglary as an accomplice, but not *completed* burglary.)

2. **Principal's conviction not necessary:** But it is not necessary that the principal be *convicted*.

    Example: A is charged with assisting B to commit a robbery. B is never arrested or brought to trial. Instead, B gets immunity and turns state's evidence against A. A can be convicted of being an accomplice to the robbery upon proof that B committed the robbery, and that A helped B carry it out — the fact that B is never charged or convicted is irrelevant.

3. **Inconsistent verdicts:** But if the principal is actually *acquitted*, the accomplice must normally be acquitted as well, according to the majority view. This is clearly true if the principal is acquitted in the *same trial*, and probably true even if the principal is acquitted in an *earlier* trial. [*People v. Taylor* (Cal. 1974)]

B. **Conviction of principal for use of innocent agent:** But in some "guilty accomplice but innocent principal" cases, the "accomplice" will in fact be, legally speaking, *a principal*. Where *A* intentionally uses *B* as an *innocent dupe*, and *B* commits what would be a crime if *B* had had the requisite mental state, then *A* will be liable for that crime not as an accomplice but as a principal. And the same will also be true if *A*, acting with intent to bring about a crime, recruits *B* who has *some culpability* but not enough to have the mental state for the crime. (See, e.g., M.P.C. §2.06(2)(a), making one person liable for the acts of another when "acting with the kind of culpability that is sufficient for the commission of the offense, he causes an *innocent or irresponsible* person to engage in such conduct.")

   Example 1: Consider again the Example on p. 47: Iago falsely tells Othello that Othello's wife Desdemona is having an affair; Iago hopes that Othello will kill her in a fit of jealousy. Othello does so, without further involvement by Iago. Assume that Othello is guilty only of voluntary manslaughter (not murder), because he acted in the heat of passion. Although according to the majority view Iago can't be guilty of murder as accessory because Othello doesn't have the mental state for murder (that's the whole point of the example on p. 47), most courts say that Iago can be found guilty of murder as a principal.

   Example 2: D wants to burglarize a house and steal its TVs. He places a ladder up against a second-floor window. Then, standing on the street in front of the house, D stops a small child, X, who is passing by, and explains (falsely) that this is D's house and that D has locked himself out. D then proposes that X climb up the ladder, open the unlocked window, climb inside, go downstairs, unlock the front door, and let D in. X, believing the truth of what D is saying, does all these things. The moment X enters the window, a police car comes along, and this causes D to flee.

   D is guilty of burglary as a principal, even though he never physically entered the house. When D induced the innocent agent X to enter for the purpose of facilitating D's felonious entry, D's guilt of burglary was complete. That is, D will be treated the same way as if he had entered the house himself with intent to commit a felony within. (At the moment X entered, the burglary by D was complete, even though no larceny ever occurred; see *infra*, p. 74.)

   1. **Liability for attempt:** By the way, the same "innocent dupe" analysis can apply to make the principal guilty of an *attempted* crime. That is, if the dupe doesn't succeed in carrying out the actus reus, the mastermind/principal will still be guilty of attempting the crime in question.

Example: Same facts as Example 2 above. Now, however, assume that X gets halfway up the ladder, then gets scared, climbs down, and runs away. D is guilty of attempted burglary as a principal.

VI. WITHDRAWAL BY THE ACCOMPLICE

A. **Withdrawal as defense:** One who has given aid or encouragement prior to a crime may *withdraw* and thus avoid accomplice liability. In other words, withdrawal is generally a *defense* to accomplice liability (in contrast to the conspiracy situation, where it is usually not a defense to the conspiracy charge itself, merely to substantive crimes later committed in furtherance of the conspiracy). But the withdrawal will only be effective if D has in some sense *undone* the effects of his assistance or encouragement.

> **Example:** X tells D that X wants to rob a gas station at gun point, and that he needs a gun to do so. D supplies X with a gun for this purpose. D then has second thoughts, and takes the gun back from X, while also telling X, "I don't think this robbery is a good idea." X gets a different gun from someone else, and carries out the same robbery of the same store. D is not guilty of being an accomplice to the robbery, because he withdrew, in a way that undid the effect of his earlier assistance and encouragement.

1. **Effect of aid must be undone:** But understand that it is not enough that D has a subjective change of heart, and gives no further assistance prior to the crime. He must, at the very least, make it *clear to the other party* that he is repudiating his past aid or encouragement.

2. **Verbal withdrawal not always enough:** If D's aid has been only *verbal*, he may be able to withdraw merely by stating to the "principal" that he now withdraws and disapproves of the project. But if D's assistance has been more *tangible*, he probably has to take *affirmative action* to undo his effects.

    > **Example 1:** On the facts of the prior example, where D supplies a gun to X, it probably would not be enough for D to say, "I think the robbery is a bad idea," while letting X keep the gun — D probably has to get the gun back.
    >
    > **Example 2:** A and B agree that A will act as driver, lookout, and getaway-car-driver while B enters and robs the First National Bank. A drives B to the location, and B enters the Bank. A thinks better of the plan, and drives away while B is in the Bank. B drops his gun during the robbery, and the gun goes off, hitting and killing a teller. A and B are both charged with felony-murder (which the jurisdiction applies).
    >
    > A has not successfully withdrawn as an accomplice. That's because he did not bring home to B the fact that he was withdrawing. (Furthermore, given that he has given the tangible assistance of dropping B off at the robbery site, A would probably have to take affirmative action to undo his aiding-and-abetting, such as by contacting the authorities.) Since A remained an accomplice while B did the actual robbery, he is substantively guilty of bank robbery. Since A is himself guilty of bank robbery, the felony-murder doctrine means that A is also guilty of murder, due to the death that has occurred during the course of the robbery (even though the death was brought about more directly by B's act than by A's.)

    a. **Warning to authorities:** Alternatively, D can almost always make an effective withdrawal by *warning the authorities* prior to commission of the crime.

3. **Not required that crime be thwarted:** Regardless of the means used to withdraw, it is *not necessary* that D actually *thwart* the crime.

    > **Example:** D encourages X to commit a particular burglary at a specified time and place. X thinks better of it, and leaves a message at the local police station alerting the police to the

place and time for the crime. He does not make any effort to talk X out of the crime, however. Due to police inefficiency, the message gets lost, and X carries out the crime. D's notice to the authorities will probably be enough to constitute an effective withdrawal, even though D was not successful in actually thwarting the crime.

VII. POST-CRIME ASSISTANCE

A. **Accessory after the fact:** One who knowingly gives assistance to felon, for the purpose of helping him *avoid apprehension* following his crime, is an *accessory after the fact*. Under modern law, the accessory after the fact is *not liable* for the *felony itself*, as an accomplice would be. Instead, he has committed a distinct crime based upon obstruction of justice, and his punishment does not depend on the punishment for the underlying felony. MBE fact patterns rarely involve an accessory after the fact.

VIII. SOLICITATION

A. **Solicitation defined:** The common-law crime of *solicitation* occurs when one *requests or encourages another* to perform a criminal act, regardless of whether the latter agrees.

   1. **Utility:** The main utility of the crime is that it allows punishment of the solicitor if the person who is requested to commit the crime *refuses*.

      Example: Wendy is unhappily married to Herbert, and has been having an affair with Bart. Wendy says to Bart, "Won't you please kill Herbert? If you do, we can live happily ever after." Bart does not respond either way, but tells the police what has happened. The police arrest Wendy before Bart takes any action regarding Herbert. On these facts, Wendy is guilty of solicitation — she has requested or encouraged another to perform a criminal act, and it does not matter that the other has refused.

B. **No overt act required:** The crime of solicitation is never construed so as to require an *overt act* — as soon as D makes her request or proposal, the crime is complete (as in the above example).

C. **Change of heart, and renunciation:** At common law, the crime of solicitation is complete as soon as the solicitor makes her request. Lafave, §6.1, p. 526. Therefore, at common law it makes no difference that the solicitor later *changes her mind and withdraws the request*.

   Example: Wife, desiring that her husband Hubby die so that Wife can get the insurance proceeds, asks her cousin Cuzz to shoot Hubby to death. Cuzz agrees to do the shooting in one week, provided that Wife pays Cuzz $10,000 two days in advance. Cuzz has no intention of shooting Hubby, and immediately tells the police about Wife's proposal. Meanwhile, Wife changes her mind, and never brings Cuzz the money. However, she doesn't say anything to Cuzz withdrawing the request.

   Under the common-law view, the crime of solicitation was complete as soon as Wife made the proposition to Cuzz. Wife's change of mind does not undo that crime.

CHAPTER 8
HOMICIDE AND OTHER CRIMES AGAINST THE PERSON

I. HOMICIDE — INTRODUCTION

A. **Different grades of homicide:** Any unlawful taking of the life of another falls within the generic class *"homicide."* The two principal kinds of homicide are *murder* and *manslaughter*.

II. MURDER — GENERALLY

A. **Definition of "murder":** There is no simple definition of "murder" that is sufficient to distinguish killings that are murder from killings that are not. At the most general level, murder is defined as the *unlawful killing* of *another person*. There are four different mental states that will suffice; see *infra*, p. 51.

B. **Elements of murder:** Here are the elements which the prosecution must prove to obtain a murder conviction:

1. *Actus reus:* There must be *conduct by the defendant* (an *"actus reus"*), either an affirmative act by D or an omission by D where he had a duty to act.

2. *Corpus delecti:* There must be shown to have been a *death* of the victim. Death is the *"corpus delecti"* ("body of the crime") of murder. But the prosecution does *not* have to produce a *corpse*. Like any element of any crime, existence of death may be proved by *circumstantial evidence*.

3. *Mens rea:* D must be shown to have had an appropriate *mental state* for murder. The required mental state is sometimes called *"malice aforethought,"* but this is merely a term of art, which can be satisfied by any of several mental states. In most jurisdictions (and on the MBE), any of the four following mental states will suffice:

    a. An intent to *kill*;

    b. An intent to *commit grievous bodily injury*;

    c. *Reckless indifference* to the *value of human life* (or a *"depraved heart,"* as the concept is sometimes put); and

    d. An intent to commit any of certain non-homicide *dangerous felonies*.

    Below, we cover each of these mental states separately.

4. **Proximate cause:** There must be a *causal relationship* between D's act and V's death. D's conduct must be both the "cause in fact" of the death and also its "proximate cause."

    a. **Year-and-a-day rule:** Most states still apply the common-law proximate cause rule that applies only in murder cases: V must die within a *year and a day* of D's conduct. (See *supra*, p. 16.)

C. **Intent-to-kill murder:** The most common state of mind that suffices for murder is the *intent to kill*.

1. **Desire to kill:** This intent exists, of course, when D has the *desire* to bring about the death of another.

2. **Substantial certainty of death:** The requisite intent also exists where D knows that death is *substantially certain* to occur, but does not actively desire to bring about V's death.

    Example: D, a terrorist, puts a bomb onto an airliner. He does not desire the death of any passengers, but knows that at least one death is almost certain to occur. D has the state of mind needed for "intent to kill" murder.

3. **Ill-will unnecessary:** The requisite intent to kill may exist even where D does not bear any *ill will* towards the victim. Thus "mercy killings" are ordinarily murder.

    Example: D's wife, V, is suffering from terminal cancer, but still has at least several weeks to live. D feeds her poison without telling her what this is, in order to spare her suffering. D has the mental state required for "intent to kill" murder — he has desired to bring about the death of another. Therefore, D is guilty of murder if V dies earlier than she otherwise would have.

4. **Compare with voluntary manslaughter:** It does not automatically follow that because D intended to kill and did kill, D is guilty of murder. For instance, most cases of *voluntary manslaughter* — generally, a killing occurring in a "heat of passion" — are ones where D intended to kill. In a prosecution for intent-to-kill murder, the mental state is an intent to kill *not accompanied by other redeeming or mitigating factors*.

D. **Intent-to-do-serious-bodily-injury murder:** At common law and in most states, the *mens rea* requirement for murder is satisfied if D intended not to kill, but to do *serious bodily injury* to V.

> **Example:** D is angry at V for welching on a debt. D beats V with brass knuckles, intending only to break V's nose and jaw, and to knock out most of his teeth. At common law, D has the mental state required for murder of the "intent to do serious bodily injury" sort. Therefore, if V unexpectedly dies of the wounds, D is guilty of murder in these states.

1. **Attack with deadly weapon:** The classic scenario on the MBE for intent-to-do-serious-bodily-injury murder is the *"assault with a deadly weapon"* fact pattern: D attacks V with some sort of potentially-deadly implement (e.g., the brass knuckles in the above example, or a baseball bat or golf club), and you're told that D merely wants to badly injure V, not kill him. If V dies, this is murder.

2. **"Serious bodily injury" defined:** D must intend to do *serious* bodily harm for this type of murder. A mere intent to commit some sort of minor bodily injury does not suffice.

> **Example:** D punches V in the face, intending merely to knock V down. V strikes his head while falling, and dies. D is not liable for "intent to do serious bodily harm" murder on these facts, because although he intended to do bodily harm to V, he did not intend harm that would be serious. (However, in most states D would be liable for *manslaughter* under the misdemeanor-manslaughter rule; see *infra*, p. 62.)

E. **"Reckless indifference to value of human life" or "depraved heart" murder:** Nearly all states hold D liable if she causes a death, while acting with such great *recklessness* that she can be said to have a *"depraved heart"* or an *"extreme indifference to the value of human life."* (We'll use the shorthand "depraved-heart murder" here.)

1. **Illustrations:** Here are some illustrations of depraved-heart murder:

> **Example 1:** D sets fire to a building where she knows people are sleeping; she does not desire their death, but knows that there is a high risk of death. One inhabitant dies in the fire.

> **Example 2:** D uses his rifle to practice shooting at a target posted to a tree 50 yards away, in what D knows is a densely-populated suburban neighborhood. One bullet misses, and goes into a nearby house, where it kills V.

> **Example 3:** D, trying to escape from pursuing police, drives her car at 75 mph the wrong way down a one-way residential street that has a 30 mph speed limit. D accidently hits and kills V, a pedestrian.

> **Example 4:** D, trying to rob a bank, fires an automatic weapon into the bank lobby's marble-covered ceiling while lots of employees are around. He does this to frighten the employees into complying with his demands. A bullet ricochets, killing V, an employee.

> **Example 5:** D, distraught at being fired from his job at a local Post Office, comes back with a shotgun and starts shooting randomly into the air. His intent is merely to get revenge on the

Post Office by "shutting the place down" for a while. One of the bullets ricochets off the wall and kills V, a friend and former co-worker of D.

2. **MBE tip:** The MBE examiners love to test on reckless-indifference murder. To hide the ball better, the correct choice typically won't refer to "reckless indifference to the value of human life" or "depraved heart." Instead, the correct choice is likely to say something more neutral, like, "D is guilty of murder because she intentionally took an act that posed a great risk of serious bodily harm or death" or "D is guilty of murder because she committed an act dangerous to life, without an intent to kill but with disregard of the consequences." It's up to you to figure out that D's conduct is so reckless that it amounts to depraved-heart murder.

   a. **No mention of theory for murder:** In fact, often the correct choice won't even give *any theory at all* for why D should be found guilty of murder. Instead, you'll be asked what the most serious crime is for which D can be convicted (choices that will typically also include voluntary and/or involuntary manslaughter), and it will be up to you to notice that because D has acted with a depraved heart, the correct choice is the one that simply reads "murder."

3. **Great recklessness required:** For depraved-heart murder, the risk of death or serious bodily injury must be so great that D can be said to have behaved with *great recklessness*. If D is merely *"negligent"* — even *"grossly negligent"* — in imposing risk on others, that *won't* suffice (for depraved-heart murder or any other form of murder except, possibly, felony-murder).

   Example: D goes deer hunting by himself, in an area frequented by other hunters. He sees a flash of orange behind a bush, and quickly fires without checking to see if it's really a deer. The movement turns out to be another hunter, who is killed.

   D is probably not guilty of depraved-heart murder. While his behavior may have been negligent, it probably does not rise to the level of extreme recklessness.

   a. **Omission to act:** Recall (*supra*, p. 8), that there are some exceptions to the general rule that D has *no affirmative duty to act*. In a situation falling within one of these exceptions, and leading to V's death, you may face the issue of whether D's failure to act can result in his conviction for depraved-heart murder. While this is logically very possible, it's an *unlikely* result, at least where D is a *non-relative* of V, and has a statutory rather than deep moral duty to act (e.g., a physician or teacher with a duty to notify authorities of cases of suspected child abuse).

   Example: D is a pediatrician who notices that V, a two-year-old, has bruises that D suspects may have been caused by child abuse on the part of V's mother's boyfriend. D has a statutory duty to report cases of possible abuse to child-welfare authorities, but decides not to report the case to the authorities because he thinks V might be taken from the mother and would fare worse in foster care. Shortly thereafter, V is beaten to death by the boyfriend. D is prosecuted for murder.

   D is unlikely to be convicted. The only possible theory for conviction is depraved-heart murder. But that requires extreme recklessness. D is unlikely to be found to have acted with extreme recklessness, even though his violation of the statute almost certainly consists of (in tort terms) negligence per se.

4. **Awareness of risk:** Courts are split as to whether D shows the requisite "depravity" where he is *not aware* of the risk involved in his conduct.

   a. **Intoxication:** If D fails to appreciate the risk of his conduct because he is *intoxicated*, all courts *allow a conviction*.

III. FELONY-MURDER

A. Generally: Under the *felony-murder rule, if D, while he is in the process of committing certain felonies, kills another (even accidentally), the killing is murder*. In other words, the intent to commit any of certain felonies (unrelated to homicide) is sufficient to meet the *mens rea* requirement for murder.

1. **Common law and today:** The felony-murder rule was applied at common law, and continues to be applied by most states today. On the MBE, you should assume that the felony-murder rule applies if the facts stipulate that common-law doctrines apply.

   Example: D, while carrying a loaded gun, decides to rob V, a pedestrian. While D is pointing his gun at V and demanding money, the gun accidentally goes off, and kills V. Even though D never intended to kill V or even shoot at him, D is guilty of murder at common law, because the killing occurred while D was in the course of carrying out a dangerous felony.

B. Dangerous felonies: Nearly all courts and legislatures today restrict application of the felony-murder doctrine to *certain felonies*.

1. **"Inherently dangerous" felonies:** Most states today apply the felony-murder doctrine only where the underlying felony is one that is *"inherently dangerous"* to life and health.

   a. **List of crimes:** For purposes of the MBE, here are the five felonies that you should regard as being sufficiently inherently dangerous that they will trigger felony murder:

   - *robbery*;
   - *rape*;
   - *arson*;
   - *kidnapping*; and
   - *burglary*

   LaFave, §7.5(b), p. 674

C. Causal relationship: There must be a *causal relationship* between the felony and the killing. First, the felony must in some sense be the "but for" cause of the killing. Second, the felony must be the *proximate cause* of the killing.

1. **"Natural and probable" consequence:** The requirement of proximate cause here is usually expressed by saying that D is only liable where the death is the *"natural and probable consequence"* of D's conduct. However, "natural and probable consequence" is given a quite broad reading in felony-murder cases. For instance, if D carries a gun that accidentally discharges and kills the person against whom the underlying crime (e.g., a robbery) is directed, most courts would say that the death was the "natural and probable consequence" of D's conduct even though it was completely accidental and undesired.

   a. **Substitute for probable cause:** So you should think of a consequence as being the "natural and probable consequence" of D's conduct as long as that conduct *"proximately caused"* the consequence, i.e., the conduct brought about the consequence without the intervention of any very bizarre additional events.

2. **Robberies, burglaries and gunfights:** Most commonly, proximate cause questions arise in the case of *robberies, burglaries and gunfights*. (We'll simplify here by just referring to the felon as being the "robber.")

   a. **Robber fires shot:** If the fatal shot is fired by the *robber* (even if accidentally), virtually all courts agree that D is the proximate cause of death, and that the felony-murder doctrine should apply. This is true whether the shot kills the robbery victim, or a *bystander*.

Example 1: On a city street, D points a gun at V, and says, "Your money or your life." While V is reaching into his pocket for his wallet, D drops his gun. The gun strikes the pavement and goes off accidentally, killing V. D's acts of robbery are clearly the proximate cause of V's death, and D is guilty of murder under the felony-murder rule.

Example 2: Same facts as above example. Now, assume that when the gun strikes the pavement and goes off, it kills B, a bystander 20 feet away. D's acts are the proximate cause of B's death, so D is guilty of murdering B under the felony-murder doctrine.

b. **Victim or police officer kills bystander:** Where the fatal shot is fired by the *robbery victim* or by a *police officer*, and a *bystander* is accidentally killed, courts are split as to whether the robber is the proximate cause of the death.

   i. **MBE tip:** At least where *someone other than D* (with D being the felon) fires the first and fatal shot, the MBE won't require you to say whether the court would or wouldn't apply felony-murder, because there's no clear majority view. You would, however, be expected to know that D has a respectable *argument* that he should not be held criminally responsible for the acts of a victim, bystander or other third person not associated with D, who fires first.

   Example: D holds up a convenience store at gun point. X, a passerby, looks through the window, sees D pointing his gun, fires her own gun through the plateglass window to try to hit D, and accidentally kills V, a customer. A court might or might not apply felony-murder to make D guilty of murder; D would at least have a respectable argument that he should not be held responsible for X's acts, since X was not associated with D's criminal venture.

c. **Victim, police officer or other non-felon kills one robber:** Where *one robber is killed* by a *non-felon* — such as by the robbery victim or by police officers attempting to make an arrest — this presents the *weakest case* for holding the other robbers liable for felony-murder. Courts disagree on whether to apply felony-murder in this situation.

   i. **Doctrine does not apply:** The *majority* approach is that the felony-murder doctrine *does not apply* in this "felon's death directly caused by an innocent non-felon" scenario. This result is sometimes justified on the rationale that the felony-murder doctrine is intended to *protect only innocent persons,* so it should not apply where a robber is killed.

   Example: D and X are co-robbers. X is killed by a police officer who is trying to apprehend the pair. Most courts would hold that D is not guilty of felony-murder. [Cf. *State v. Sophophone.*]

   Note on "depraved-heart" as alternative: In any robbery situation, in addition to the possibility of "felony-murder" as a theory, examine the possibility of using "*depraved-heart*" murder as an alternate theory. For instance, if D, while committing a robbery, initiates a gun fight, and a police officer shoots back, killing a bystander, it may be easier to argue that D behaved with reckless indifference to the value of human life (thus making him guilty of "depraved-heart" murder) than to find that the felony-murder doctrine should apply (since many courts hold that the felony-murder doctrine applies only where the killing is by the defendant's own hand or the hand of his accomplice).

d. **V's response, including fear, attempt to escape:** V's death can trigger felony-murder even if it comes about as the result of V's own response to the felony. Thus if V struggles, attempts to escape, or suffers great fear at the felony, and V's death stems directly from one of these responses, the scenario will usually qualify for felony-murder.

Example: At gunpoint, D robs a 7/11 owned and operated by V. D does not threaten V's safety, or desire that any harm come to V. Nonetheless, V is so terrified by the robbery that 10 minutes after D leaves, V has a fatal heart attack. This can and will be felony-murder — it's a death that is proximately related to the commission of a dangerous felony, robbery.

3. **Arson:** On the MBE, be on the lookout for felony-murder whenever D starts a *fire*, and this leads to someone's *death*. Arson is always considered a dangerous felony, so as long as D intended to burn a building or recklessly disregarded the risk of burning a building, he's likely to be guilty of felony-murder if the jurisdiction applies that doctrine.

   Example: D, in an act of vandalism, sets fire to a seemingly-abandoned building not owned by D. Unbeknownst to D, V, a homeless person, is sleeping inside, and dies of smoke inhalation. If the jurisdiction applies felony-murder, D is guilty of murder. That's because D has committed arson, the death was proximately caused by the arson, and arson is one of the inherently-dangerous felonies.

D. **Accomplice liability of co-felons:** Frequently, the doctrine of felony-murder combines with the rules on *accomplice* liability. The net result is that if two or more people work together to commit a felony, and one of them commits a killing during the felony, the others may also be guilty of felony-murder.

   1. **"In furtherance" test:** In most courts, all of the co-felons are liable for a killing committed by one of them, if the killing was: (1) committed *in furtherance of the felony*; and (2) a *"natural and probable" result* of (i.e., proximately caused by) the felony. (For more about (2), see *supra*, p. 54.)

      a. **Accidental killing:** Thus one felon (call her D1) will commonly be guilty of murder based on the *accidental* killing of V by another felon (call her D2) during the course of the felony they're committing together. And that's true even if the way the accidental killing comes about is very much against the express prior agreement between D1 and D2 (e.g., they agree to be unarmed, but D2 violates their agreement).

         Example: Bob wants to rob a bank. He asks Jill to serve as the driver of the getaway car, in return for 10% of the profits. Jill agrees, but says "You know I'm a pacifist, so you have to promise me that you won't hurt anyone, or even carry a gun." Bob agrees, but secretly brings a small pistol on the robbery. While Jill waits in a getaway car, Bob goes inside, pulls the gun, and tells V, a cashier, to hand over the money. Bob accidentally drops the gun, which when it hits the floor discharges, killing V. Can Jill be convicted of murder in a jurisdiction that follows common-law principles on all matters?

         Yes. Jill is clearly an accomplice to the robbery (she aided and abetted its commission). So she, too, is substantively liable for robbery, since an accomplice is liable for the substantive crime being aided (see *supra*, p. 42). Since V's death was proximately caused by the robbery, the robber(s) are guilty of murder under the felony-murder doctrine whether or not the death was a reasonably foreseeable consequence of their initial decision to rob. This means that even if Jill had no reason to foresee that Bob would disobey their agreement about carrying a gun, she's guilty of felony-murder.

         Note: The above example illustrates how, on the MBE, the felony-murder rule can be used to move an accomplice's liability for murder from the "possible" category to the "certain" category. For a discussion of how the basic principles of accomplice liability alone, without felony-murder, might — but would not necessarily — make an accomplice in Jill's position guilty of murder, see the convenience store example on p. 46 *supra*.

E. **"In commission of" a felony:** The felony-murder doctrine applies only to killings which occur *"in the commission of"* a felony.

1. **Causal:** There must be a *causal relationship* between felony and killing.

2. **Escape as part of felony:** If the killing occurs while the felons are attempting to *escape*, it will probably be held to have occurred "in the commission of" the felony, at least if it occurred reasonably close, both in *time and place*, to the felony itself.

3. **V dies while trying to escape peril:** Similarly, if V has been confined by D (while D commits, say, robbery or burglary), and dies while trying to *escape the confinement*, the death will probably be found to be "in the commission of" the felony.

   Example: D breaks into V's house, ties V up in a chair, and robs V's safe. After D returns home with the loot, V suffers a fatal heart attack while trying to remove his bonds. This will be felony-murder because a court will conclude that the death occurred "during the commission of" the robbery.

4. **No requirement that felony be completed:** The death has to happen in the "course of the commission" of a dangerous felony. But there's *no* requirement that D actually *complete* the underlying felony. So if, as often happens both in real life and on the MBE, the death occurs before the felony is complete, D is still guilty of felony-murder.

   Example: D walks into Bank, points his gun at Tell, a teller, and says, "Give me all your cash." Tell gets so frightened that he has an immediate fatal heart attack. D is so stunned that he walks out of the bank without taking a dollar.

   D has committed felony-murder, since Tell's death occurred during the course of the dangerous felony of robbery. The fact that this never became actual robbery (which requires a "taking" of another's property; see *infra*, p. 77) doesn't matter.

F. **Felony must be independent of the killing:** For application of the felony-murder doctrine, the felony must be *independent* of the killing. This prevents the felony-murder rule from turning virtually any attack that culminates in death into automatic murder.

   Example: D, without provocation, intends to punch V in the jaw, but not to seriously injure him or kill him. V, while falling from the blow, hits his head on the curb and dies. Even though D was committing the dangerous felony of assault or battery, this will not be upgraded to felony-murder, because the felony was not independent of the killing.

1. **Assault:** This "felony must be independent of the killing" rule is why it's *not* felony-murder when D commits an *assault or battery* against V (but doesn't intend to kill V), and V unexpectedly dies as a result. The above Example illustrates this principle.

IV. DEATH PENALTY AS PUNISHMENT FOR MURDER

A. **Death penalty:** At least 35 states now authorize the *death penalty* for some kinds of murder.

1. **Not necessarily "cruel and unusual":** The *Eighth Amendment* prohibits *"cruel and unusual punishment."* The Supreme Court has held that the death penalty is not necessarily a "cruel and unusual" punishment, and thus does not necessarily violate the Eighth Amendment. [*Gregg v. Georgia*]

2. **Mandatory sentences not constitutional:** It is generally *unconstitutional* for a state to try to avoid undue jury discretion by making a death sentence *mandatory* for certain crimes (e.g., killing of a police officer, or killing by one already under life sentence). The Supreme Court has held that the states must basically allow the jury to consider the *individual circumstances*

of a particular case (e.g., the presence of extenuating circumstances), and a mandatory-sentence scheme by definition does not allow this. [*Woodson v. North Carolina*]

3. **Racial prejudice:** A defendant can avoid a death sentence by showing that the jury was motivated by *racial* considerations, in violation of his Eighth Amendment or equal protection rights. However, the Supreme Court has held that any proof of impermissible racial bias must be directed to the *facts of the particular case*, and may not be proved by large-scale *statistical studies*. [*McCleskey v. Kemp*]

4. **Non-intentional killings:** The Eighth Amendment forbids use of the death penalty against a defendant who *does not himself kill, attempt to kill or intend that a killing take place*, or that *lethal force* be employed. [*Enmund v. Florida*]

    a. **No felony-murder death penalty:** This means that where D's guilt of murder stems solely from the application of the *felony-murder* doctrine, and D did not directly precipitate the killing, attempt to kill or desire to kill, D can't be subjected to the death penalty. *Enmund, supra.*

    Example: D drives a getaway car while his two accomplices go into a farm house and murder the inhabitants. *Held*, since D did not commit the killing or desire it, he may not be executed, even though he is guilty of murder by virtue of the felony-murder doctrine and the rules on accomplice liability. [*Enmund, supra*]

5. **Execution of the mentally retarded:** The Court has held that execution of the *mentally retarded violates* the Eighth Amendment. [*Atkins v. Virginia*]

6. **Juveniles:** Similarly, the Court has held that the execution of persons who were *juveniles* (under 18) at the time the crime was committed violates the Eighth Amendment. [*Roper v. Simmons*]

V. MANSLAUGHTER — VOLUNTARY

A. **Two types of manslaughter:** In most states, there are two types of manslaughter: (1) *voluntary manslaughter*, in which there is generally an *intent to kill*; and (2) *involuntary manslaughter*, in which the death is *accidental*. Here, we consider voluntary manslaughter.

   1. **Two kinds:** There are also two basic ways in which voluntary manslaughter can be committed:

      [1] D kills in the *"heat of passion,"* i.e., under a provocation that would cause a reasonable person to lose some degree of control; and

      [2] D kills under an unreasonable mistake about the need for *self-defense* (*"imperfect self-defense"*).

      We consider "heat of passion" first, then "imperfect self-defense" (*infra*, p. 60).

B. **"Heat of passion" manslaughter:** The most common kind of voluntary manslaughter is that in which D kills while in a *"heat of passion,"* i.e., an extremely *angry* or disturbed state.

   1. **Four elements:** Assuming that the facts would otherwise constitute murder, D is entitled to a conviction on the lesser charge of voluntary manslaughter if he meets four requirements:

      a. **Reasonable provocation:** He acted in response to a *provocation* that would have been sufficient to cause a *reasonable person* to *lose his self-control.*

      b. **Actually act in "heat of passion":** D was *in fact* in a "heat of passion" at the time he acted;

      c. **No time for reasonable person to cool off:** The lapse of time between the provocation and the killing was not great enough that a *reasonable person* would have *"cooled off,"* i.e., regained his self-control; and

      d. **D not in fact cooled off:** D did not *in fact* "cool off" by the time he killed.

MANSLAUGHTER — VOLUNTARY

2. **Consequence of missing hurdle:** If D fails to clear hurdles (a) or (c) above (i.e., he is actually provoked, and has not cooled off, but a reasonable person would have either not lost his self-control or would have cooled off), D will likely be convicted of murder, but not of a degree of murder that requires premeditation (as first-degree murder requires in many states).

    a. **D has cooled off:** But if D trips up on hurdles (b) or (d) (i.e., he is not in fact driven into a heat of passion, or has in fact already cooled off), he is likely to be convicted of *first-degree* murder, since his act of killing is in "cold blood." See *infra*, p. 60.

3. **Provocation:** As noted, D's act must be in response to a *provocation* that is: (1) sufficiently strong that a *"reasonable person"* would have been *caused to lose his self control*; and (2) strong enough that *D himself* lost his self-control.

    a. **Lost temper:** The provocation need not be enough to cause a reasonable person to kill. The provocation merely needs to be enough that it would make a reasonable person *lose his temper*.

    b. **Objective standard for emotional characteristics:** Courts generally do *not* recognize the peculiar *emotional* characteristics of D in determining how a reasonable person would act.

        Example: All courts agree that the fact that D is unusually bad-tempered, or unusually quick to anger, is not to be taken into account.

    c. **Particular categories:** Courts have established certain rules, as a matter of law, about what kind of provocation will suffice:

        i. **Battery:** More-than-trivial *battery* committed on D is usually considered to be sufficient provocation.

            Example: V, a man, slaps D, a man, because D has failed to pay back a debt. This will probably constitute adequate provocation, so if D then flies into a rage and kills V, this will be manslaughter rather than murder.

        ii. **Mutual combat:** If D and V get into a *mutual combat*, in which neither one can be said to have been the aggressor, most courts will treat this as sufficient provocation to D.

        iii. **Adultery:** The classic voluntary manslaughter situation is that in which one spouse surprises the other in the act of *adultery* with a lover, and kills either the spouse or the lover. The discovery of the adultery will almost always be sufficient provocation.

        iv. **Words alone:** Traditionally, *words alone* cannot constitute the requisite provocation — no matter how *abusive, insulting or harassing* V's words are, D will be guilty of murder, not manslaughter, if he kills in retaliation for the words.

            Example: D and V, drinking in a bar, get into an argument about the upcoming Presidential election. V calls D a moron, and then insults D's mother's chastity. D becomes enraged, pulls out a knife, and without deliberation stabs V in the stomach, intending to kill him. V dies.

            D has committed murder, not voluntary manslaughter. No words of insult, standing alone, will be deemed sufficiently provocative as to cause the target's homicidal rage to be "reasonable."

    d. **Effect of mistake:** If D *reasonably* but *mistakenly* reaches a conclusion which, if accurate, would constitute sufficient provocation, courts will generally allow manslaughter.

Example: Based on circumstantial evidence, D reasonably but erroneously suspects that his wife has been sleeping with his best friend, V. Probably this will suffice as provocation, making D's killing of V voluntary manslaughter rather than murder.

    e. Actual provocation: Remember that the provocation must be not only sufficient to cause a reasonable person to lose his self-control, but also sufficient to have *in fact* enraged D.

    Example: D finds his wife together with V, his best friend. D has suspected the affair for some time, and now coolly says to himself, "This is my chance to kill V and get off with just voluntary manslaughter." He cold-bloodedly shoots V in the heart. Even though the provocation would have been sufficient to cause a reasonable person to lose control, D does not qualify for manslaughter here because he was not in fact enraged at the moment of the shooting.

4. "Cooling off" period: The *time* between D's discovery of the upsetting facts and his act of killing must be sufficiently short that a *reasonable person* would not have had time to "cool off."

    a. D has actually cooled down: Furthermore, D himself must not have cooled off — even if a reasonable person would not have had time to cool off, if D cooled off and killed the provoker anyway, this is murder, not voluntary manslaughter.

    Example: D comes home to find his wife in bed with another man, V, whom D has known for years and who is D's business rival. 10 minutes later, acting with cool calculation rather than emotion, D says to himself, "I have the perfect excuse to get rid of a competitor," and shoots V to death. This is murder, not voluntary manslaughter — D has in fact cooled down, so he hasn't killed in the heat of passion even though under comparable facts a reasonable person in D's position might still have been in the heat of passion.

    b. Rekindling: But even if there is a substantial cooling-off period between the initial provocation and the killing, if a *new provocation* occurs which would *rekindle* the passion of a reasonable person, the cooling-off rule is not violated. This is true even if the new provocation would not *by itself* be sufficient to inflame a reasonable person.

C. "Imperfect" self-defense: The second type of voluntary manslaughter occurs where D acts with might be described as *"imperfect self-defense."*

1. Where applicable: That is, most states entitle to have a murder charge lowered to voluntary manslaughter if D *killed to defend himself* but is not entitled to an acquittal because:

    [1] he was unreasonably mistaken about the *existence of danger*;

    [2] he was unreasonably mistaken (perhaps because of *intoxication*) about the *need for deadly force*, or the proper level of non-defense required; or

    [3] he was the *aggressor*.

2. Imperfect defense of others: Similarly, if D uses deadly force in *defense of another*, but does not meet all of the requirements for exculpation, some courts give him the lesser charge of voluntary manslaughter.

    Example: If D witnesses a fight between V and X, and honestly but unreasonably concludes that X was the aggressor, D may be entitled to manslaughter for killing V.

VI. MANSLAUGHTER — INVOLUNTARY

A. Involuntary manslaughter based on gross negligence: A person whose behavior is *grossly negligent* may be liable for *involuntary manslaughter* if her conduct results in the accidental death of another person.

1. **Gross negligence required:** Nearly all states hold that *something more than ordinary tort negligence* must be shown before D is liable for involuntary manslaughter. Most states require *"gross negligence."* Usually, D must be shown to have disregarded a very substantial danger not just of bodily harm, but of *serious* bodily harm or death.

    a. **MBE Tip:** Obviously, this means that if D behaves reasonably, she certainly can't be convicted of involuntary manslaughter. The MBE examiners will sometimes give you a fact pattern in which D's conduct leads directly to V's death, but there's no affirmative evidence that D behaved with the required gross negligence. In that scenario, of course, assuming that D did not desire V's death, D can't be guilty of involuntary manslaughter (or any other form of homicide apart from, perhaps, felony-murder).

        Example: D, who lives alone, hears what she reasonably believes is a burglar entering through an unlocked rear door late at night. She retrieves a pistol which she is licensed to own. She points the pistol at the intruder, hoping to frighten him away but not intending to fire. She shouts, "Get out." The intruder says nothing, and keeps walking in the darkness. D is so frightened that she drops the pistol, and it goes off, killing the intruder. The intruder turns out to be a drunk neighbor, who mistook D's house for his own.

        D can't be liable for even involuntary manslaughter. She has not behaved negligently, and involuntary manslaughter requires at least gross negligence.

2. **Intent not required:** D can be convicted of involuntary manslaughter *even though D did not intend to bring about a death, or even intend to bring about serious bodily harm.* The MBE examiners like to try to trick you with this one — they give you a case in which V dies in a way that is somehow related to D's conduct, and then give you a (false) choice that says that D will be acquitted of manslaughter "because D did not intend to cause V's death" or "because D did not act with malice."

    a. **Drunk driving:** Be especially on the lookout for involuntary manslaughter when D gets into a *drunk driving* accident that kills someone. As long as the intoxication contributed significantly to the accident, D is almost certainly guilty of involuntary manslaughter. That's because even a state with a narrow definition of involuntary manslaughter will not require a mental state more culpable than recklessness (gross negligence is enough in most states; see *supra*, p. 61), and driving while drunk constitutes recklessness. (Alternatively, in a jurisdiction applying misdemeanor-manslaughter, see *infra*, 62, drunk-driving is certainly at least a misdemeanor.)

        i. **D's mistake of fact:** Apart from the standard scenario of a traffic accident caused by D's lack of coordination while drunk, D's intoxication can also cause the accident by *wrecking D's judgment.*

            Example: D gets drunk at a bar, then drives home. A police car sees him drive erratically and starts to follow him. D, because his judgment has been impaired by the alcohol, thinks that the car following him contains criminals who will hijack his car. (A reasonable sober driver would have recognized the car as a police car.) Therefore, D speeds away, and kills V, a pedestrian.

            D has committed involuntary manslaughter — his drunk driving constituted recklessness (the most culpable mental state ever required for involuntary manslaughter), and the intoxication proximately caused the crime by leading to his mistake of believing he was being chased by criminals.

3. **Contributory negligence of V:** The fact that the victim may have been *contributorily negligent* is not a defense to involuntary manslaughter (or to most other crimes).

Example: D gets drunk, and drives home. While en route, he has a collision with a car driven by V, who dies in the accident. If D's intoxication was a cause in fact and proximate cause of the accident, the fact that V may have driven negligently won't negate D's liability for involuntary manslaughter.

4. **Causal link required:** The gross negligence must be *causally related* to the death. So, for instance, if the death would have occurred *even if D had not been grossly negligent,* she won't be guilty of involuntary manslaughter.

    Example: Same basic facts as in the above Example, in which D gets drunk, drives home, and has a fatal collision with a car driven by V. But now suppose that D drove at a correct speed, obeyed all other traffic regulations, and hit V when V went through a red light. If the accident would have happened the same way had D not been drunk (which seems likely), then D won't be guilty of involuntary manslaughter — in that event, his drunken driving, though grossly negligent, wouldn't be the cause in fact or the proximate cause of V's death.

B. **The misdemeanor-manslaughter rule:** Just as the felony-murder rule permits a *murder* conviction when a death occurs during the course of certain felonies, so the *"misdemeanor-manslaughter"* rule permits a conviction for *involuntary manslaughter* when a death occurs accidentally during the commission of a misdemeanor or other *unlawful act*.

    1. **Most states apply:** Most states continue to apply the misdemeanor-manslaughter rule.

    2. **Substitute for criminal negligence:** The theory behind the rule is that the unlawful act is treated as a *substitute for criminal negligence* (by analogy to the "negligence *per se*" doctrine in tort law).

    3. **"Unlawful act" defined:** *Any misdemeanor* may serve as the basis for application of the misdemeanor-manslaughter doctrine. Also, some states permit the prosecution to show that D violated a *local ordinance* or *administrative regulation*. And if a particular *felony* does not suffice for the felony-murder rule (e.g., because it is not "inherently dangerous to life"), it may be used.

        a. **Battery:** The most common misdemeanor in misdemeanor-manslaughter cases is *battery*.

            Example: D gets into an argument with V, and gives him a light tap on the chin with his fist. D intends only to stun V. V slips, falls, and fatally hits his head on the sidewalk. Since D has committed the misdemeanor of simple battery, and a death has resulted, he is guilty of manslaughter under the misdemeanor-manslaughter rule.

        b. **Traffic violations:** The violation of *traffic laws* is another frequent source of misdemeanor-manslaughter liability.

            Example: D fails to stop at a stop sign, and hits V, a pedestrian crossing at a crosswalk. V dies. Even if D does not have the "gross negligence" typically required for ordinary voluntary manslaughter, D's violation of the traffic rule requiring that one stop at stop signs will be enough to make him guilty of manslaughter under the misdemeanor-manslaughter rule.

    4. **Causation:** There must be a *causal relation* between the violation and the death.

        a. **Licensing requirements:** On the MBE, this principle is sometimes tested with respect to *licensing* requirements: If the jurisdiction requires a license to pursue some activity, but D would be entitled to the license as a matter of right, his conducting of the activity without a license, coupled with a harm (a death) stemming from the activity, *won't trigger* the misdemeanor-manslaughter rule because the failure to get a license is not deemed to be the proximate cause of the harm.

            Example: After D's license expires, D fails to renew it, and continues driving. Driving without a currently-valid license is a misdemeanor in the jurisdiction. While D is driving non-negligently, D's car collides with V, a pedestrian, when V darts out from between two parked cars. V dies. D is not guilty of misdemeanor-manslaughter because his misdemeanor of driving without a currently-valid license was not the proximate cause of the accident.

VII. ASSAULT AND BATTERY

A. **Battery:** The crime of *battery* exists where D intentionally or recklessly causes either: (1) *bodily injury*; or (2) *offensive touching*.

1. **Injury or offensive touching:** Any kind of physical injury, even a bruise from a blow, will meet the physical harm requirement. Also, in most states an *offensive touching* will suffice.

    Example: D, without V's consent, kisses V. Since this is an offensive touching, it will constitute battery in most states even though V was not physically injured.

2. **Mental state:** D's *intent* to inflict the offensive touching or the injury will suffice, of course. But also, in most states, if the contact is committed *recklessly*, or with gross negligence, this will also suffice. LaFave, §7.15(c), p. 740.

    Example: D throws a baseball with a friend, in a crowded city street. The ball strikes V, a passerby. If a court finds that D behaved recklessly, he will probably be guilty of battery, even though he did not intend to touch or injure V.

B. **Assault:** The crime of *assault* exists (in most states) where either: (1) D *attempts to commit a battery*, and fails; or (2) D intentionally places another in *fear of imminent injury*.

1. **Attempted-battery assault:** In every state, D is guilty of assault if he *unsuccessfully attempts* to commit a battery.

    Example: D shoots at V, attempting to hit him in the leg. The bullet misses. D is guilty of the attempted-battery form of assault.

2. **Intentional-frightening assault:** Most states also recognize a second form of assault, that in which D intentionally *frightens his victim* into fearing *immediate bodily harm*.

    Example: During an attempted bank robbery, D points his gun at V, a customer at the bank, and says, "One false step and I'll fill you full of lead." This is assault of the intentional-frightening variety; the fact that D's threat is conditional does not prevent the crime from existing.

3. **MBE Tip:** On the MBE, you should assume that the crime of assault can be committed via *either* of the two above mental states: (1) intent to commit a battery; and (2) successful attempt to frighten the victim.

4. **Intent required:** Even in states recognizing both forms of assault, the crime requires an intent — it *cannot be committed recklessly*.

    Example: D drives recklessly, and nearly runs over V, who is frightened and believes she will be struck. This is not assault, because D neither intended to make harmful contact with V nor intended to frighten her by making her think she would suffer a harmful contact.

5. **Words alone:** *Words alone* will *not* suffice for assault. The words must be accompanied by some overt gesture (e.g., the pointing of a gun) or other *physical act*.

    Example: D walks into a 7/11, and says to V, the owner, "Give me all the cash in the register, or you'll get hurt." D does not make any gesture, and does not brandish any weapon.

V faints, and hits his head on the floor, sustaining a skull fracture. D has not committed assault. First, he did not intend to commit a harmful contact, so he didn't have the intent for the attempted-battery version of assault. Second, he didn't make any frightening or menacing gesture (e.g., brandishing a weapon), so his words alone will not constitute the intent needed for the intentional-scaring version of assault.

VIII. RAPE

- **A. Rape defined:** Rape is defined at common law as *unlawful sexual intercourse with a female, not one's wife, without her consent.*

  1. **The spousal exception:** Common-law rape requires that the victim be one *other than the defendant's wife.*

  2. **Without consent:** The intercourse must occur without the woman's *consent.*

     a. **Victim drunk or drugged:** If D causes V to become *drunk, drugged* or *unconscious,* the requisite lack of consent is present. In some but not all states, consent is lacking if the woman is drunk, drugged or unconscious even if this condition was not induced by D.

     b. **Mistake no defense:** At common law (which is what is typically tested on the MBE), D's *mistake about whether V consented is not a defense.* This stems from the fact that most courts have generally viewed rape as a crime of *"general intent."* In other words, most courts require the prosecution to prove only that D voluntarily committed an act of sexual intercourse — consequently, the fact that D mistakenly thought the woman consented is irrelevant. LaFave, §§7.18, pp. 753-54; 7.18(e), p. 758.

        i. **Assault with intent to rape:** But don't confuse a prosecution for rape with a prosecution for *"assault with intent to rape,"* which you will sometimes see on the MBE. Assault with intent to rape is essentially "attempted rape," and a prosecution for attempt generally requires a showing that D had an intent to bring about each element of the completed crime (see *supra,* p. 28). Consequently, D generally *can't* be convicted of assault with intent to rape unless he *believed that the woman wasn't consenting to the sex act.*

           Example: D and V go out on their first date, then V agrees to come back to D's apartment. There, D undresses himself and V, believes that V has consented to have sex with him, and pushes V onto the bed. At that point, V shouts "No," gets dressed, and leaves.

           D cannot be convicted of assault with intent to rape — since completed rape requires unconsented-to sexual intercourse, assault with intent to rape cannot exist unless D intended to have unconsented-to sexual intercourse. Therefore, D's mistake about consent will negate liability (even though, at common law, that same mistake about consent would not negate D's liability for the completed act of rape).

- **B. Statutory rape:** All states establish an *age of consent,* below which the law regards a minor's consent as *impossible.* One who has intercourse with a minor below this age is punished for what is usually called *"statutory rape."*

  1. **Reasonable mistake:** In most states, even a *reasonable belief* by D that the minor was over the age of consent is *not a defense.* That is, in most states, with respect to the element of the minor's age, statutory rape is a strict liability crime.

     a. **Attempted liability is blocked:** But if D does not realize that the girl is underage, D cannot be convicted of *attempt* to violate the statutory-rape statute, if no intercourse takes place. That is, just as attempt liability in general requires intent (see *supra,* p. 28), and just as a mistake about consent negates "assault with intent to commit [ordinary] rape" (see *supra,* p. 64), so such a mistake about age negates both attempted statutory rape and assault with intent to commit statutory rape.

Example: The jurisdiction makes it statutory rape to have sex with a minor under 16. D and V go on a date, and then back to D's apartment. V is 15, but looks 19 (and D believes that she is 19). D asks V to have sex. She says yes. He undresses her, and is about to have sex, when she says that she has changed her mind, dresses, and leaves.

D cannot be convicted of attempted statutory rape, because his belief that V was over 16 blocks him from having the required intent to have sex with a minor.

2. **Encouragement by girl:** The fact that the minor has *encouraged* the sex is irrelevant. Also, the fact that the minor has lied about her age is no defense (unless it contributes to D's reasonable mistake as to age, in a state following the minority rule recognizing reasonable mistake as a defense to statutory rape).

   a. **Prostitution:** Nor will the fact that the minor is a *prostitute* make any difference.

IX. KIDNAPPING

A. **Definition of kidnapping:** Kidnapping is the *unlawful confinement* of another, accompanied by either a *moving* of the victim or a *secreting* of him.

1. **Model Penal Code:** The MBE examiners sometimes test you on the particulars of the *Model Penal Code's* somewhat-elaborate definition of kidnapping. (Perhaps they do this because the common-law definition of kidnapping is hard to test, due to its vague contours and narrow scope.) Under M.P.C. §212.1, a person is guilty of kidnapping "if he unlawfully *removes* another *from his residence or business*, or *a substantial distance from the vicinity where he is found*, or if he unlawfully *confines another for a substantial period in a place of isolation*, with any of the following *purposes*:

   (a) to hold for *ransom or reward*, or as a *shield or hostage*; or

   (b) to facilitate *commission of any felony* or *flight* thereafter; or

   (c) to inflict *bodily injury* on or to *terrorize* the victim or *another*; or

   (d) to interfere with the performance of any *governmental or political function*."

   (We'll look in more detail below at how the M.P.C. provision on moving a person works.)

2. **Asportation:** Assuming that the crime does not involve secret imprisonment, the prosecution must show that the victim was *moved* (the "*asportation*" requirement).

   a. **Large distance not required:** In many states, the asportation need not be over a substantial distance.

   Example: D accosts V on the street, and makes her walk 20 feet to his car, where he detains her. In many (but by no means all) states, the requisite asportation will be found despite the short distance.

   b. **Must not be incidental to some other offense:** However, even in states that don't require the asportation to be over a substantial distance, the asportation must not be merely *incidental to some other offense*.

   Example: D, in order to rob V, forces him to stand up and put his hands against the wall, while D empties V's pockets. There is probably no asportation since there was no independent purpose to the confinement and movement; therefore, there is probably no kidnapping. But if V had been taken 20 feet away from the robbery site, bound and gagged and left in a secluded and dark place to allow D time to escape, this probably *would* be kidnapping, since the movement of V would not be "incidental" to the robbery.

- c. **M.P.C. "substantial distance" rule:** Under the Model Penal Code, the asportation requirement is met only if the defendant either (1) "removes" the victim from his "place of residence or business" or (2) moves the victim "a *substantial distance* from the vicinity where he is found." M.P.C. §212.1. The Code Commentary says that the "substantial distance" requirement is designed to "preclude kidnapping convictions based on *trivial changes of location* having no bearing on the evil at hand. Thus, for example, the rapist who forces his victim into a parked car or dark alley may be punished quite severely for the crime of rape, but he does not thereby also become liable for kidnapping." *Id.* at Comm. 2.

    Example: While V is stopped at a red light late at night, D opens V's car door, gets into the car, points a gun at V's head, and says, "Take me to whatever bank A.T.M. you use." V drives several blocks to a nearby bank and parks. D escorts V at gunpoint up to the A.T.M., demands that D withdraw $100, and runs away with the money. In a jurisdiction that has adopted the Model Penal Code definition of kidnapping, has D kidnapped V?

    Yes. Here, D has caused V to move a "substantial distance," not merely compelled V to make a "trivial change of location having no bearing on the evil at hand." That is, forcing V to go to some specific other place, in order that the particular method of robbery could take place, was an integral part of the scheme, not an incidental by-product of the scheme. And since the asportation was done in order to "facilitate commission of any felony" (robbery), it satisfies the full M.P.C. definition of kidnapping.

3. **Confinement must be against V's will:** If the crime does involve a "secreting" of the victim, D must imprison or confine the victim against her will — if the victim is *free to go,* and knows it, the crime has not been committed *even though a third person thinks that the victim is being confined.*

    Example: D and V, boyfriend and girlfriend, go away for a weekend together. Early Sunday morning, D leaves V in their hotel room, telling her he is going for a walk. He calls V's father F from a pay phone and says that he has kidnapped V, whom he will kill if F does not wire D $10,000 immediately. F wires the money. D is immediately tracked down and arrested. Until the moment of D's arrest, V has no idea of D's plot.

    D has not committed kidnapping (or even attempted kidnapping). Kidnapping requires secreting or movement of the victim against the victim's will. Since V was always free to leave the hotel room, she was never moved or secreted against her will. Nor did D intend to move or secret her against her will, so he can't be guilty of attempted kidnapping (since an attempt to commit crime X requires a person to intend to carry out each element of crime X; see *supra*, p. 28).

CHAPTER 9
THEFT CRIMES

I. INTRODUCTION

A. **List of theft crimes:** There are five crimes that can loosely be called "theft" crimes, and that are tested with regularity on the MBE:

1. *Larceny*

2. *Embezzlement*

3. *False pretenses*

4. *Burglary*

5. *Robbery*

B. **Distinguishing the basic three:** The three "basic" theft crimes are *larceny, embezzlement* and *false pretenses*. Most MBE questions relating to theft focus on the distinctions among these three categories. Therefore, you must focus on two particular dividing lines:

1. **Larceny vs. embezzlement:** First, focus on the dividing line between *larceny* and *embezzlement*. This comes down to the question, "Was possession originally obtained unlawfully [larceny] or lawfully [embezzlement]?"

2. **Larceny vs. false pretenses:** Second, focus on the dividing line between *larceny* and *false pretenses*. This comes down to the question, "What was obtained unlawfully, mere possession [larceny] or title [false pretenses]?"

II. LARCENY

A. **Definition:** Common-law larceny is defined as follows:

1. The *trespassory*

2. *taking* and

3. *carrying away* of

4. *personal property*

5. of *another* with

6. *intent to steal*.

> **Example:** D, a pickpocket, removes V's wallet from V's pocket, and runs away with it, without V discovering for some time what has happened. D has committed common-law larceny. That is, he has taken property that belonged to another and that was in the other's possession, and has carried it away, with an intent to steal it.

B. **Trespassory taking:** The requirement of a "trespassory taking" means that if D is *already in rightful possession* of the property at the time he appropriates it to his own use, he *cannot* be guilty of larceny.

1. **Concurrence is required:** On the MBE, *concurrence* between the *act* (taking possession) and the *mental state* (intending to permanently deprive), is *often tested*. Before you pick "larceny" as the answer, make sure that *at the moment D got possession*, D *intended to steal* the property. At common law, it's not enough for larceny that D got possession at one moment, then made the decision to steal at some materially later moment. (In this scenario, the original taking is not "trespassory.")

> **Example (not larceny):** D rents a car from V, a car-rental agency. At the time D consummates the rental transaction, he intends to use the car for one week (and so notifies V), then return it. After the week has passed, D decides to keep the car permanently, without paying any further rental fee. At common law, D is not guilty of larceny. This is because at the time he made the decision to appropriate the car, he was already in rightful possession pursuant to the rental contract. (But if at the moment D rented the car he had already intended to steal it, this *would* be a "trespassory taking" and thus larceny.)

2. **Taking by use of innocent agent:** Larceny, like any crime, can be committed by use of an *innocent agent*.

> **Example:** D tells her neighbor, a 9-year-old boy, Brian, that D lent an iPod to V (another neighbor), and that V has refused to return the iPod. D therefore asks Brian to go to V's house at a time when D knows Brian is not home, see if the door is unlocked, and if it is, retrieve the iPod from V's bedroom dresser. Brian does all this, and is in the process of bringing the iPod back to D when V discovers what's going on, and retrieves the iPod from Brian.
>
> D has committed larceny by use of an innocent agent (Brian). Brian's acts will be treated as if they had been committed by D. Since D had the requisite mental state (intent to steal), and Brian committed the rest of the elements of larceny (trespassory taking and carrying away of the personal property of another), D fulfills all requirements for larceny even though D never herself got possession of the object.

3. **Larceny by trick:** If D gains possession of property by *fraud or deceit*, the requisite trespassory taking takes place. The larceny in this situation is said to be *"by trick"* — larceny by trick is simply one way in which larceny may be committed, not a separate crime.

> **Example:** D rents a car from V, a car rental agency. At the moment of the rental transaction, D has already decided that he will not return the car, and will not pay for it. D has committed larceny of the "by trick" variety, because his initial taking of possession was obtained by fraud or deceit.

   a. **Distinguished from false pretenses:** Distinguish the taking of possession by fraud or deceit (leading to larceny by trick) from the taking of *title* by fraud or deceit (which is not larceny at all). If title passes, the crime is theft by false pretenses.

   b. **MBE Tip:** On the MBE, you should be a little skeptical of a choice that refers to "larceny by trick" — Sometimes this is indeed the correct answer (as in the above Example), but often the examiners try to fool you with this choice.

   c. **Intent to steal required:** In any event, for larceny-by-trick scenarios, as for any other kind of larceny, make sure that *at the moment D took possession*, she had an intent to steal. Any intent to steal (or to not return) that is formed *after* the moment D takes possession will not count as larceny. For instance, if D *borrows money* or property with a promise to return/repay, if at the moment of the borrowing D genuinely intends to repay/return the property, the fact that she later has a change of mind won't convert this into larceny, whether of the by-trick variety or not.

   > **Example:** Same facts as the above car-rental Example. Now, however, assume that at the moment of rental, D intends to return the car to V at the scheduled time. Thereafter, he decides to keep it. This is not common-law larceny (whether "by trick" or otherwise), because D did not have the required intent to steal at the time he took possession of the car.

C. **Carrying away ("asportation"):** D, to commit larceny, must not only commit a trespassory taking, but must also *carry the property away*. This is called *"asportation."*

   1. **Slight distance sufficient:** However, as long as every portion of the property is moved, even a *slight distance* will suffice. The MBE examiners like to test this element.

   > **Example 1:** D sees V lying in the gutter, apparently drunk. D reaches into V's pocket, pulls out V's wallet, and starts to walk away with it. After a few steps, he hears a police siren, quickly puts the wallet back into V's pocket, and runs away.
   >
   > D has met the asportation requirement, so he can be convicted of larceny. It was enough that D moved the wallet a few feet before abandoning his plan and returning the wallet.

Example 2: D enters V's department store. D sees an iPod that V has left out on display. D slips the iPod in his coat pocket, then takes a few steps towards the exit, intending to take the device without paying for it. At that moment, V's security guard detains D until the police can come.

D has met the asportation requirement, so he can be convicted of larceny. It was enough that D moved the item a few feet, and it doesn't matter that he did not take the item outside of V's premises.

    a. **D changes mind:** This principle that a slight movement is enough means that D can be guilty of larceny even though she *quickly changes her mind and doesn't carry the item from the owner's premises.* The MBE examiners like to trick you with this kind of fact pattern: D picks up and moves the item with an intent to steal it, then thinks better of it and returns it to its original place. In this scenario, D has *already committed larceny the instance she moved the item*, and nothing she does thereafter can change this.

D. Property of another: The property taken, to constitute larceny, must be property *belonging to another*.

  1. **Recapture of chattel:** If D is attempting to *retake* a *specific chattel* that belongs to him, D will not be guilty of larceny, because he is not taking property "of another."

    a. **Mistaken claim of right:** In most states (and on the MBE), this is also true if D is genuinely *mistaken* (even if unreasonably) in thinking that the thing he is taking belongs to himself rather than the other person.

Example: D's bicycle is stolen. Two days later he sees what is apparently the same bike, chained to a lamp post. D genuinely believes that this is his own stolen bike. He cuts the chain and removes the bike. If the bike was in fact his own, D is clearly not guilty of larceny, because he has not taken the property "of another." If D genuinely believes that the bike was his — even if this belief is unreasonable — most courts will similarly hold that he has not committed larceny.

E. Intent to steal: Larceny is a crime that can only be committed *intentionally*, not negligently or recklessly.

  1. **Intent to permanently deprive owner:** D must thus generally be shown to have an intent to *permanently deprive* the owner of his property. An intent to take property *temporarily* is not sufficient.

Example: D enters V's car, intending to take it on a three-mile "joy ride." After one mile, D crashes the car, destroying it totally. At common law, D is not guilty of larceny, because he did not intend to permanently deprive V of his property.

    a. **Substantial deprivation:** But if D intends to use the property for such a long time, or in such a way, that the owner will be deprived of a *significant portion of the property's economic value*, the requisite intent to steal exists.

Example: D takes a lawnmower belonging to V, with an intent to keep it all summer and fall. This probably constitutes larceny, because D intends to deprive V of a substantial part of the useful life of the mower.

  2. **Claim of right:** If D takes another's property under a *claim of right*, D will not be found to have had the requisite guilty intent.

    a. **Money taken to satisfy claim:** Thus if D takes V's property with an intent to *collect a debt* which V owes D, or to satisfy some other kind of *claim* which D has against V, D will not be guilty of larceny. D is especially likely to have a good defense where D's claim against V is a "liquidated" one, that is, one is with a fixed monetary value.

Example: D works for V. V fires D, and illegally refuses to pay D D's last week of wages, equaling $100. D reaches into V's cash register and removes $100 and walks out with it. D is not guilty of larceny, because his intent was to collect a debt which V owed him.

  i. **Mistake:** Most significantly, D lacks the requisite intent for larceny even if he is *mistaken* about the validity of his claim against V. And this is true even if D's mistake is *unreasonable*, so long as it is sincere.

    Example: D works for V. V fires D, and refuses to pay him for three weeks of vacation pay, which D genuinely believes is owed to him. Assume that under applicable legal principles, and as any reasonably knowledgeable employee would understand, D was not entitled to any vacation pay, because D had taken all the vacation to which he was entitled up to the moment he was fired. D nonetheless reaches into V's cash register and removes three weeks' pay. D is not guilty of larceny, because he took pursuant to an honest, though unreasonable and mistaken, belief that he had a legally-enforceable claim against V for the money.

 b. **Grievance not enough:** But the "claim of right" defense requires that D be taking the property in a mistaken belief that she is *entitled to that property* or that money. The mere fact that D feels *aggrieved by some unfair treatment* on the part of V won't suffice; D must be acting on the belief that D has a "*claim*," not merely a grievance.

    Example: D works in the office of a nightclub owned by V. V unjustly accuses D of theft of some petty cash. D, angered by the false and unfair accusation, decides to quit. On the way out, D takes $100 from the petty cash box, saying "Those [expletives deleted], I'll get even with them."

    D has committed larceny. Even though D correctly felt aggrieved, he was not taking the money in a genuine belief (whether reasonable or not) that he had a "claim" or was legally entitled to it. Therefore, he has intentionally taken property of another.

III. EMBEZZLEMENT

 A. **Definition:** Embezzlement is defined as follows:

  1. A *fraudulent*

  2. *conversion* of

  3. the *property*

  4. of *another*

  5. by one who is *already in lawful possession* of it.

 B. **No overlap with larceny:** Embezzlement *does not overlap* with larceny — a given fact pattern cannot be both larceny and embezzlement.

 C. **Conversion:** For most larceny, D needs only to take and carry away the property. But for embezzlement, D must *convert it*, i.e., deprive the owner of a significant part of its usefulness. If D merely uses the property for a short time, or moves it slightly, he is not guilty of embezzlement (regardless of whether he *intended* to convert it.)

    Example: D's boss lends D the company car to do a company errand, and D decides to abscond with it or sell it. The police stop D after he has driven the car for one mile. D is not guilty of embezzlement, since he has not yet deprived the company of a significant part of the car's usefulness, and thus has not converted it.

D. **Property of another:** The property must be property belonging to *another* rather than to D.

   a. **D to pay from own funds:** Thus if D has an obligation to *make payment from his own funds*, he *cannot embezzle* even if he fraudulently fails to make the payment.

   Example: D, a coal mine operator, has his employees sign orders directing D to deduct from their wages the amount that each owes to a grocery store. D deducts the amount, but then fails to pay the store owner. D is not guilty of common-law embezzlement, because he did not misappropriate the employees' money, but rather, failed to make payment from his own funds. Therefore, he is civilly liable but not criminally liable. [*Commonwealth v. Mitchneck* (1938)]

E. **"By one in lawful possession":** The main distinction between larceny and embezzlement is that embezzlement is committed by one who is *already in lawful possession* of the property before he appropriates it to his own use.

   Example 1 (embezzlement): D, a lawyer, is appointed trustee of a trust for the benefit of V. The trust principal consists of $10,000, held by D in a bank account named "D in trust for V." D takes the money and buys a new car for himself. D is guilty of embezzlement, because he converted to his own use property of which he was already in lawful possession.

   Example 2 (not embezzlement): D rents a car from V for one week. At the moment that D signs the rental contract, D intends never to return the car. D nonetheless signs the rental contract, which as he knows contains his promise to return the car in one week. After the week is over, D follows through on his plan, by not returning the car.

   D has not committed embezzlement, because at the moment D first gained possession, his intent was already wrongful. That is, because D got possession by telling a lie (that he intended to return the car after one week), his initial possession was unlawful; embezzlement requires that D's initial possession be lawful.

   1. **MBE Tip:** This principle — that D can't be guilty of embezzlement unless D was first in lawful, non-fraudulent possession of the property — means that the substantial majority of the time on the MBE, "embezzlement" will be the *wrong* answer.

   2. **Employees:** Most commonly, embezzlers are *employees* who misappropriate property with which their employer has entrusted them.

      a. **Bailees:** *Bailees* — people who are holding property for the rightful owner — are also likely to be embezzlers if they sell or otherwise dispose of the property without authorization. A lender who has possession of collateral (e.g., a pawnbroker), for instance, will likely be an embezzler if she sells the collateral when she is not authorized to do so.

      Example: V borrows $500 from Pawn, a pawnbroker, by giving Pawn possession of V's Rolex watch as collateral. Their agreement says that Pawn will hold the watch for 90 days, and will during this period give it back to V if V pays back the $500 plus interest. After 60 days, Pawn knowingly sells the watch to X for $1,000. When V tenders the $500 plus interest on the 75th day, Pawn admits that he has sold the watch.

      Pawn has committed embezzlement. He obtained possession lawfully (at the time of the loan). He then converted it by making an unauthorized sale.

F. **Fraudulent taking:** For embezzlement, the taking must be *"fraudulent."*

1. **Claim of right:** Thus if D honestly believes that he has a *right* to take the property, this will usually negate the existence of fraud. So, for instance, if D mistakenly believes that the property is *his*, or that he is authorized to use it in a certain way, this will be a defense (probably even if the mistake is unreasonable).

IV. FALSE PRETENSES

A. **Definition:** The crime of obtaining property by false pretenses — usually called simply *"false pretenses"* — has these elements:

1. A *false representation* of a
2. *material present or past fact*
3. which *causes* the person to whom it is made
4. to *pass title to*
5. his *property* to the misrepresenter, who
6. *knows* that his representation is false, and *intends to defraud*.

B. **Nature of crime:** Thus false pretenses occurs where D uses fraud or deceit to obtain not only possession but also *ownership* (title). The crime differs from larceny with respect to what is obtained: in larceny, D obtains possession only, not title.

C. **False representation of present or past fact:** There must be a *false representation* of a *material present or past fact*.

D. **Reliance:** The victim must *rely* upon the representation.

1. **Belief required:** Thus if the victim does *not believe* the representation, there is no crime of false pretenses.

2. **Materiality:** Also, the false representation must be a *"material"* one. That is, it must be a representation which would play an important role in a *reasonable person's decision* whether to enter into the transaction.

E. **Passing of title:** Remember that *title*, not merely possession, must pass for false pretenses. Generally, this turns on what the *victim intends* to do.

1. **Mere transfer of possession:** If D merely induces V to give D what V regards as *possession* of the property, that's *not false pretenses* even if D makes a material misrepresentation to induce the turn-over. Only if V thinks she's *passing title* can the crime exist.

    Example: D goes to V's bicycle store, and, pointing to an expensive model, says to V, "I'm a rich guy and also an avid biker. Can I borrow the bike for a couple of hours, and if I like it I'll buy it?" D is in fact broke, and plans to steal the bike, not buy it or return it. V says yes, and D rides the bike away.

    Even though the transaction was brought about by D's lie, it's not false pretenses. That's because V thought he was turning over mere possession, not title, to D. (This is therefore larceny by trick; see *supra*, p. 68.)

F. **MBE Tip:** "False pretenses" is *very rarely the correct answer* to an MBE question. Therefore, think long and hard before choosing this as the answer.

V. BURGLARY

A. **Common-law definition:** The common-law crime of burglary is defined as follows:

1. The *breaking* and
2. *entering* of
3. the *dwelling of another*
4. at *night*
5. with *intent to commit a felony* therein.

B. Breaking: At common law, there must be a *"breaking."* This means that an *opening* must be *created* by the burglar.

> **Example:** If Owner simply leaves his door or window *open*, the requisite breaking does not exist. However, no force or violence is needed; the mere opening of a closed but unlocked door, followed by entry, suffices.

> **1. No consent:** Also, breaking does not exist at common law if D is *invited* into the house. The MBE examiners love to test on this point.

>> **Example 1:** O, owner of a house, hires D to burn the house down so O can collect insurance proceeds. D opens the rear door, enters, then burns down the house. Even if D has committed arson, D hasn't committed burglary, because his breaking and entry was with the consent of the owner.

>> **Example 2:** D enters a museum during the hours in which it's open to the public, intending to steal a painting. D has not committed burglary, because there is no breaking (or entering) if the defendant's presence in the building was authorized. And the fact that D intended to commit a felony while inside doesn't change this fact.

> **2. Constructive breaking:** Breaking can be *"constructive"* — if D makes a *threat* that induces the occupant to let D into the building, this will satisfy the breaking element.

>> **Example:** D follows V as V drives home. When V is outside V's house, D grabs him, points a gun at V's temple, and tells V that if V doesn't let him in the house, D will shoot him. V complies, allowing D to enter. D intends to steal items from the house.
>> This is burglary. By using threats, D has constructively broken (and entered) the house.

C. Entry: There must also be, at common law, an *entry* following a breaking. However, it is sufficient that *any part* of D's anatomy enters the structure, even for a moment.

> **Example:** D opens a closed window on the first floor of V's house, then reaches his hand through the window to try to grab an item just on the inside. If D intends to take and carry the item away, as soon as D has reached the hand through D has "entered" (and also "broken"). Therefore, D has committed burglary. (And that's true even if D is unable to pick the item up and carry it away — the crime is complete as soon as the breaking-and-entering-with-intent-to-commit-a-felony-therein occurs.)

D. Dwelling of another: The common-law definition requires that the structure be the *dwelling of another*. Thus a place of business does not suffice.

E. Nighttime: At common law, the breaking and entering has to occur *at night*. But on the MBE, fact patterns may be burglary even though the entry is not at night. That's because the examiners will often give you a "burglary" statute that more-or-less mimics the common-law definition, but without the requirement of entry being at night (or, perhaps, without the requirement that the structure be a "dwelling.")

F. Intent to commit felony therein: At common law, the burglar must, at the time she entered, have *intended to commit a felony* once she got inside.

>   **Example:** D, a homeless person, breaks into V's unoccupied house at night. D does this so she can sleep where's it dry and warm. This is not burglary — there is no felony that D intends to commit once she gets inside the premises (since sleeping in someone else's premises is not a felony).

> **1. Most-often tested:** "Intent to commit a felony therein" is the element *most often tested on the MBE*. The examiners love to give you fact patterns in which D breaks and enters a dwelling, but where she does not have the intent to commit a felony inside.

>   **a. Intent to reclaim own property:** Most common scenario for testing intent-to-commit-felony-within on the MBE: D intends to *reclaim* property that she thinks is her own. Since even an *unreasonable and/or mistaken belief* that the property one is going to take or retake is one's own, this will prevent the person from intending to commit larceny in the dwelling she breaks into.

>   **Example:** D breaks into V's house at night by opening the unlocked rear door. D intends to take back a laptop computer that he thinks (honestly but unreasonably and inaccurately) V stole from him some time before. After D enters, he doesn't find the laptop, but decides on the spur of the moment to steal a piece of silverware, which he takes with him out of the house.

>   D has not committed burglary. What counts is whether D had a felonious intent *at the moment of the breaking-and-entering*. Taking back one's own property — or even what one unreasonably and mistakenly *believes* is one's own property — is not larceny. Therefore, an *intent* to take back what one thinks is one's own property cannot be an intent to commit larceny. So D had no felonious intent at the moment of entry. And the fact that D later, post-entry, developed a felonious intent regarding the silverware, does not change this key fact. So D hasn't committed burglary.

>   **b. MBE Tip:** Therefore, before selecting a choice that makes D guilty of burglary on the MBE, be sure you know exactly what felony D intended to commit once he got inside. And be especially skeptical of a choice that turns on D's alleged intent to commit larceny or robbery inside the premises — larceny-like fact patterns are especially easy for the MBE examiners to manipulate so that there's no larcenous intent.

> **2. Need not carry out felony:** Keep in mind that D must merely *intend*, at the moment of breaking-and-entering, to commit a felony inside — there's *no requirement that D actually carry out the felony*. So once D *enters with felonious intent*, the burglary is *complete*, and D can't "undo" it by changing his mind and not committing that intended (or any) felony inside. The MBE examiners like to test you on this sort of change-of-mind scenario; just be sure to answer that the burglary is complete at the moment of entry if D intended a felony.

>   **Example:** D intends to steal jewelry from V's house. He opens the front door and steps inside. V's dog barks, and D immediately leaves without taking anything. D has committed burglary — the crime was complete the instant D opened the door and stepped inside with an intent to steal something. The fact that D never stole, or committed any felony inside the house, is irrelevant.

VI. ROBBERY

A. Definition: Robbery is defined as *larceny* committed with two additional elements:

  1. The property is taken from the *person or presence* of the owner; and

2. The taking is accomplished by using *force* or putting the owner in *fear*.

   Example: D accosts V on the street at night, and says to V, "Give me your wallet or I'll punch you in the face." V complies, and D carries the property away. D has committed robbery, because D has committed larceny (the taking and carrying away of the property of another with intent to permanently deprive him of it), and has done so by taking the property from V's person, and putting V in fear of what would happen if he did not comply with D's demand.

   Note on importance of robbery on MBE: For some reason, the MBE examiners love to test on robbery. Therefore, we'll spend more time on it here than you might expect.

B. **Presence or person of V:** The property must be taken from the *presence or person* of its owner.

   1. **"Presence" of victim:** Most robberies take place directly from the victim's "person." But it is enough that the taking is from V's *"presence."* The test for "presence" is whether V, if he had not been intimidated or forcibly restrained, could have prevented the taking.

      Example: D enters V's house and bedroom. While pointing a gun at V, who is on the bed, D takes V's purse from her dresser, and carries it away. Since the property was taken from V's "presence" — V could have prevented the taking if not intimidated — robbery has taken place even though the taking was not from V's "person."

C. **Use of violence or intimidation:** The taking must be by use of *violence* or *intimidation*.

   Example 1: V is walking down the street, and is momentarily distracted by a near collision. D stealthily plucks V's wallet out of V's half-open purse. V does not realize what has happened until some time later. D has committed larceny but not robbery, because D did not use violence or intimidation.

   Example 2: Same basic fact pattern as prior example, except that D simply snatches V's purse from her grasp. V has no chance to resist, though she is aware for a fleeting second of what is happening. This is not robbery, because there has been no violence or intimidation. (But if V had been able to put up even a brief struggle, the requisite violence would exist for robbery.)

   1. **Intimidation:** A *threat of harm* may suffice in lieu of violence. V must be placed in *apprehension* of harm.

      Example: D pulls a gun on V, and says, "Your money or your life." This is robbery even though no actual force is used.

      a. **Threat that D would not carry out:** The element of intimidation is satisfied if V is put in fear, even if D makes a threat of violence that D *cannot or would not carry out*.

         Example: D enters a bank, puts his finger in his coat pocket, points it towards V (a teller) and says, "Give me the money in the cash drawer, or I'll shoot." V thinks that D probably doesn't really have a gun, but she's not sure, and doesn't want to take any chances. She gives D the contents of the cash drawer.

         D has committed robbery. Even though D could not have made good on his threat to shoot, and did not intend violence, he has intentionally and successfully created fear, and that's enough to satisfy the "force or intimidation" requirement.

   2. **Lack of force or intimidation:** If D *does not use force*, and V is *not put in fear*, then there *cannot be robbery*, even if D commits larceny from the person or presence of V.

Example: D picks V's pocket. Even if V realizes what has happened seconds later as D runs away, D has not committed robbery, because he has not used force or created fear in the victim.

    a. **Threat that V does not believe:** If D makes a threat of force that the victim V *does not believe* — so that V is *not put in fear* — there can't be robbery, even if D takes money.

    Example: D, a 17-year-old who is known in the neighborhood for being a coward and a blusterer, walks into a candy store owned by V, who has known D for years. D says, "Give me $10 from the register, or I'll shoot you with the gun I've got in my pocket." V believes that D doesn't have a gun, and wouldn't shoot or harm V even if he had one. However, V feels sorry for D, and hands him $2, saying, "Go home to your momma, sonny."

    D has not committed robbery, because he did not actually induce fear (or use actual force) against V. That's true even though D attempted to induce fear. (By the way, it's not even clear that this is larceny — V probably voluntarily gave the $2 to D, so it's not a "taking" of V's property.) But D *has* committed *attempted* robbery, since he tried to take another's property by force or fear.

    b. **Threat to third person:** The "force or intimidation" requirement can be met by D's use of force or threats to A, while taking property from the person or presence of B. In other words, threats to do *harm to someone other than the owner of the property being taken* will suffice.

    Example: An unmarried couple, Al and Betty, park a car belonging to Al. Al stays in the car, and Betty gets out. D stops Betty a few steps away, puts a gun to her head, and says to Al through the car window, "Give me the keys to the car, or I'll shoot the girl." Al hands over the keys, and D hijacks the car. Even though D made the threat of violence only as against Betty, D has taken Al's property from Al's presence, by means of force and/or intimidation. Therefore, D has committed robbery of Al.

3. **Force needed at moment of gaining possession:** D must use force or threat of harm *at the moment D first gets possession*. If D gets possession without force or threat (whether with intent to steal or not), the fact that she *later* uses force or threat to keep possession won't constitute robbery.

    Example: D spots a bicycle belonging to V chained to a lamppost, with the owner nowhere nearby. D cuts the lock, and takes the bike. One week later, D is standing next to the bike when V recognizes the bike as his own. He tries to grab the bike, but D holds on tight, and says, "If you take this from me, I'm going to smash your head in." D then rides away.

    D has not committed robbery. When she originally took possession, she did not take it "from the person or presence" of the owner. Although D used force and threats to regain possession, this doesn't constitute robbery, because the force and threats did not coincide with the original taking of possession.

    a. **"Reasonable person" standard not applied:** It is irrelevant that a *"reasonable person"* would not have been apprehensive of bodily harm. Thus if V is frightened of bodily harm due to his unusual timidity, robbery will exist even though most people would not have been afraid.

D. **No simultaneous larceny and robbery:** The same transaction *cannot* give rise to *simultaneous convictions* for larceny and robbery. This is because robbery is a form of larceny, with the additional element of force present. To put it another way, larceny is a *lesser-included offense* within robbery.

    Example: D enters Bank, and says to Teller, "Give me the money in the cash drawer, or I'll shoot you." Teller feels fear, and gives D the cash in the drawer. D can be convicted of robbery, or larceny, but not both, because larceny is a lesser included offense in the robbery charge.

1. **Requires larceny:** The fact that larceny is a lesser included offense within robbery means that if you think your MBE fact pattern may involve robbery, you must check to make sure that the elements of larceny are all satisfied.

    a. **"Taking" must be completed:** This means that if D makes a threat or uses force in an attempt to take property, but then doesn't succeed in taking the property, there can't be robbery. In other words, for robbery the *larceny must be completed.*

    Example: D walks into a bank, points a gun at the teller, and says, "Give me the cash in your drawer or I'll shoot." The teller says, "I don't have any cash, my drawer was just emptied." D looks, and sees that this is true. D decides to flee, rather than approach a different teller.

    D hasn't committed robbery — there was no completed larceny, so there can't be robbery, even though D used force in an attempt to commit larceny. (But this *is attempted* robbery.)

    b. **Reclaiming of D's own property:** Similarly, the fact that robbery includes larceny means that if D is *reclaiming his own property*, then even if he's using force or intimidation and taking the property back from the possession of another, D isn't committing robbery. The same is true if D honestly but mistakenly (even unreasonably) believes that what he is taking is his own property.

    Example: D's bicycle is stolen. Two weeks later, D sees V standing on the street, holding what D thinks he recognizes as his stolen bicycle. He grabs it from V, saying "If you don't give it to me, I'll shoot you." D is in fact mistaken — it's not his bicycle, just a look-alike.

    D has not committed robbery because he hasn't committed larceny. He hasn't committed larceny because he is taking (back) his own property, not property of "another." (See *supra*, p. 69.)

VII. ARSON

A. **Nature of offense:** At common law, arson is the *malicious burning* of the *dwelling* of *another*.

1. **Act posing great risk of fire:** The mens rea requirement for arson is *"malice,"* not "intent." Therefore, D need *not* be shown to have intended to create a burning — it's enough that D intentionally took an action under circumstances posing a *large risk* of a burning. In other words, *"recklessness"* with respect to the risk of fire suffices.

    Example: D, a sailor, intends to steal rum from the hold of a ship. He lights a match to see better, and the rum catches fire. Since D's act is reckless — D disregarded a large risk of a burning of the dwelling of another (people live on the ship) — D can be found guilty of arson, even though he did not intend the burning. [*Regina v. Faulkner*]

    a. **Failure to take action:** Furthermore, in an arson scenario, the rule that one who brings about a risky condition has an obligation to *use reasonable efforts to avoid harm* (p. 9) is likely to be important. (This is an exception to the general rule that omission to act will generally not bring criminal liability.)

        i. **Failure to put out fire D started:** So one who *brings about a serious risk of fire —* even if *non-negligently —* then has *an obligation to take reasonable affirmative steps to put out the fire.* If the person doesn't take such steps, and the person also had a desire that property be destroyed (or even recklessness with regard to the risk of destruction by fire), she can be liable for arson even though she didn't intentionally or negligently start the fire.

Example: For some time, D has wished that his warehouse would burn down, so that D could collect the insurance on it. But D has never acted on this wish. One day, D drops a match by accident (non-negligently). A small fire starts. D could put out the fire. Instead, he decides to let nature take its course, and walks away. The building is destroyed. Assume that a statute makes it arson to "intentionally cause the destruction of a building by fire" (even if it's one's own building).

D can be convicted of arson. Even though he started the fire unintentionally (indeed, non-negligently), once he created the risk of fire and knew it, he had the obligation to use reasonable means to stop the fire. When he didn't do that, and had a mental state of desire that the building burn, he became guilty of arson just as if he had intentionally started the fire.

2. **Dwelling:** At common law, the property burned must be a *dwelling*.

   Example: D starts fire to an office building. Because this is not a dwelling, D cannot be guilty of common-law arson.

   a. **"Of another":** Furthermore, the dwelling must be "of *another*," i.e., must not belong to the defendant.

   Example: D sets fire to his own house, in order to collect the insurance proceeds. If only D's house burns, he's not guilty of common-law arson. That's true even if the house is co-owned by D's wife W. (But if the fire spreads to another house, D is guilty, even if he didn't expect or desire the spreading.)

   b. **MBE tip:** But on the MBE, the examiners will often tell you the text of the arson statute you are to assume is in force. That statute may well omit either the "dwelling" or "of another" requirements. In that case, the crime could include a scenario in which D burns down his own business premises to collect insurance, and is guilty of statutory arson.

CRIMINAL PROCEDURE OUTLINE

TABLE OF CONTENTS
CRIMINAL PROCEDURE OUTLINE

Chapter 1
CONSTITUTIONAL CRIMINAL PROCEDURE GENERALLY

I. CRIMINAL PROCEDURE ON THE MBE........................ 85

Chapter 2
ARREST; PROBABLE CAUSE; SEARCH WARRANTS

I. GENERAL PRINCIPLES 86

II. AREAS AND PEOPLE PROTECTED BY THE FOURTH AMENDMENT 87

III. THE "PLAIN VIEW" DOCTRINE 90

IV. PROBABLE CAUSE GENERALLY 92

V. PARTICULAR INFORMATION ESTABLISHING PROBABLE CAUSE 94

VI. SEARCH WARRANTS — ISSUANCE AND EXECUTION 94

Chapter 3
WARRANTLESS ARRESTS AND SEARCHES

I. INTRODUCTION.. 96

II. WARRANTLESS ARRESTS 96

III. SEARCH INCIDENT TO ARREST............................. 97

IV. EXIGENT CIRCUMSTANCES 100

V. AUTOMOBILE SEARCHES 100

VI. CONSENT SEARCHES GENERALLY 103

VII. CONSENT BY THIRD PERSONS............................. 104

VIII. STOP-AND-FRISK AND OTHER BRIEF DETENTION 106

IX.	INSPECTIONS AND WEAPONS SEARCHES	108

Chapter 4
ELECTRONIC SURVEILLANCE AND SECRET AGENTS

I.	ELECTRONIC SURVEILLANCE	109
II.	SECRET AGENTS	110

Chapter 5
CONFESSIONS AND POLICE INTERROGATION

I.	INTRODUCTION	111
II.	VOLUNTARINESS	111
III.	*MIRANDA* GENERALLY	111
IV.	WHAT IS A "CUSTODIAL" INTERROGATION	113
V.	MINOR CRIMES	113
VI.	WHAT CONSTITUTES INTERROGATION	113
VII.	THE "PUBLIC SAFETY" EXCEPTION TO *MIRANDA*	115
VIII.	WAIVER OF *MIRANDA* RIGHTS	115
IX.	OTHER *MIRANDA* ISSUES	116

Chapter 6
LINEUPS AND OTHER PRE-TRIAL IDENTIFICATION PROCEDURES

I.	I.D. PROCEDURES GENERALLY	117
II.	THE PRIVILEGE AGAINST SELF-INCRIMINATION	117
III.	THE RIGHT TO COUNSEL AT PRE-TRIAL CONFRONTATIONS	119
IV.	DUE PROCESS LIMITS ON I.D. PROCEDURE	120

TABLE OF CONTENTS

Chapter 7
THE EXCLUSIONARY RULE

- I. THE RULE GENERALLY 120
- II. STANDING TO ASSERT THE EXCLUSIONARY RULE 121
- III. DERIVATIVE EVIDENCE 122
- IV. COLLATERAL USE EXCEPTIONS 124
- V. THE "GOOD FAITH WARRANT" EXCEPTION 124

Chapter 8
THE RIGHT TO COUNSEL

- I. THE INDIGENT'S RIGHT TO COUNSEL 125
- II. WAIVER OF THE RIGHT TO COUNSEL 126
- III. ENTITLEMENTS OF THE RIGHT TO COUNSEL 127

Chapter 9
FORMAL PROCEEDINGS

- I. GRAND JURY PROCEEDINGS 127
- II. RIGHT TO BAIL 129
- III. PLEA BARGAINING AND GUILTY PLEAS 129
- IV. THE RIGHT TO A JURY TRIAL 131
- V. THE TRIAL 132
- VI. DOUBLE JEOPARDY 135

CRIMINAL PROCEDURE OUTLINE

This Outline attempts to cover only topics that have been repeatedly tested on actual MBE exams. References to "L&I" are to LaFave & Israel, *Criminal Procedure* Hornbook (2d Ed., West, 1992).

CHAPTER 1
CONSTITUTIONAL CRIMINAL PROCEDURE GENERALLY

I. CRIMINAL PROCEDURE ON THE MBE

A. Meaning of "criminal procedure": The MBE's questions on Criminal Procedure account for about 40% of total Criminal Law and Procedure questions (i.e., about 13 questions out of 33).

These questions focus almost exclusively on the federal constitutional requirements that state and federal prosecutions must meet. Here are the main topics that the examiners test:

1. The *Fourth Amendment's* rules on *when and how the police may make arrests,* and may *search and seize* people's premises and possessions.

2. The *Fifth Amendment's* limits on the *interrogation* of suspects and the obtaining of *confessions*, especially the *Miranda* rule.

3. The use of *line-ups* and other pre-trial *identification procedures*.

4. The *exclusionary rule*, and how it affects the admissibility of evidence obtained through methods that violate the Constitution.

5. The Sixth Amendment *right to counsel*.

6. *Grand jury* proceedings.

7. *Plea bargaining* and the making of *guilty pleas*.

8. The right to, and conducting of, a *jury trial*.

9. The *Double Jeopardy* clause.

Of these topics, the most important two are Nos. 1 and 2 (in particular, Fourth Amendment limits on searches and seizures and *Miranda* rules on confessions).

B. Applicability of Bill of Rights to states: In deciding how the federal constitution applies to state criminal prosecutions, the Supreme Court follows the *"selective incorporation"* approach. Under this approach, not all rights enumerated in the Bill of Rights are applicable to the state, but if *any aspect of a right* is found to be so necessary to fundamental fairness that it applies to the states, then *all aspects* of that right apply. Thus if a right is applicable in state courts, its *scope* is the same as in federal courts.

1. **Nearly all rights applicable to states:** Virtually all of the rights given to criminal defendants under the U.S. Constitution apply — and apply the same way — whether the investigation and trial are done by federal or by state authorities.

    a. **Grand jury indictment:** The one exception relevant to the MBE is that Fifth Amendment's right to a *grand jury* indictment applies only to federal charges, not state ones. (Therefore, a state may decide to begin a prosecution by using an "information" prepared

Chapter 2
ARREST; PROBABLE CAUSE; SEARCH WARRANTS

by the prosecutor rather than a grand jury indictment, whereas federal prosecutions must always be brought by indictment.)

I. GENERAL PRINCIPLES

A. **Fourth Amendment:** The Fourth Amendment to the U.S. Constitution provides, "The right of the people to be secure in their persons, houses, papers, and effects, *against unreasonable searches and seizures*, shall not be violated, and *no Warrants shall issue, but upon probable cause*, supported by Oath or affirmation, and *particularly describing* the place to be searched, and the persons or things to be seized."

B. **Applies to both searches and arrests:** The Fourth Amendment thus applies both to *searches and seizures* of *property*, and to *arrests* of persons.

   1. **Invalid arrest no defense:** Generally, the fact that D was *arrested in an unconstitutional manner* makes *no difference*: a defendant may generally be tried and convicted regardless of the fact that his arrest was made in violation of the Fourth Amendment. However, when evidence is seized as part of a *warrantless search* conducted *incident to an arrest*, the evidence will be excluded as inadmissible if the arrest was a violation of the Constitution (e.g., the arresting officer did not have probable cause to believe that D had committed a crime).

   2. **Probable cause for issuance of warrant:** Where a search or arrest warrant is issued, the Fourth Amendment requires that the warrant be issued only based on *"probable cause."* This requirement is quite strictly enforced.

   3. **Where warrant required:** A warrant is usually *required* before a *search or seizure* takes place, unless there are "exigent circumstances." An *arrest* warrant, by contrast, is usually *not* constitutionally required.

   4. **Search must always be "reasonable":** Whether or not there is a search warrant or arrest warrant, the arrest or search *must not be "unreasonable."*

C. **Protects against government action only:** The Fourth Amendment protects only against searches and seizures that are *carried out by (or on behalf of) the government.*

   1. **Purely private search or seizure:** Therefore, if a *private person, acting alone,* does something that if done by government would constitute a search or seizure, then *forwards* the resulting evidence to the government, the Fourth Amendment has not been violated.

   > **Example:** D has a guest, G, staying at his house. G is aware of a recent murder, in which an unusual gold-and-diamond bracelet engraved with the victim's initials was stolen. G, who suspects that D may have committed the murder, rummages through D's bedroom closet while D is away, and discovers what G recognizes as the missing bracelet. G forwards the bracelet to the police, who promptly arrest D for the murder. D moves to suppress the bracelet on the theory that its seizure violated D's Fourth Amendment rights.
   >
   > D will lose. The Fourth Amendment protects only against seizures and seizures by or on behalf of government. G was acting here solely as a private citizen, and the fact that G turned the evidence over to the government after seizing it doesn't change this.

a. **Distinctions:** But the "purely private action" scenario in the above Example must be *distinguished* from two other situations in which the Fourth Amendment *will* be implicated:

[1] The private citizen has suspicions, goes to the police, and the police *actively encourage the private citizen to make the search.* If the private citizen does so, this probably will now be government action — action taken on behalf of the government — that can violate the Fourth Amendment.

Example: On the facts of the above Example, suppose that before rummaging in D's closet, G went to the police and said, "I suspect D of the murder — do you think I should look through his closet?" The police say, "Yes, by all means, because we agree with you that D may well have done it." Now, if G does the closet-rummaging, this is effectively state action, and the performance of the warrantless search violates D's Fourth Amendment rights.

[2] The private citizen finds suspicious materials that she seizes without having fully searched, and forwards them to the government. The government then *examines the materials more extensively* than the private citizen did. Anything "extra" that the government discovers will be deemed the product of a Fourth Amendment search, and potentially suppressed. Cf. L&I, §3.1, p. 118; [*Walter v. U.S.*].

Example: Same basic facts from the example on p. 86, in which G suspects D of the murder, and rummages through D's closet. Now, however, assume that G finds only a closed box with a note on it in D's handwriting, "souvenir of my night with V.G." (the victim's initials). G doesn't open the box, but forwards it to the police. The police open it and find the bracelet that they recognize as having come from the victim. The bracelet will be suppressible. That's because the police conducted a new, wider, search than G did, and the new information they discovered — the existence and appearance of the bracelet — was the fruit of the wider government search. Since that new search took place without a warrant (and probably without probable cause), D is entitled to have it suppressed as a violation of his Fourth Amendment rights.

Note: But a government search that merely replicates what the private individual already did will not be a government search. Thus if on the above example G had found the box, opened it, discovered the bracelet, resealed the box, and forwarded the re-closed box to the government, the government *wouldn't* commit a Fourth Amendment search or seizure by re-opening the box and examining the bracelet. [*U.S. v. Jacobsen*]

II. AREAS AND PEOPLE PROTECTED BY THE FOURTH AMENDMENT

A. *Katz* **"expectation of privacy" doctrine:** A Fourth Amendment search or seizure only takes place when a person's *"reasonable expectation of privacy"* has been violated. [*Katz v. U.S.*]

1. **Waiver of privacy right:** A person's conduct may mean that he has *no* reasonable expectation of privacy in a particular situation. If so, no Fourth Amendment search or seizure will result, even if the police are doing something that a non-lawyer would think of as being a "search" or "seizure."

   a. **Contexts:** Some types of evidence that are likely to be found *not protected* by any "reasonable expectation of privacy" are:

   [1] *abandoned property*, such as *trash*;

[2] things that can be seen from an *aerial overview*, or from the perspective of a person *stationed on public property* (e.g., a police officer who stands on a sidewalk and looks through binoculars into a window at the front of D's house);

[3] things a person says or does while *in public* (e.g., D1 talks to D2 in a restaurant, while a police officer is eavesdropping nearby); and

[4] information the police learn by use of *other senses* while the police are in a place they have a right to be (e.g., the police use dogs to smell luggage in airports and, thus, detect drugs).

2. **Significance of trespass:** If the police have committed a *trespass* or a *physical intrusion* against a person's property, their conduct is *more likely* to be found to *violate* the person's reasonable expectation of privacy than if no trespass or physical intrusion takes place.

   a. **Presence or absence of trespass not dispositive:** But presence or absence of physical intrusion or trespass is *just one factor* — it's not dispositive. So the "reasonable expectation of privacy" rule means that police conduct may still be a Fourth Amendment search or seizure even though the police do *not* commit a trespass — if the facts are such that D had a reasonable expectation that his possessions, conduct, or words would remain private, the absence of police trespass will be irrelevant.

   Example: FBI agents place electronic eavesdropping equipment on the outside of a public telephone booth from which D, a bookmaker, conducts his business. *Held*, even though D made his phone calls on public property, and the agents did not commit trespass in installing their devices, D's reasonable expectation of privacy was violated, so the agents conducted a Fourth Amendment search. "The Fourth Amendment protects people, not places." [*Katz v. U.S.*, supra, p. 87.]

   i. **Remote entry via computer:** Because no physical trespass is necessary, it can and often will be a violation of D's Fourth Amendment rights for government to seize or search the contents of D's *computer by remote means.*

   Example: Agent, a government law-enforcement agent, heads a government program to detect child-pornographers. Agent puts up a Website offering what appear to be (but are not) child-pornographic images. When a person downloads one of the images, the image contains a secret "Trojan Horse" that mails back to Agent's computer a sample of images on the user's hard drive. D downloads an image from Agent's site, and the Trojan Horse causes pornographic images from D's computer to be uploaded to Agent. D is prosecuted for illegally possessing the images, and seeks to have them suppressed as having been obtained in violation of his Fourth Amendment right not to be subjected to warrantless searches.

   D will win. D had a reasonable expectation of privacy in the contents of his computer, and the secret use by government of the software to sample his computer's contents impaired that expectation. Since the government did not have a warrant (or probable cause), the taking of the contents was a violation of D's Fourth Amendment rights.

B. **Standard for determining:** For the defendant to get Fourth Amendment protection in a particular situation, two tests must be satisfied: (1) she must show an *actual, subjective,* expectation of privacy; and (2) the expectation must be one that *society* recognizes as being *"reasonable."*

   1. **"Reasonable expectation of privacy":** The two concepts are expressed together by saying that D must *"have a reasonable expectation of privacy"* in the place or thing being searched or seized.

C. **Curtilage:** The "reasonable expectation of privacy" concept intersects with the concept of *"curtilage."* The curtilage of a building typically refers to the *land and ancillary buildings* that are associated with a dwelling. In the case of a typical private house, for instance, the front yard, backyard and garage are all parts of the curtilage.

1. **Significance of curtilage:** In general, a person has a *reasonable expectation of privacy with respect to the curtilage*, but *not* with respect to *open fields outside the curtilage*. (This is always subject to the exception that a person does not have a reasonable expectation of privacy as to things that can be *seen from public property*.)

    Example 1: D fences in his backyard with a 10-foot high wall, and grows marijuana in the backyard. Officer climbs over the wall and takes photos of the marijuana bushes. Since the backyard is part of D's curtilage, he has a reasonable expectation of privacy with respect to that area, and Officer has carried out a Fourth Amendment search (which will be invalid unless done with probable cause, and which may be invalid because no warrant was procured).

    Example 2: D owns a 100-acre farm, with a farmhouse near one edge. D grows marijuana in the very middle of the 100 acres. The fields (except perhaps those that are immediately adjacent to the farmhouse) are not part of the curtilage. Therefore, if Officer enters D's property and photographs the marijuana plants, he is not infringing on D's reasonable expectation of privacy, and is thus not committing a Fourth Amendment search. This is probably true even if D has fenced in the entire 100 acres, and placed "No Trespassing" signs throughout. [*cf. Oliver v. U.S.*]

D. **Trash and other abandoned property:** *Trash* or other *abandoned* property will normally *not* be material as to which the owner has a reasonable expectation of privacy. Therefore, when a person puts trash out on the curb to be picked up by the garbage collector, the police may *search that trash without a warrant*. [*California v. Greenwood*]

E. **Guests:** *Guests* — persons visiting or staying in premises that are *not their own residence* — may or may not have a legitimate expectation of privacy in the premises being visited. Generally, an *overnight guest will* have an expectation of privacy, but a *casual social visitor* who is *not staying overnight* is *less likely* to have such an expectation.

1. **Guest staying in hotel room:** A person who is staying *overnight* in a *hotel room* normally has a reasonable expectation of privacy in that room. Therefore, the police will need a search warrant (or some exception to the need for one) before they conduct a search of the room. Furthermore, the manager of the hotel does not have actual or apparent *authority* to consent to a search of the hotel room before the guest has permanently checked out (see *infra*, p. 105 for more about third-party consent to search).

    Example: Muni police have long suspected D of being the murderer of V, found shot to death two years before. The Muni police get a tip from an informant known to be reliable that: (1) D is in town to visit relatives, and has just checked in to the local Holiday Inn; and (2) D has brought with him on the trip a gun that was used in the shooting of V. The police go to the Holiday Inn, and are told that D seems to have left the hotel for the evening, but has not checked out. They ask the hotel manager to let them into D's room, which she does. There, on the desk, they spot a gun that they seize, and that turns out to have been the one used in the shooting of V. At his murder trial, D moves to suppress the gun on the grounds that it was obtained in violation of his Fourth Amendment rights.

    The court must *grant* D's suppression motion. An overnight hotel guest has a reasonable expectation of privacy in the rented room, up until the time the guest checks out. Furthermore, the hotel management does not have actual or apparent authority to consent to a search of the premises while the guest is checked in (since the hotel has, by renting the room to the guest, given the guest exclusive right to possess the room during the stay, except for housekeeping purposes). Therefore, the fact that the manager let the police into D's room does not prevent their entry from being an interference with D's privacy expectations. Consequently, even though the police probably had probable cause to believe that evidence of criminality would be found in the room, the Fourth Amendment required them either to get a search warrant, or to establish some exception to the need for such a warrant. Here, the only plausible exception was the one for "exigent circumstances" (see *infra*, p. 100), but that exception would not apply here — the police could have posted a guard outside the room to secure it, while they went to a magistrate to get a warrant, so the circumstances were not truly exigent.

2. **Overnight social guest:** Similarly, an *overnight social guest* normally *has* a legitimate expectation of privacy in the home where he is staying. Therefore, the police may normally not make a warrantless arrest or warrantless search of the premises where D is staying as an overnight guest. (But if the owner of the premises consents to a search, the guest is out of luck.) [*Minnesota v. Olson*]

   a. **Social guest not staying overnight:** A social guest who is *not staying overnight* probably *also has* a legitimate expectation of privacy in the premises, although the Supreme Court has not definitively decided this question yet.

3. **Business guest:** A guest who is at the premises on *business* is *less likely* than a social guest to be found to have a legitimate expectation of privacy in the premises. Where the business visit is a relatively *brief* one, the court is especially likely to find that there is no legitimate privacy expectation.

   Example: D visits X's apartment for a couple of hours, for the purpose of bagging cocaine that D and X will later sell. The police snoop while the visit is going on. *Held*, the shortness of the visit and the business-rather-than-personal nature of what D did at the apartment meant that D had no legitimate expectation of privacy in the apartment. Therefore, D's Fourth Amendment rights couldn't have been violated, even if *X*'s rights were violated. [*Minnesota v. Carter* (1998)]

III. THE "PLAIN VIEW" DOCTRINE

A. **The plain view doctrine, generally:** In general, the police do not commit a Fourth Amendment search where they see an object that is in the *plain view* of an officer who has a *right to be in the position to have that view*. This is the "plain view doctrine."

   Example: While Officer is walking down the street, he happens to glance through the picture window of D's house. He spots D strangling V to death with a stocking. Because D's conduct took place in "plain view" of Officer — that is, Officer perceived the conduct while being in a place where he was entitled to be — Officer can give testimony at D's trial about what he saw, with no Fourth Amendment problem. By contrast, if Officer had without a warrant secreted himself in D's house, then observed the murder, Officer would not be permitted to testify about what he saw, because the view would not have occurred from a place from where Officer had a right to be.

   1. **Police must be entitled to be in place from which they have view:** Keep in mind that the plain-view doctrine applies only if the police are, at the time they have the plain view, *in a position that they are legally entitled to be in*. So if they've committed, say, some Fourth Amendment violation to get in that position, the doctrine won't apply.

Example: Officer files with a magistrate an affidavit seeking a warrant to search D's basement for a rifle believed to have been used in the murder of V. Officer knowingly falsifies some of the material information in the affidavit. The magistrate issues the warrant. Officer conducts the search pursuant to the warrant. While Officer is in the basement, she sees, in plain view on a work bench, marijuana, which she seizes. At D's drug possession trial, D moves to suppress the marijuana as the fruit of an illegal search and seizure.

D will win. It's true that at the moment Officer saw the marijuana, the drugs were in "plain view" from Officer's position. But Officer only got to that physical position by lying about material facts on the warrant application, so the warrant was improperly issued, and the basic entry into D's house violated his Fourth Amendment rights. Since the plain view doctrine only applies when the police are legally the position from which they have the view, the doctrine doesn't apply here.

a. **Violation of some third party's right to get in position for view:** When you are applying the rule that police must be "in a position that they are legally entitled to be in" at the time they have the plain view, keep in mind that *standing principles* (see *infra*, p. 121) dictate that "legally entitled" refers *only to the legal rights of the defendant*, not to the rights of *some third person*. In other words, if the police get themselves in a position to have the plain view of D's wrongdoing not by violating D's rights but by violating the rights of some third person, that will *not negate* the police's use of the plain-view doctrine as against D.

   i. **Trespass on neighbor's property to get the plain view:** So, for instance, if the police gain the plain view of D's activities by *trespassing on the property of D's neighbor N*, the fact that the police violated N's legal rights won't prevent the plain view doctrine from applying against D.

   Example: Officer gets an anonymous tip from an informant of unknown reliability that D, who lives at a particular address, appears to be growing marijuana plants under bright lights in the den of D's home. Officer determines that, although the den cannot be viewed from the street, it can be viewed from a vantage point in the backyard of N, a neighbor whose backyard backs up to D's backyard. Officer, without notifying N, crosses N's front yard into his backyard, and from a position in N's backyard, sees into D's den, and spots what look like a large number of marijuana plants being cultivated under very bright lights. Officer uses this information to get a search warrant, serves the warrant, and seizes the marijuana plants from the den. D moves to suppress the plants as being the fruit of a Fourth Amendment violation.

   D's motion will be denied. It is true that Officer probably violated the Fourth Amendment rights of *N*, by trespassing on N's property to get into position to have the view of D's den. But the principle that the police may apply the plain view doctrine only when they are "legally entitled to be in the position to have that view" means only that the police must not be violating the rights *of the person against whom the view is directed*. So the fact that Officer violated *N*'s rights doesn't matter as against *D*, due to the rule preventing the assertion of the constitutional rights of third parties (see *infra*, p. 121).

   What about any violation of D's own rights? The fact that D cultivated the plants within plain view of his neighbor N means that D did not have a reasonable expectation of privacy as to that cultivation — a person does not have a reasonable expectation of privacy as to activities that may be observed by, say, a non-relative X standing on X's own property. (Nor does it matter that, due to the informant's unknown reliability, the informant's tip did not give Officer *probable cause* to suspect wrongdoing by D — when the plain view doctrine properly applies, it negates the applicability of *both* the requirement of a search warrant to obtain that view, and the requirement of probable cause to obtain that view, since no Fourth Amendment search is deemed to occur.) Therefore, the plain view doctrine applied to validate Officer's view through D's window, and the fruits of that view were properly relied on by Officer in getting the subsequent search warrant.

2. **Distinguish from seizure:** The fact that the police may have a plain view of an item does not mean that they may necessarily *seize* that item as evidence. Unless the officer is already legally in a place where he can *touch* the item, the mere fact that he *sees* it will not dispense with the need for a warrant to seize the item.

> **Example:** On the facts of the above marijuana-cultivation example, the fact that Officer has properly looked through the den window to see D's marijuana plants wouldn't entitle Officer to then enter D's house without a warrant and to seize the plants. (That's why the problem was set up to have Officer use what he learned via the plain view to get a search warrant.)

B. **Use of mechanical devices, generally:** The "plain view" doctrine will often apply where the police stand on public property, and use *mechanical devices* to obtain the view of D or his property.

1. **Flashlights:** Thus if a police officer, standing on public property, uses a *flashlight* to obtain a view of D or his property, this will nonetheless be a "plain view" and will, therefore, not be a Fourth Amendment search. [*Texas v. Brown*]

2. **Electronic "beeper":** Similarly, the police may attach an electronic *"beeper"* on a vehicle, and use the beeper to follow the vehicle — this does not violate the driver's reasonable expectation of privacy, and thus does not constitute a Fourth Amendment search.

3. **High-tech devices not in general public use:** But if government obtains special *high-tech devices, not in general civilian use,* and employs them from public places to gain "views" that could *not* be had by the naked eye, the use of such devices will be *considered a search*. [*Kyllo v. U.S.*]

> **Example:** Police point a "thermal imager" at the outside of D's house from across the street. The device detects heat escaping from D's house, and shows the relative amounts of heat as black and white images, so that police can see that the garage is much hotter than the rest of the house (indicating that it's being used to grow marijuana). *Held*, because the imager has not been in general civilian use, what it shows is not in "plain view." [*Kyllo v. U.S.*]

C. **Aerial observation:** When the police use an *aircraft* to view D's property from the air, *anything the police can see with the naked eye* falls within the "plain view" doctrine (as long as the aircraft is in *public, navigable* airspace). [*California v. Ciraolo; Florida v. Riley*]

D. **Police on defendant's property:** The plain view doctrine applies not only where the police obtain a view from public property, but also where they are *lawfully on the owner's property*.

> **Example:** The police come to D's house to make a lawful arrest of him. Any observation they make while in the ordinary process of arresting him does not constitute a Fourth Amendment search. (But this does not allow the police to open closed containers or packages while they are making the arrest, or even move items to get a better view — this would not fall within the plain view doctrine, and would be a Fourth Amendment search.)

IV. PROBABLE CAUSE GENERALLY

A. **Where requirement of probable cause applies:** The requirement of "probable cause" applies to two different situations: (1) before a judge or magistrate may issue a *warrant* for a search or arrest, she must be satisfied that probable cause to do so exists; and (2) before the police may make a *warrantless* search or arrest (permissible only in special circumstances described below), the officer must have probable cause for that search or arrest.

1. **Source of requirement:** Only case (1) above — the requirement of probable cause prior to issuance of a warrant — is expressly covered in the Fourth Amendment. But the Supreme Court has, as a matter of constitutional interpretation, held that probable cause must normally exist before a warrantless search or arrest as well, to avoid giving the police an incentive to avoid seeking a warrant.

B. **Requirement for probable cause:** The meaning of the term "probable cause" is not exactly the same in the search context as in the arrest context.

1. **Probable cause to arrest:** For there to be probable cause to *arrest* a person it must be *reasonably likely* that:

    a. a *violation of the law* has been committed; and

    b. the *person* to be arrested *committed* the violation.

2. **Probable cause to search:** For there to be probable cause to *search* particular premises, it must be reasonably likely that:

    [1] the specific items to be searched for are *connected* with *criminal activities;* and

    [2] these items will be *found in the place to be searched.*

C. **No admissibility limitation:** Any trustworthy information may be considered in determining whether probable cause to search or arrest exists, *even if the information would not be admissible at trial.*

D. **Only evidence heard by magistrate used:** Probable cause for the issuance of a warrant must be judged only by reference to the *facts presented to the magistrate* who is to issue the warrant. (Usually, information for a warrant will be in the form of a police officer's affidavit, not oral testimony.)

> **Example:** Officer asks for a warrant to search Dwight's apartment for the fruits of a recent specified burglary. Officer's supporting affidavit asserts Officer's belief that such fruits will be found in the apartment, but does not mention to Magistrate his basis for that belief. Magistrate grants the warrant, the search takes place, fruits of the burglary are found, and Dwight is tried for the burglary. At Dwight's trial, Dwight can successfully move to have the fruits of the search excluded, because the Magistrate was not presented with specific facts that would have given Magistrate probable cause to believe that the fruits would be found at Dwight's premises.

1. **Perjured affidavit:** If D can show, by a preponderance of the evidence, that (1) affidavits used to obtain the warrant contained *perjury* by the affiant, or (2) the affiant *"recklessly disregarded"* the truth or falsity of the information used in the affidavit, the warrant will be *invalidated* (assuming that the rest of the affidavit does not contain materials sufficient to constitute probable cause). [*Franks v. Delaware*] But D can't knock out the warrant merely because it contains *inaccurate* material; he must show actual perjury or reckless disregard of the truth by the affiant himself (not merely by the affiant's sources, such as informers).

    a. **Honest police error:** So if the police make an *honest error* — they honestly and reasonably, but erroneously, believe certain information and assert it in affidavits to get a warrant — the warrant will not be rendered invalid when the error later comes to light. [*Maryland v. Garrison*] (See infra, p. 125.)

V. PARTICULAR INFORMATION ESTABLISHING PROBABLE CAUSE

A. **Information from informants:** When the information on which probable cause is based comes from *informants* who are themselves engaged in criminal activity, courts closely scrutinize the information. Whether the informant's information creates probable cause for a search or arrest is to be determined by the *"totality of the circumstances."* [*Illinois v. Gates*]

 1. **Two factors:** The magistrate will consider two factors in evaluating the informant's information:

 [1] whether the informant is a generally *reliable witness*; and

 [2] whether facts are set forth showing the informant's *"basis of knowledge,"* that is, the particular means by which the informant came upon the information that he supplied to the police.

 a. **Strong factor can buttress weak factor:** But a strong showing on one of these factors can make up for a weak showing on the other one.

 Example: If a particular informant is known for being unusually reliable, her failure to explain the basis of her knowledge in a particular case will not be a bar to a finding of probable cause based on her tip.

 b. **Prediction of future events:** Also, if later events help *corroborate* the informant's story, these events can be combined with the informant's story to establish probable cause, even though neither by itself would suffice.

 2. **MBE tip on informant's info:** If information from an informant meets this "totality of the circumstances" test, it can *suffice* for issuance of a warrant *even without any other, non-informant-supplied, information.* The MBE examiners like to test you on this — they give you a (wrong) choice that asserts that a warrant can't be issued based solely on an informant's information.

B. **"Stale" information not sufficient:** Information submitted to the magistrate in support of a search warrant may not be *"stale,"* i.e., *too old to have much predictive value* about whether the items will still be found when the warrant is issued. Information more than a couple of weeks old presents a serious staleness issue. MBE examiners like to test on this. [*Sgro v. U.S.*]

 Example: Officer submits an affidavit in support of a search warrant request. The affidavit says that Informant, who has previously given Officer reliable information, said that Informant visited the home of X two months ago and purchased narcotics. Officer therefore requests a warrant to search X's home now for narcotics.

 The magistrate should refuse to issue the warrant, on the grounds that the information is too stale to constitute probable cause to believe that drugs will be found on the premises now.

VI. SEARCH WARRANTS — ISSUANCE AND EXECUTION

A. **Who may issue:** A search warrant must be issued by some sort of *judicial officer*, usually either a judge or a magistrate. (We'll use the term "magistrate" here.)

 1. **Neutrality:** The magistrate must be a *neutral party*, detached from the law-enforcement side of government.

B. **Affidavit:** Normally, the police officer seeking a search warrant must put the facts establishing probable cause into a *written, signed affidavit*.

C. **Requirement of particular description:** The Fourth Amendment requires that a warrant contain a *particular description of the premises to be searched, and the things to be seized*. This means that the warrant must be specific enough that a police officer executing it, even if she had no initial connection with the case, would know where to search and what items to seize.

D. Execution of warrant: The Fourth Amendment places some limits on how a validly-issued search warrant may be *executed*:

1. **Knock and announce:** Except under exigent circumstances, the police must *"knock and announce"* themselves before they enter the premises. However, if they do so and do not receive a response, they may then *break into* the premises to execute the warrant. And that's true even if there are no exigent circumstances that would make it likely that evidence would be destroyed if the police waited and came back at a different time.

2. **Limited to plausible locations:** When the police are executing the warrant, they may only search in places where the items covered in the warrant *might plausibly be located*.

    Example: If the warrant is solely for a specified automobile thought to be located in or at D's house, the police cannot roam through, say, D's kitchen or living room, because the automobile is so big that it couldn't plausibly be there. If they roam beyond the places the item might plausibly be, and find something incriminating (drugs, say), they can't seize the item even though it's in plain view, because the plain view doctrine (see *supra*, p. 90), applies only to items seen and seized by the police from a position they have a right to be in.

    a. **End of search when object is found:** Similarly, if the warrant lists a particular item, the police must ordinarily *stop their search as soon as the item is found*. The MBE examiners like to give you scenarios in which the police are validly executing a search (or arrest) warrant, but then *go beyond the scope* of the warrant, perhaps because they've already found the item(s) covered by the warrant. In general, what the police find after they have gone beyond the scope of the warrant will be inadmissible against the defendant.

    Example: The police receive a reliable tip from an informant that D is in possession of cocaine in a ruby-encrusted jewel box located somewhere in the living room of D's house. They procure a warrant to search the house for the jewel box. They knock at the front door, and D allows them to enter the house. They find the jewel box in the living room, open it, see that it contains a substance that appears to be cocaine, and seize the substance. They immediately arrest D, who is standing nearby, on drug possession charges. They then continue to search the rest of the house for other drugs. In the basement, they find a closed briefcase. They open the briefcase, see it contains plastic bags of marijuana, and seize those bags. D moves to suppress the marijuana on Fourth Amendment grounds.

    D's motion to suppression must be granted. Once the officers found the jewel box and seized its contents, they had completed the execution of the warrant. Therefore, no further searching they did was justified by the warrant. It's true that they then had probable cause to arrest D for drug possession, and the consequent right to search the area around his person (and probably the entire room he was in) incident to the arrest. (See *infra*, pp. 97-98.) They probably also had the right to do a protective sweep of the house to discover whether other dangerous persons might be there (see *infra*, p. 98); but this protective-sweep right extended only to look in places where a person might be hiding, not to examine closed containers found in rooms where no one was present. So the contents of the briefcase were fruits of an extended search conducted in violation of the Fourth Amendment, and will be suppressed.

CHAPTER 3
WARRANTLESS ARRESTS AND SEARCHES

I. INTRODUCTION

A. **Warrant not always required:** The Fourth Amendment mentions warrants specifically, but does not actually *require* warrants — the amendment merely says that "no warrants shall issue, but upon probable cause, supported by Oath or affirmation, and particularly describing the place to be searched, and the persons or things to be seized." So going by the literal text of this amendment, a warrant might *never* be constitutionally required.

   1. **Judicial interpretations sometimes required:** But the Supreme Court has *interpreted* the Fourth Amendment to sometimes require a warrant. In very general terms, the rules for when a warrant is required may be summarized as follows:

      a. **Arrest warrants:** An *arrest* warrant will *rarely* be required. Only when the police need to *enter a private home* to make the arrest, and there are *no exigent circumstances*, does the Fourth Amendment require the police to procure an arrest warrant before they make the arrest.

      b. **Search warrant:** But just the converse is true in the case of a *search*: the *general rule* is that a warrant is *required*. Only if some special exception applies will the requirement of a search warrant be dispensed with. Some of the more common exceptions are:

         [1] a search *incident to a valid arrest*;

         [2] a search motivated by *exigent circumstances* (e.g., to avoid destruction of evidence);

         [3] certain types of *automobile* searches (e.g., a search of a car when the driver is arrested and both driver and car are taken to the police station);

         [4] searches done after the person to be searched or the owner of the property to be searched *consents*;

         [5] partial searches done pursuant to the *"stop-and-frisk"* doctrine; and

         [6] certain *inspections* and *regulatory searches* (e.g., immigration searches at U.S. borders, sobriety checkpoints on highways, etc.).

      Note: The fact that in a particular situation no search warrant is required does *not* necessarily mean that *probable cause* is not required. In some but not all of the above listed situations (e.g., exigent circumstances), the police must have probable cause to believe that a search will furnish evidence of crime, even though they are not required to get a warrant. In others of the above situations, something less than probable cause, and perhaps no real suspicion at all, will be needed.

II. WARRANTLESS ARRESTS

A. **Not generally required:** An *arrest* warrant is *not* generally required by the Constitution. This is true even where the police have sufficient advance notice that procurement of a warrant would not jeopardize the arrest. [*U.S. v. Watson*]

B. **Entry of dwelling:** The only situation in which an arrest warrant *is* likely to be constitutionally required is where the police wish to enter *private premises* to arrest a suspect. In that instance, the requirement for a warrant will depend on whether exigent circumstances exist.

1. **No exigent circumstances:** If there are no exigent circumstances, the police *may not enter a private home* to make a warrantless arrest. [*Payton v. New York*]

    a. **Result of invalid arrest:** A warrantless arrest made in violation of *Payton* will not prevent D from being brought to trial (since he can always be re-arrested after a warrant has been issued). However, if the police make an in-house arrest that required a warrant because there were no exigent circumstances, then any evidence seized as a result of a *search* incident to the arrest will be excluded.

2. **Exigent circumstances:** If there *are* exigent circumstances, so that it is impractical for the police to delay the entry and arrest until they can obtain an arrest warrant, no warrant is necessary, at least where the crime is serious.

    a. **Destruction of evidence:** For instance, if the police reasonably believe that the suspect will *destroy evidence* if they delay their entry into the dwelling until they can get a warrant, the requisite exigent circumstances exist.

    b. **Hot pursuit:** Similarly, if the police are pursuing a felony suspect, and he runs into his own or another's dwelling, a warrantless entry and arrest may be permitted under the *"hot pursuit"* doctrine.

III. SEARCH INCIDENT TO ARREST

A. **Search-incident-to-arrest generally allowed:** In general, when the police are making a lawful arrest, they may *search* the area within the arrestee's *control*. This is known as a *"search incident to arrest."* Search-incident-to-arrest is the most important exception to the general rule that a search warrant is required before a search takes place.

> **Example:** Officer watches D run out of a coin shop at night, while the shop's alarm is ringing. Assuming that Officer has probable cause to arrest D (which she almost certainly does), Officer may conduct a fairly full search of D's person after the arrest. For instance, Officer can require D to empty his pockets to show that there are no weapons, contraband, or stolen property from the coin shop on his person. If on these facts Officer had arrested D while D was driving a car, Officer would also be permitted, under the search-incident-to-arrest doctrine, to search the passenger compartment of the car for weapons, contraband, etc.

1. **Limited area around defendant:** Only the area that is at least theoretically within D's *immediate control* may be searched incident to arrest. (The basic idea is that only the area that D might get to in order to destroy evidence or gain possession of a weapon may be searched.)

    > **Example:** Officers come to arrest D at his house for a recent robbery. They have an arrest warrant but no search warrant. After arresting D, the police conduct a full-scale search of D's three-bedroom house. They discover some of the stolen property in one of the bedrooms, not the room in which they arrested D. *Held*, the property may not be admitted against D because it was found pursuant to a search that was unnecessarily widespread. Only the area within D's immediate control could be searched incident to the arrest. [*Chimel v. California*]

    a. **MBE scenario:** A common scenario on the MBE (and in real life) is that the police procure a warrant to arrest D, they go to D's house, they properly enter the house (perhaps by breaking in after there is no answer), they search for and find D, and they then search the area within his possible control. As long as the arrest warrant was properly issued, and the search incident to the arrest was indeed limited to an area within D's reasonably-immediate presence (e.g., the *same room*), the search incident to arrest will be *valid*. (But if the police go beyond the areas within D's immediate control, the search will be invalid.)

> **Example:** Officers get a properly-issued warrant to arrest D for murdering his wife. They come to his house, and ring the bell. They reasonably believe that he's present (because what they know to be his car is in the driveway), and that he's likely to flee the jurisdiction. There's no answer. They give a warning ("Open up for the police") and then break in. They find D in the attic, with a paper bag by his side. They arrest and handcuff D, and search the paper bag. There, they find drugs. D moves to suppress the drugs as the fruits of an illegal search.
>
> D will lose. The police acted properly in breaking in, finding D and then arresting him. Once they arrested him, they were permitted to search the area within his immediate control. The bag was within that area, entitling the police to open it and inspect its contents.

B. Protective sweep: The Supreme Court also upholds *"protective sweeps"* under the search-incident-to-arrest doctrine. That is, where the arrest takes place in the suspect's *home*, the officers may conduct a protective sweep of *all or part of the premises*, if they have a *"reasonable belief"* based on *"specific and articulable facts"* that *another person* who might be dangerous to the officer may be present in the areas to be swept. [*Maryland v. Buie*]

1. **Adjoining spaces:** But "specific and articulable facts" are *not* needed for the officers to search in *closets* and other sizeable spaces *immediately adjoining* the place of an arrest, to make sure that no possible attacker lurks there.

2. **Can't search too-small spaces:** The police can't use the protective-sweep rationale to look in places that are *too small to possibly contain a human*. Thus searches of small *closed containers* can't be justified on this rationale. Therefore, even if the police are validly making an arrest or executing a search warrant, they can't look in small containers that are neither covered by a search warrant nor within the control of the arrestee.

   > **Example:** The police arrive at D's house with a warrant to arrest D on charges of murdering V with a rifle, and a separate warrant to search for only one specified item, "A Remington Model 7615 pump rifle." The police arrest D in the kitchen, handcuff him to a post, then fan out through the house. One officer opens a bedroom closet, sees a 6-inch-cube wooden box, opens it, and finds drugs. D is charged with drug possession and moves to suppress the contents of the box as having been taken in violation of the Fourth Amendment.
   >
   > D's motion will be granted. The arresting officers were entitled to search (incident to the lawful arrest of D) the area within his immediate control. They were also entitled, under the protective-sweep rationale, to search any place where a human could be. And they were entitled, pursuant to the search warrant, to search any place where a rifle could be. But none of these rationales applied to the opening (which is a form of search) of a 3-inch-cube box, which could not have held either a human or a rifle.

C. Automobile search-incident-to-arrest: Where the police have made a lawful "custodial arrest" of the occupant of an *automobile*, they may, incident to that arrest, search the car's *entire passenger compartment*, and the *contents of any containers* found in that compartment. [*New York v. Belton; Thornton v. U.S.*]

1. **Container found in compartment:** The right to search the contents of any container found in the compartment means that the police may search closed or open *glove compartments*, as well as any *luggage*, boxes, bags, etc. found in the car.

   > **Example:** In *Belton, supra*, the police were permitted to search through the zipped-up pocket of D's jacket found in the car.

a. **MBE Tip:** The MBE examiners like to test you on this point — they give you a lawful arrest of the driver of a car, and then ask you whether the police can search small containers found somewhere in the passenger compartment. The answer is "yes."

Example: The police properly stop D for travelling 30 miles over the speed limit. They have him exit the car. They observe his gait, and decide he is drunk. They arrest him for drunk driving, handcuff him and place him in the squad car. They then search the passenger compartment. There, they find a small plastic box whose outside gives no clue to its contents. They open the box, and discover that it contains marijuana. D is charged with marijuana possession, and moves to suppress the marijuana under the Fourth Amendment.

D's suppression motion will be denied. The police properly made a custodial arrest of D. Once they did so, the bright-line rule of *Belton, supra* (and the later case of *Thornton v. U.S.*) means that they can search the entire passenger compartment, including any small containers in it. That's true even if the police have immobilized D (and any other passengers) so that there is no realistic chance that D could get away and either attack the police or destroy evidence.

2. **Trunk not included:** The rule permitting search of the passenger compartment incident to arrest does *not* cover searches of the *trunk* of the car.

3. **Consent to search of another's possessions:** An automobile search may be validated by the *consent of the driver*. This follows from the general principle that a search of premises controlled by a person is valid based on that person's consent (see *infra*, p. 103).

   a. **Consent by driver to search of another's car or possessions:** The driver's consent to a search of the car will be valid as to the car's *entire contents,* if the *driver is the only person present*. And that's true even if the car (or an item in the car) *belongs to a third person not present*. The MBE examiners like to test you on this sort of third-party consent-by-driver scenario. The search will be valid even though the owner or the car, or of the car's contents, was not present and didn't consent.

   Example: X borrows D's car. Unbeknownst to X, D has a container of marijuana in the trunk. X is stopped for speeding. The officer asks if X will consent to a search of the trunk. D says yes. The officer finds the marijuana, and D is charged with possessing it. D moves to suppress.

   The motion will be denied, and the marijuana admitted against D. It's true that D, the owner of both the car and the marijuana, did not consent to the search. But where police properly stop a car, they can presume that the driver has authority to consent to a search of the car's contents, even if the driver doesn't own the car. (It would likely be different if D were present and protesting — then X's consent wouldn't authorize a search of the trunk of a car that the police knew was owned by D, if D protested. But D's absence lets the police presume that the driver X has authority to consent.)

   Note: When you are given facts involving the search of an automobile, consider, in addition to the search-incident-to-arrest exception to the search warrant requirement, the automobile-impoundment exception (*infra*, p. 101), by which once the police stop a car, arrest its owner and *impound* the car, they may then search the entire car, including the trunk.

D. **Legality of arrest:** The search-incident-to-arrest exception to the search warrant requirement applies only where the arrest is *legal*. Thus if the arrest turns out to have been made without probable cause, the search incident to it cannot be justified on the search-incident-to-arrest rationale, and the arrest must be suppressed unless some other exception to the warrant requirement (e.g., prevention of destruction of evidence) justifies it.

E. **Must be custodial arrest:** For the search-incident-to-arrest doctrine to apply, the arrest must be a *"custodial"* one. That is, the officer must be planning to take D to the station-house for booking.

> **Example:** Officer stops D, a driver, for driving with an expired registration sticker. Assume that this is a misdemeanor, and that under local police department procedures, a driver stopped for such an offense is virtually never arrested, but is instead given a summons to be answered at a later date. On these facts, D is not being subject to a "custodial arrest." Therefore, neither D's body, nor his car, may be searched incident to arrest.

IV. EXIGENT CIRCUMSTANCES

A. **Exigent circumstances generally:** Even where the search-incident-to-arrest exception to the search warrant requirement does not apply, there may be *exigent circumstances* that justify dispensing with the warrant requirement. The most common exigent circumstances are: (1) preventing the imminent *destruction of evidence*; (2) preventing *harm to persons*; and (3) searching in *"hot pursuit"* for a suspect.

B. **Destruction of evidence:** The police may conduct a search or seizure without a warrant provided that they have probable cause, and provided that the search or seizure is necessary to prevent the possible *imminent destruction of evidence.*

> **Example:** The police obtain probable cause to believe that D has hidden a small quantity of marijuana in his trailer. While D is outside the trailer, the police refuse to let him re-enter the trailer unaccompanied while they get a warrant. In less than two hours, they get the warrant, and do the search, where they find drugs.
>
> *Held*, for the prosecution. The police's refusal to let D in his trailer without a police escort was a "seizure" for Fourth Amendment purposes. But because the police had probable cause to believe that the trailer contained contraband or evidence of crime, and also had reasonable fears that D would destroy the evidence if left in the trailer alone, they were entitled to make that seizure without a warrant for the length of time reasonably needed to get the warrant. [*Illinois v. McArthur*]

C. **Danger to life:** A warrantless search may be allowed where *danger to life* is likely if the police cannot act fast.

> **Example:** At 3 a.m., police respond to a call that a loud party is taking place at a house. When they arrive, they hear shouting and see, through a screen door, a fight taking place in the kitchen. They open the screen door, enter, announce themselves, and arrest several people for fighting.
>
> *Held*, the police entry, though warrantless, did not violate the Fourth Amendment, because the entry was justified by the exigent circumstances. The police may make a warrantless entry into a home to assist an injured occupant or prevent imminent injury. [*Brigham City v. Stuart*]

D. **Hot pursuit:** If the police are pursuing a felony suspect, and have reason to believe that he has entered particular premises, they may enter those premises to search for him. While they are searching for him, they may also search for weapons which, since he is still at large, he might seize. This is called the *"hot pursuit"* exception to the search warrant requirement.

1. **Other items:** The "hot pursuit" exception is often combined with the "plain view" exception (discussed *supra*, p. 90). That is, while the police are engaged in a hot pursuit of a suspect and any weapons he might have, they may seize any other evidence of criminal behavior that they stumble upon in plain view.

V. AUTOMOBILE SEARCHES

A. **Relation to general exceptions:** We look now at two special exceptions to the warrant requirement in the context of *automobile searches*. Keep in mind, however, that the *general* exceptions discussed above will frequently apply in the case of cars:

1. **Incident to arrest:** For instance, recall (*supra*, p. 98) that a car's *passenger compartment* may be searched *incident to the custodial arrest* of the driver or passenger.

2. **Exigent circumstances:** Similarly, *exigent circumstances* will often cause the warrant requirement to be suspended where a car search is involved.

    Example: Officer spots a car known to be owned by a fugitive drug dealer, and reasonably believed to be used by the dealer in his drug operations. Officer may stop the car and search it even without a warrant, because of the risk that the car will otherwise be driven away or hidden.

    a. **No general "exigent circumstances" exception for vehicles:** But there is *no general doctrine* "vehicular exigent circumstances" doctrine. That is, there's no doctrine that says that when the police have properly stopped a car, the mobility of the car automatically makes the circumstances exigent, entitling the police to search it. The MBE examiners will sometimes try to mousetrap you into thinking that there is such a "vehicle equals exigent circumstances" rule.

    Example: Officer properly stops D on suspicion of speeding. Assume that local practice dictates that speeders normally not be subjected to custodial arrest, and merely given a ticket. Officer does this. Officer knows that a search of the passenger compartment is not allowed under the incident-to-arrest exception if no custodial arrest is made (see *supra*, p. 100). But Officer decides to search the passenger compartment anyway, just because D looks to him like the sort of guy who might have drugs. He finds a closed container in the back seat, which when he opens it turns out to contain marijuana. D moves to suppress the marijuana. The prosecution claims that since D could and would have simply driven the car away after the ticket, the circumstances were "exigent" and made the search reasonable.

    D will win. There's no general "exigent circumstances" exception that applies just because a car is involved. If the police don't have strong reason (at least probable cause) to believe the search will turn up evidence of criminality, they can't just rely on exigent circumstances to make the warrantless search reasonable.

B. **Two special exceptions:** There are two major *automobile-specific* exceptions that have developed to the warrant requirement:

    [1] when the driver is properly arrested, the police may *impound* the car, transport it to *the station house,* and search it there, all without a warrant; and

    [2] if the police reasonably believe that a car is carrying *contraband*, it may be subjected to a full warrantless search in the field.

    We discuss each in turn.

    1. **Search at station house after arrest:** Where the police arrest the driver, take him and his car *to the station*, and search the car there, no search warrant is generally required. [*Chambers v. Maroney*]

    2. **Field search for contraband:** Where the police have probable cause to believe that a car is being used to transport *contraband*, and they stop it, they may conduct a warrantless search not only of the car but of *closed containers* in the car. They may do this *on the scene*, without even impounding the car (as they have to do in the above "search at the station house after arrest" scenario). [*U.S. v. Ross; Calif. v. Carney*]

Example: The police get a tip — which under the circumstances seems credible — that a red-haired man in a blue 2006 Dodge van has been selling in front of City Hall. Five minutes later, the police arrive at that location, and see a blue 2006 Dodge van being driven away by a red-haired man. They stop the van, and find that in addition to the driver (D1), the van contains a passenger, D2, a young woman. The police ask both to exit the vehicle, and one officer escorts them to wait nearby. The police then search the van, discover a locked tool box in the back seat, and break into it. Inside the box they discover methamphetamines. At D1's trial, he moves to suppress the meth at his trial. (Ignore D2 for a moment; we'll be considering her *infra*, p. 102.)

D1 will lose. Based on the combination of the tip, and the fact that the van and driver matched the tipper's description, the police had probable cause to believe that the van contained contraband. Given that this was so, they had the right to stop the vehicle, and then search any closed containers in it, even if they are not deemed to have arrested the driver (D1). So the police right to search the vehicle and all its contents stemmed not from search-incident-to-arrest (*supra*, p. 97), but from right to stop and search a vehicle without a warrant if police have probable cause to believe it is transporting contraband.

    a. Passenger's belongings: Once the police have probable cause to believe that the car contains contraband, they may search closed containers inside it that could hold that type of contraband, even if those containers belong to a *passenger*, and even if there is no probable cause to believe that the passenger has been involved in carrying the contraband or any other illegality. [*Wyoming v. Houghton*]

    Example: On the facts of the above Example involving the Dodge van, suppose the police found a woman's purse on the back seat. Since the police had probable cause to believe that the driver of the vehicle, D1, was carrying drugs, they were entitled to search the purse. This is true even though all the following statements are true: (1) the police knew or suspected that due to parties' gender, the purse was owned by the passenger (D2) not the driver (D1); (2) the police had no particular reason to suspect that the purse (as opposed to the car in general) contained drugs; and (3) the police had no reason to suspect D2 of any wrongdoing. [*Wyoming v. Houghton*]

        i. Can't search passenger: But the mere fact that the police are entitled to search all items in the vehicle stopped for contraband-carrying doesn't give the police the right to search the *person* of a *passenger*, if there's no independent evidence that the person is carrying contraband.

        Example: Same facts as above Example involving D1, D2 and the Dodge van. Now, assume that there is no purse in the car. After the police find meth in the glove compartment, they go over to D2 (the passenger), and search her purse, looking for drugs. They find heroin. D2 moves to suppress it.

        D2 will win. The mere fact that the police had probable cause to believe that the van was being used to transport drugs (giving the police the right to stop and search it without a warrant), and even the follow-on fact that the police knew based on the glove-compartment search that their suspicions had been correct, did not give them the right to search the person of D2, since they had no probable cause either to arrest her or to search her person for drugs.

C. Traffic stop followed by ticket: Don't make the mistake of thinking that every time the police validly stop a motorist, they may search that motorist's car. There are times when no warrantless search is allowed *even though the stop was proper*. In particular, if the officer properly stops a car to write a *traffic ticket*, and does not make an arrest, the officer is *not allowed, merely by virtue of the stop, to search the car*. This is true even if under local law the officer *could* have made a custodial arrest for the traffic violation. [*Knowles v. Iowa*]

> **Example:** Officer Jones observes Goodman's car change lanes without signaling. Jones stops Goodman and begins to write a summons (a ticket), the proper procedure under local department rules. Jones demands that Goodman step out of the car while the ticket is being written, and then solely on a "hunch" decides to search Goodman's car. Jones finds cocaine under the front passenger seat. While the stop was proper, there's no applicable exception to the warrant requirement, so the search is invalid.

VI. CONSENT SEARCHES GENERALLY

A. Consent generally: The police may make a warrantless search if they receive the *consent* of the individual whose premises, effects, or person are to be searched.

> **Example:** D, who is wanted on an outstanding arrest warrant, is making a week-long visit to his friend F. The police get a call from D's ex-wife telling them, "You can find D at F's house, here's the address." The police ring F's doorbell, and ask if they can search the house because they have reason to believe that a person with an outstanding arrest warrant may be inside. F, eager to keep on the good side of the police, agrees. The police search F's house, and soon spot and recognize D sitting in the living room. They immediately arrest him, and search his jacket pursuant to that arrest. In the jacket, they find drugs. D moves to suppress the drugs, on the grounds that the search was incident to an invalid arrest, and that the arrest was in turn invalid because it came pursuant to an invalid search of the living room.
>
> D will lose. F, as owner of the living room, had authority to consent to the search. Therefore, the search of the living room was valid, the ensuing arrest was valid, and the search of D's jacket incident to that arrest (see *supra*, p. 97) was also valid.

B. D need not know he can refuse consent: A person's consent will be *effective* even if the person *did not know she had a right to refuse to consent* to the search. [*Schneckloth v. Bustamonte*]

1. **Must be voluntary:** The consent, to be effective, must be *"voluntary,"* rather than the product of duress or coercion. But the Court measures voluntariness by a *"totality of the circumstances"* test, and the fact that the consenter did or did not know she had a right to refuse consent is merely *one factor* in measuring voluntariness.

   a. **Ignorance of police motive:** Similarly, the fact that the consenter *didn't know what the police were looking for* (or didn't know that the consenter or a relative was a suspect) *won't* negate the consent. And that's true even if the consenter's lack of knowledge about these issues stems from some *disease or mental defect*.

   > **Example:** H and W are married. The police suspect H of murdering V. They come to the couple's house while (as they know) H is at work. They say to W, "We've gotten a tip that your basement may contain evidence of a serious crime. May we search it?" (Assume that it's true that the police got such a tip.) W has no idea that the police visit concerns a murder, let alone the specific murder of V, or that H is a police suspect. She gives permission to search. The police find evidence incriminating H in the basement.
   >
   > The consent will be found valid because it was "voluntary" under the totality of the circumstances. (For instance, there's no evidence that the police procured it by coercing W.) The fact that W didn't know what crime they police were investigating, and didn't know that they suspected H of crime, is irrelevant to the validity of the consent. The same would be true even if the reason W didn't know that H was a suspect in the murder of V

was because W was unusually stupid or mentally ill (as long as W had enough intelligence and awareness to give a voluntary consent to the search).

C. Physical scope of search: Where D's consent is reasonably interpreted to apply only to a *particular physical area*, a search that extends *beyond* that area will not be covered by the consent, and will be invalid unless it falls within some other exception to the warrant requirement.

> **Example:** Officer asks D for permission to search D's living room for certain evidence. D responds, "O.K.," and leaves the room. Officer then, unbeknownst to D, goes into the kitchen and basement, and finds incriminating evidence. Since Officer went beyond the scope of the consented-to search, the evidence will be suppressed if no other exception to the search warrant requirement applies.

> **1. Plain view exception:** But always keep in mind the *"plain view"* exception to the warrant requirement — if while the searching officer is standing within part of the consented-to area, she spots evidence in another part of the premises, she can seize that evidence under the plain view doctrine.

VII. CONSENT BY THIRD PERSONS

A. The problem generally: Be careful of consent issues raised when the police seek the consent of *one person* for the search of the *property of another*, or for the search of an area as to which another has an expectation of privacy — the mere fact that the first person has voluntarily consented does not mean that the police may conduct the search and introduce evidence against the second person. In general, *A may not consent to a search that would invade B's expectation of privacy* — only if special circumstances exist (e.g., both *A* and *B* have *authority over the premises*) will *A's* consent be in effect binding on *B*.

B. Joint authority: In cases in which the defendant and a *third person* have *joint authority* over the premises, that third party's consent will often be binding on the defendant. We will consider two separate scenarios: (1) where D is *absent* at the time the third person consents; and (2) where D is *present*, and *refuses to consent*, while the third person consents.

By "joint authority," we mean a situation in which D and the third party have some sort of *joint access to*, and some sort of *joint expectation of privacy in*, the place to be searched. Common examples of joint authority are:

- ❏ *roommates*, as to the common areas of the dwelling or any shared bedroom;
- ❏ *husband and wife*, as to the marital dwelling;
- ❏ a *homeowner* (or tenant) and his *social guest*, where the homeowner gives the consent and the evidence is then used against the guest.

All of these scenarios are evaluated according to the same basic set of rules.

> **1. D is absent when third person consents:** Where D is *absent*, and the police ask for and receive consent of the third person to search the jointly-controlled premises, the basic rule is that the third party's consent is *effective*, if that third party either (a) *actually* has or (b) is *reasonably believed* by the police to have, joint authority over the premises.

>> **Example:** G cohabits in a house together with D. The police show up at this house one day, arrest D in the front yard, and put him in a squad car nearby. They then knock on the front door, and G answers. They explain that they are looking for money and a gun from a recent bank robbery, and ask if they can search the house. G gives consent to the police to search the

house, including her and D's bedroom. In the bedroom, the police find money and the gun from the robbery.

Held, G's consent was valid as against D. G had joint authority over the bedroom. In such a joint-authority scenario, "it is reasonable to recognize that *any of the co-inhabitants* has the right to permit the inspection in his own right and that the others have *assumed the risk* that one of their number might permit the common area to be searched." [*U.S. v. Matlock*]

    a. Reasonable mistake: The third-party consent will be binding on the absent defendant even if the police were *mistaken* about whether the consenter in fact had joint authority over the premises, as long as the *mistake was a reasonable one.* For instance, if the consenting third person falsely tells the police that she lives in the premises to be searched, and the police reasonably believe her, the lie will not invalidate the consent. [*Illinois v. Rodriguez.*]

2. **D is present and objecting when third person consents:** Now, let's consider the second scenario: D is *present* when the third party consents to a search of the premises over which the two have joint authority, and D makes it clear that he, D, is *not consenting*. Here, the third party's consent is *not binding on D*, at least where it appears to the police that the third person and D have *equal claim* to the premises.

    Example: W, who is estranged from her husband D, returns to the former marital residence. There, she calls the police. They arrive without a warrant and meet W. D then arrives back at the house. W tells the police that there are items showing D's drug use in the house. The police ask D for his consent to a search of the house, and he refuses. The police then ask W for consent and she gives it. In D's bedroom, the police find cocaine.

    Held, W's consent was not effective as against D. Where as here the two parties are not living within some "recognized hierarchy" (like a household with parent and child), the co-tenant who wishes to open the door to a third person "has no recognized authority in law or social practice to prevail over a present and objecting co-tenant." Consequently, even though W may have had joint authority with D over the house, the police's warrantless entry in the face of D's express refusal to consent made this an unreasonable search. [*Georgia v. Randolph*]

C. Assumption of risk: Even where the person doing the consenting does not have joint authority over the premises, the relationship between the third party and D may be such that D will be found to have *"assumed the risk"* that the third party might see or scrutinize D's property, in which case the third party may also consent to a search.

    Example: D shares a duffle bag with X, his cousin. X consents to a police search of the bag. *Held*, this consent was binding on D, because D assumed the risk that X or others would look in the bag, and thus D had no expectation of privacy in the bag's contents. [*Frazier v. Cupp*]

D. Other situations: Here are some situations that frequently arise regarding third-party consent:

1. **Landlords:** Generally, a *landlord* may not consent to a search of his tenants' rooms, even though the landlord has the right to enter them for cleaning. But the landlord *may* consent to a search of the areas of "common usage," such as hallways and common dining areas.

    a. Hotel room: Similarly, the manager of a *hotel* may generally not consent to a search of the guest's room while the guest is still registered, even though the manager and his staff have the right to enter for housekeeping purposes. (The hotel is viewed as being a landlord that has given temporary but exclusive occupancy rights to the guest.) But after the guest *checks out*, the manager *does* have the right to consent to a search of the room, since the checking out means that the guest no longer has an expectation of privacy in the room.

2. **Employer:** An *employer* probably may consent to a search of his employee's work area if the search is for items *related to the job*. But probably the employer cannot consent to a search of areas where the employee is, by the terms of the job, permitted to store personal effects (e.g., a locker given to the employee to store his street clothes at a factory).

3. **Non-paying guest:** When a *social (non-paying) guest* is present, the consent of the owner will generally be *binding*. That's especially true as to *common areas* of the premises like kitchens and living rooms, i.e., areas as to which the guest would have a limited expectation of privacy because these are shared areas. So if the owner consents to the search of such an area, the guest will lose in a suppression motion not because the guest doesn't have an expectation of privacy in the room (and not because the guest doesn't have standing; see *infra*, p. 121), but because the owner also has rights to the room, and has authority to consent.

    Example: Recall the Example on p. 103: D is staying overnight at F's house, and F consents to a police search of the premises; D is found in the living room (a common area). F's consent will be valid and binding on D, since F's authority over the common-areas of the house will override any privacy expectations of D, a non-paying guest.

VIII. STOP-AND-FRISK AND OTHER BRIEF DETENTION

A. **Problem generally:** Sometimes the police, when they encounter a suspect, do not want to make a full arrest, but merely want to *briefly detain* the person. This happens most typically when the police are not investigating any particular crime, and are simply performing routine patrolling functions. The two questions which the "stop-and-frisk" doctrine deals with are: (1) When may the police *briefly detain* a person even though they *do not have probable cause* to arrest him or to search him? and (2) to what extent may the police conduct a protective, limited *search* for weapons on the suspect's person?

B. **General rule:** In general, the stop-and-frisk doctrine lets the police do *both* of the above things in appropriate circumstances:

1. **Right to stop:** Where a police officer *observes unusual conduct* which leads him reasonably to conclude that criminal activity is afoot, he may briefly detain the suspect in order to make inquiries. Probable cause is not required — *reasonable suspicion*, based on *objective facts*, that the individual is involved in criminal activity, will suffice. (The stop is a seizure under the Fourth Amendment, but it does not require probable cause, merely reasonable suspicion.)

2. **Protective frisk:** Once the officer conducts a stop as described above, then assuming nothing in the initial encounter dispels his reasonable fear for his or others' safety, the officer may conduct a *carefully limited search* of the *outer clothing* of the suspect in an attempt to discover *weapons*. This limited *"frisk"* or *"pat-down"* is a Fourth Amendment search, but is deemed "reasonable." Consequently, any weapons seized may be introduced against the suspect. [*Terry v. Ohio*; *Brown v. Texas*]

C. **No *Miranda* warnings required:** If the officer makes a proper *Terry* stop-and-frisk, *no Miranda warnings are required* during or following the procedure, as long as the suspect is not properly viewed as being in custody. So at the end of the stop-and-frisk, as long as the officer has not expressly or implicitly communicated to the suspect that he is not free to leave, the officer may ask questions without triggering the need for *Miranda* warnings. (The example following Par. (D)(1) below illustrates this principle.)

D. How stop-and-frisk appears on MBE: When stop-and-frisk is tested on the MBE, the examiners will usually give you a situation in which *both* a stop and a pat-down occur, and in which both of these are *valid* (i.e., they meet the requirements of the stop-and-frisk doctrine).

  1. **Less-than-probable-cause specified:** Often, the examiners will *specify* that, at the moment of the stop, the officer had reasonable suspicion of wrongdoing but less than probable cause. Why do they do this? Well, it's very hard for the examiners to come up with a fact pattern that unambiguously signals "reasonable suspicion but not probable cause," so the examiners will usually *have* to tell you explicitly that there is no probable cause. That's a strong tip-off that the problem will turn on whether the requirements for the stop-and-frisk doctrine are satisfied (which they usually will be).

     Example: There have been a number of recent holdups of different convenience stores in Muni. Witnesses to these holdups report that in each case, the robber has turned out to be a man wearing a New York Yankees baseball cap and windbreaker who seemed to be nervously watching the cashier while standing in the beer section at about 1 a.m. One night at about 1 a.m., Officer happens to be standing in a convenience store when he notices that a man wearing a New York Yankees baseball cap and windbreaker, and standing in the beer section, seems to be nervously watching the cashier. Officer asks the man what he is doing in the store; the man looks nervously around, then mumbles, "Just hanging out, man." Officer then pats the outside of the man's windbreaker to determine whether he is carrying a weapon. Officer finds no weapon, and says to the man that he conforms to the description of the man who has recently been robbing convenience stores. Officer then asks the man, "Are you in fact that guy?" After a few seconds pause, the man confesses. At trial, the man moves to suppress his confession as the fruit of a Fourth Amendment and/or *Miranda* violation. The trial court initially and properly determines that at the moment that Officer first approached the man, Officer had reasonable grounds — but not probable cause — to suspect the man of being the perpetrator of the prior holdups. How should the court rule on the suppression motion?

     The court should *deny* the motion, because both the stop and the frisk were justified under the *Terry v. Ohio* stop-and-frisk doctrine, and because *Miranda* was never triggered. First, the facts expressly tell us (and plausibly so) that Officer had reasonable suspicion, based on objective facts, that the man was the convenience-store holdup artist. That reasonable suspicion, even though less than probable cause, justified Officer in briefly detaining the suspect in order to make inquiries. Then, when the man answered evasively (thus not dispelling Officer's suspicions but not confirming them either), Officer still didn't have probable cause, but had the limited right to *protect himself* by doing a carefully limited pat-down of the outer part of the man's clothing, solely to determine whether he was carrying a weapon. That's all Officer did, so he still had not violated the man's rights.

     At the moment just following this stop-and-frisk, Officer still had not arrested the man (i.e., he had not communicated to the man that the man was no longer free to leave, which is the test for whether there has been a custodial arrest and thus a duty to give *Miranda* warnings — see *infra*, p. 113). Therefore, Officer was entitled to interrogate the man, at least briefly, without giving him *Miranda* warnings. Consequently, Officer's stop-and-frisk of the man did not violate the Fourth Amendment, and his *Miranda*-less question to him did not violate *Miranda*, so the confession will not be suppressed.

IX. INSPECTIONS AND WEAPONS SEARCHES

A. Summary: *Inspections* and *regulatory searches*, which are not focused on investigating a particular crime or apprehending a known criminal, pose Fourth Amendment questions. In this context: (1) *probable cause* to conduct the inspection or regulatory search usually is *not* required; and (2) a search warrant may or may not be required.

B. Inspections: For most types of inspections — *health, safety, and fire inspections*, for instance — a *search warrant is required*. [*Camara v. Municipal Court*]

   1. Probable cause not required: However, in order to obtain the warrant, the inspector does *not* have to demonstrate *probable cause* to believe that a violation will be discovered in the premises to be searched. Instead, the inspector merely needs to show that the inspection is part of a *general area* inspection (i.e., the inspector has not singled out a particular premises).

   2. Heavily-regulated businesses: Where a business is subject to unusually heavy *governmental regulation*, a *warrantless* inspection search is *permissible*, at least if the inspection program is relatively unintrusive compared with the danger, and thus "reasonable."

   > **Example:** A state heavily regulates pawnshops, because the legislature has concluded that pawnshops often serve as fences for stolen goods. The regulatory scheme includes the requirement of a special license following an investigatory into the owners' moral character, and a requirement that the owners allow random searches of their premises and inventory. Officer randomly, and without a search warrant specifically naming D, shows up at D's pawnshop, demands to examine gold jewelry that D is keeping in his safe, recognizes one of the pieces as stolen, and arrests D. D moves to suppress the jewelry from this receipt-of-stolen-goods trial.
   >
   > D will lose. The pawnshop industry is heavily regulated, and subjected to unusual licensing requirements. Furthermore, if there were not random warrantless inspections, pawnshops would have a good opportunity to fence stolen goods. Consequently, the random search here did not require a warrant or probable cause, and was not "unreasonable" under the Fourth Amendment.

C. Immigration searches: At the *border, immigration, customs* and *drug-enforcement officials* may search baggage and vehicles (and to a limited extent, the traveler's own person) *without probable cause* to believe that there is an immigration violation or smuggling, and *without a warrant*. [*Almeida-Sanchez v. U.S.*]

D. Routine traffic stops: Apart from the border-search and immigration scenarios, the police may wish to stop cars for regulatory purposes (e.g., to make sure that the driver is *licensed* and the car is *registered*).

   1. Random stops: If the police want to *randomly* stop cars to do this checking, they may not make a particular stop unless they have a *suspicion* of wrongdoing based upon an "objective standard." That is, a practice of making *totally random* stops, where a stop is made even though the officer has no objective grounds for suspicion, violates the Fourth Amendment. [*Delaware v. Prouse*]

   2. Check-point: However, the police may set up a *fixed checkpoint* on the highway to test for compliance related to driver-safety. Thus they can stop all cars — or every *n*th car — to check for *drunkenness* [*Mich. Dept. of State Police v. Sitz*], or to see that the *driver is licensed* and the vehicle is registered. [Dictum in *Delaware v. Prouse*]

   > **a. Seeking of eyewitnesses to crime:** Similarly, the police may set up a fixed roadblock or checkpoint to *find witnesses* to a recent crime, if that's a reasonable method of finding such witnesses.

3. **No general crime-fighting:** But police may *not* set up a fixed checkpoint to pursue *general crime-fighting objectives*, such as *narcotics detection*.

E. **Searches in schools:** A *school official* may search the person and possessions of a student *without a warrant*. All that is required is that the official have *"reasonable grounds* for *suspecting* that the search will turn up evidence that the student has violated or is violating either the *law* or the *rules of the school."* [*New Jersey v. T.L.O.*]

1. **Law enforcement agencies involved:** But it seems highly probable that this right of school authorities to search based on "reasonable suspicion of violation of law or school rules" *doesn't apply* where the school authorities are *acting at the request of law enforcement agencies*.

    Example: Police inform Principal, a public-school principal, that they believe that D, a student, has been dealing drugs. They request that Principal search D's person. Assume that the police do not have either probable cause or a search warrant. Principal pulls D out of class and searches his pockets and his backpack, finding drugs.

    It seems very likely that D can have the drugs suppressed, on the theory that the right (given in *T.L.O., supra*) to search a student without a warrant or probable cause doesn't apply where the school authorities are acting at the request of law enforcement.

Chapter 4
ELECTRONIC SURVEILLANCE AND SECRET AGENTS

I. ELECTRONIC SURVEILLANCE

A. **Wiretapping and bugging generally:** There are two main techniques of "electronic surveillance" often used by law enforcement officials, on which the Fourth Amendment places strict limits. These two techniques are *"wiretapping"* and *"bugging."*

1. **Wiretap:** In a *wiretap*, the listener (in our context, the government) places electronic equipment on the *telephone wires*, and uses this equipment to listen to conversations that take place on the telephone.

2. **Bugging:** In *"bugging"* (also known as *"electronic eavesdropping"*), the listener puts a microphone in or near the place where a conversation is to occur, and uses this equipment to listen directly to the conversation. (An example of bugging would be the placement of a microphone inside a lamp inside the suspect's bedroom, where the microphone is used to pick up and transmit conversations taking place in that room.)

B. **Requires warrant and probable cause:** Both wiretapping and bugging normally constitute *Fourth Amendment searches*, and must therefore satisfy the requirements of *probable cause* and a *warrant*. That is, so long as the conversation that is intercepted is one as to which both participants had a *reasonable expectation of privacy*, the fact that the microphone or wiretapping equipment is located outside the suspect's premises makes no difference.

1. **Participant monitoring:** But where the wire-tapping or eavesdropping occurs with the *consent* of one of the parties to the conversation, then there is *no Fourth Amendment problem*.

    Example: The FBI learns that D and X will be having a conversation in which D is likely to implicate himself in a crime. They ask X for permission to place a wiretap on X's phone; X agrees. The conversation takes place, and the agents record it without a warrant. This wiretapping is not a violation of the Fourth Amendment, because it occurred with the permission of one of the participants. Therefore, the recording can be introduced against D at his criminal trial.

II. SECRET AGENTS

A. **Secret agents generally:** Fourth Amendment questions can also arise where the police make use of *"secret agents."* A secret agent is, in essence, a person who has *direct contact* with a suspect, under circumstances in which the suspect *does not realize* that he is dealing with someone who is helping the government. A secret agent can either be "bugged" (i.e., equipped with an electronic device that records and/or transmits conversations) or "unbugged."

1. **Summary of law:** In brief, *neither "bugged" nor "unbugged" secret agents pose Fourth Amendment problems* — so long as the target is aware that a person (the agent) is present, the fact that the target is unaware that the agent is indeed a secret agent or informer (as opposed to being the suspect's friend, for instance) does not turn the mission into a "search" or "seizure" under the Fourth Amendment.

B. **Bugged agents:** Thus the Supreme Court has held several times that "bugged agents" — secret agents equipped with *electronic surveillance* equipment — are not eavesdropping and thus cannot possibly violate the Fourth Amendment. [*On Lee v. U.S.*; *U.S. v. White*]

   Example: Informer is wired to transmit to narcotics agents conversations that Informer hears or is a part of. Informer then has conversations with D in a restaurant, in D's home, and in Informer's car. Tapes of these transmitted conversations are introduced at D's criminal trial. *Held*, no Fourth Amendment right has been triggered. When a person misplaces his trust and makes incriminating statements to an informer, he does not have any justifiable expectation of privacy which has been violated — there is no Fourth Amendment protection given to "a wrongdoer's misplaced belief that a person to whom he voluntarily confides his wrongdoing will not reveal it." This is true whether the informer is bugged or not. [*U.S. v. White, supra.*]

   1. **Recording devices:** An informant's use of *recording devices* (as opposed to electronic transmission devices) is treated the same way — that recording won't violate the speaker's Fourth Amendment rights as long as the informant is physically present in the room and known to the speaker to be present.

      Example: Same facts as above example, except that Informer personally tapes the conversations he has with D, rather than transmitting them to agents who record them. D's Fourth Amendment rights are not violated by the recordings, and the recordings may therefore be admitted against D.

C. **Unbugged agents:** Similarly, the use of *unbugged* agents does not violate the Fourth Amendment either.

   Example: A Teamster-turned-informant visits Jimmy Hoffa's hotel room and overhears conversations concerning Hoffa's plan to bribe jurors. The informant testifies about these conversations in Hoffa's later jury-tampering trial.

   Held, Hoffa's Fourth Amendment rights were not even implicated, let alone violated, by introduction of these statements. Hoffa's "misplaced trust" was his own fault, and did not vitiate his consent to the informant's entry into the hotel suite. [*Hoffa v. U.S.*]

   Note on the right to counsel: But the use of a bugged or unbugged informer against a suspect who has already been *indicted* may violate the suspect's *Sixth Amendment right to counsel*, as discussed below (p. 127).

Chapter 5
CONFESSIONS AND POLICE INTERROGATION

I. INTRODUCTION

A. **Two requirements for confessions:** In both state and federal courts, a *confession* may be introduced against the person who made it only if the confession satisfies *each* of the following two requirements:

1. **Voluntary:** The confession must have been *voluntary*, i.e., not the product of *coercion* by the police; and

2. *Miranda* **warnings:** The confession must have been obtained in *conformity* with the *Miranda* decision — in brief, if the confession was given by the suspect while she was in custody and under interrogation by the authorities, the suspect must have been warned that she had the right to remain silent, that anything she said could be used against her, and that she had the right to have an attorney present.

II. VOLUNTARINESS

A. **Voluntariness generally:** Regardless of whether *Miranda* warnings are given to the suspect, her confession will only be admissible against her if it was given *voluntarily*.

1. **Must be police coercion:** But the test for determining the "voluntariness" of a confession is one that is fairly easy to satisfy. Apparently the only thing that can now prevent a confession from being found to be "voluntary" is *police coercion*. Thus neither coercion by non-government personnel, nor serious *mental illness* on the suspect's part, is relevant to this question.

    Example: Suspect is in a psychotic schizophrenic state. He confesses to a crime because the "voice of God" tells him he should do so. *Held*, this confession is admissible against Suspect, because there was no police or other governmental wrongdoing. [*Colorado v. Connelly*]

2. **Collateral use:** If a confession *is* obtained by police coercion (and is thus "involuntary"), it must be excluded not only from the prosecution's case in chief, but also from use to *impeach* D's testimony. (This makes involuntary confessions quite different from confessions given in violation of *Miranda*, which may be admitted to impeach D's testimony on the stand.)

III. *MIRANDA* GENERALLY

A. *Miranda:* The main set of rules governing confessions in both state and federal courts derive from *Miranda v. Arizona*. In general, *Miranda* holds that when a suspect is questioned in custody by the police, his confession will be admissible against him only if he has received the "*Miranda* warnings."

B. **Three requirements for application:** Before *Miranda* will be found to apply, *three requirements* must be satisfied:

1. **Custody:** First, *Miranda* warnings are necessary only where the suspect is taken into *custody*. (Thus if the police ask a question to someone they meet on the street, without formally detaining him, *Miranda* is not triggered.)

2. **Questioning:** Second, the *Miranda* rule applies only where the confession comes as the result of *questioning*. (Thus statements that are truly *"volunteered"* by the suspect are not covered.)

3. **Authorities:** Finally, *Miranda* applies only where both the questioning and the custody are by the *police* or other *law enforcement authorities*. (Thus if a private citizen, acting independently of law enforcement officials, detains a suspect and questions him, any resulting confession is not covered.)

C. **Warnings required:** There are *four warnings* that are required once *Miranda* applies at all. The suspect must be warned that:

1. He has the right to *remain silent*;

2. Anything he says can be *used against him* in a court of law;

3. He has the right to the *presence* of an *attorney*; and

4. If he cannot *afford* an attorney, one will be *appointed for him* prior to any questioning if he desires.

D. **Inadmissibility:** Any statement obtained in violation of the *Miranda* rules will be *inadmissible* as prosecution evidence, even if the statement is in a sense "voluntary."

1. **Impeachment use:** But a confession given in violation of *Miranda*, although not admissible as part of the prosecution's case in chief, may generally be introduced for purposes of *impeaching* testimony that the defendant has given. This "impeachment exception" to *Miranda* is discussed on p. 116 *infra*.

E. **Rights may be exercised at any time:** The suspect may exercise his right to remain silent, or to have a lawyer present, at *any time* during the questioning. Thus even if the suspect at first indicates that he waives his right to silence and to a lawyer, if he *changes his mind* the interrogation must *cease*.

F. **Waiver:** The suspect may *waive* his right to remain silent and to have a lawyer. However, this waiver is effective only if it is *knowingly and intelligently made*. The suspect's *silence* may not be taken as a waiver.

1. **Suspect already aware of rights:** The police must give the *Miranda* warnings even if they have reason to believe that the suspect is already *aware* of his rights.

G. **Right to counsel:**

1. **Right to appoint counsel applies only where questioning occurs:** If the suspect says that he wants his own lawyer present, or that he cannot afford a lawyer and wants one appointed for him, the police do *not* have an absolute duty to provide the previously-retained lawyer or a newly appointed one — the rule is merely that the police *must not question the suspect* until they get him a lawyer. So the police can avoid the need for procuring counsel by simply not conducting the interrogation.

2. **Right to have lawyer present during questioning:** The right to counsel imposed by *Miranda* is not merely the right to *consult* a lawyer prior to the questioning, but the right to *have the lawyer present* while the questioning occurs.

H. **Fifth Amendment basis for:** The basis for *Miranda* is the *Fifth Amendment's* privilege against *self-incrimination*, *not* the Sixth Amendment's right to counsel. The basic idea is that when a suspect is questioned while in custody, this questioning is likely to induce confessions made in violation of the Fifth Amendment.

I. **MBE Tip:** Failure to give *Miranda* warnings, when it's an issue on the MBE, is more likely to be the *wrong* answer than the right answer. But when it *is* the right answer, the examiners will often try to *obscure this fact* by *not* mentioning "*Miranda*" or "*Miranda* rights" anywhere in either the fact pattern or any choice. (They seem to think that if they mention *Miranda*, that will clue in some students who otherwise would have missed the *Miranda* issue.)

1. **Consequence:** Therefore, where *Miranda* applies and supplies the solution, the correct choice may say something non-*Miranda*-specific like "The court should grant D's suppression motion because he *did not voluntarily waive his right to silence.*"

IV. WHAT IS A "CUSTODIAL" INTERROGATION

A. **"Custody" required:** *Miranda* warnings must be given only when police questioning occurs while the suspect is in *"custody."*

1. **"Focus of investigation" irrelevant:** In deciding whether the suspect is in "custody," the fact that the police investigation has (or has not) *"focused"* on that suspect is *irrelevant*.

2. **Objective "reasonable suspect" test:** Whether a suspect is or is not in "custody" as of a particular moment is to be determined by an objective *"reasonable suspect"* test: the issue is *whether a reasonable person in the suspect's position would believe that he was (or was not) in custody — i.e., free to leave — at that moment.*

3. **Undercover agent:** One consequence of the "reasonable suspect" rule is that if D talks to an *undercover agent* or to a government *informant*, and D does not know he is talking to a law enforcement officer, no "custodial interrogation" has taken place. This is true even if D is *in jail.* [*Illinois v. Perkins*]

   Note: However, the use of undercover agents, although it will never cause a *Miranda* violation, may lead to a violation of the suspect's *Sixth Amendment* right to *counsel* — once a suspect has been indicted, it violates her right to counsel for a secret agent to deliberately obtain incriminating statements from her in the absence of counsel. See *infra*, p. 127.

4. **Stop-and-frisk:** When an officer makes a *Terry "stop-and-frisk"* of a suspect (see *supra*, p. 106), based on *reasonable suspicion* of wrongdoing but not probable cause, the officer may briefly *question the suspect* about his activities, *without* giving *Miranda* warnings. That's because, while the stop-and-frisk is going on, the officer by definition does not have probable cause to arrest, has not made an arrest, and is therefore *not holding the suspect in custody* (so that the interrogation is not "custodial"). [*Berkemer v. McCarty* (1984)] See *supra*, p. 107, for an example of a typical stop-and-frisk-accompanied-by-interrogation that does not trigger the need for *Miranda* warnings.

V. MINOR CRIMES

A. **No "minor crimes" exception:** There is *no "minor crimes" exception* to the *Miranda* requirement. That is, if an interrogation meets all of the standard requirements for *Miranda* warnings (especially the requirement that the suspect be "in custody"), these warnings must be given *no matter how minor the crime*, and regardless of the fact that *no jail sentence* may be imposed for it. [*Berkemer v. McCarty, supra.*]

1. **Traffic stops:** This means that if the suspect is charged with a *minor traffic violation*, but is then taken into custody, he is entitled to *Miranda* warnings.

VI. WHAT CONSTITUTES INTERROGATION

A. **Volunteered statements:** A *"volunteered statement"* is not covered by *Miranda*. That is, if a suspect, without being questioned, *spontaneously* makes an incriminating statement, that statement may be introduced against him, despite the absence of *Miranda* warnings.

1. **Voluntary custodial statements:** This is true even if the statement comes from a suspect who is *in custody*. So long as the statement is not induced by police questioning, the fact that the suspect is in custody is not enough to trigger *Miranda*.

    Example: The police arrest D at his house, pursuant to a validly-issued arrest warrant. The arrest is for holding up a 7/11 with Zeke, in which (the prosecution alleges) both men wore masks. After they handcuff him, D blurts out, "You never would have caught me if it wasn't for that snitch Zeke who pulled the 7/11 heist with me." At trial, the prosecution offers this statement to show that D committed the crime. D moves to suppress on the grounds that he made the statement in custody after not being given *Miranda* warnings.

    D will lose — even though he was in custody, his un-Mirandized statement is admissible, because it was volunteered, instead of being given in response to interrogation.

B. **Indirect questioning:** But "interrogation" for *Miranda* purposes includes more than just direct questioning by the police. Interrogation will be deemed to occur whenever a person in custody is subjected to either express questioning, or to words or actions on the part of the police that the police "*should know* are *reasonably likely* to *elicit* an *incriminating response* from the suspect." [*Rhode Island v. Innis*] So "indirect questioning" will count as interrogation.

   1. **No interrogation found:** Application of this "should know are reasonably likely to elicit an incriminating response" test will often mean that even though the police make comments that lead directly to an incriminating result, no "interrogation" is found.

        Example: D is arrested for a murder committed by use of a sawed-off shotgun, which has not been found. While D is being transported near the crime scene, Officer comments to his colleagues in front of D that there is a school for handicapped children nearby, and that "God forbid one of the children might find a weapon with shells and they might hurt themselves." D then directs the officers to the place where the gun can be found. *Held*, Officer's comment did not constitute interrogation of D, so D was not entitled to *Miranda* warnings (and D's comments are admissible against him). [*Rhode Island v. Innis, supra.*]

C. **Police allow situation to develop:** The requirement of "interrogation" means that even if the police allow a situation to develop that is likely to induce the suspect to volunteer an incriminating remark, no *Miranda* warnings need be given if the police do not directly interact with the suspect. For instance, if the police merely *allow (but don't promote) a meeting* between D and his spouse in which D is likely to incriminate himself while under covert observation, probably no "interrogation" occurs. [*Arizona v. Mauro*]

   1. **Police set up situation:** But if the police *intentionally set up a compromising situation* for the *purpose* of inducing D to incriminate himself, interrogation is likely to be found, triggering the need for *Miranda* warnings (and for compliance with any request by D for a lawyer after he receives the warnings).

        Example: The police suspect D of arranging the murder of his business rival, V. The police arrest D on murder charges and give him his *Miranda* warnings. D asks for a lawyer. The police say that they are arranging one. Instead of obtaining a lawyer, however, the police phone X, who they know is D's mistress, and ask her to come to the police station. They tell X, "D is feeling really lonely and vulnerable. Why don't you talk to him?" They then show X into a room in which D is sitting, and in which there is a concealed camera. As the police hoped, D makes a remark to X that incriminates him in the murder of V. D moves to suppress the remark.

        There is a good chance that D's remark to X will be ordered suppressed. Given that D was in custody and in receipt of his *Miranda* warnings, once he asked for a lawyer no "interrogation" could occur until a lawyer was obtained. The police's hope and intent that D would incriminate himself to X, coupled with the use of the concealed camera and the police's request that X talk to D, would likely cause the court to conclude that the police had "constructively interrogated" D in violation of D's request for a lawyer.

D. **Questions by non-police:** Where questions are asked by people other than the police, these will invoke *Miranda* only if asked by other *law enforcement* officials.

1. **Investigator or victims:** Thus questions asked of a suspect by a *private investigator*, or by a *victim* of the crime, will not be covered by *Miranda*.

2. **Government officials:** But questions by *probation officers*, *IRS agents* conducting tax investigations, or a court-ordered psychiatrist evaluating D's sanity for purposes of penalties, are all likely to be found to trigger a requirement of *Miranda* warnings.

VII. THE "PUBLIC SAFETY" EXCEPTION TO *MIRANDA*

A. **The public safety exception generally:** *Miranda* warnings are *unnecessary* where the questioning is "reasonably prompted by a concern for the *public safety*." [*New York v. Quarles*]

> **Example:** Officer and three colleagues accost D, a suspected rapist, in a grocery store. When he sees the officers, D runs towards the back of the store, where he is caught and handcuffed. Officer, without giving D *Miranda* warnings, asks him whether he has a gun and where it is. D answers, "Over there." The gun is found, and D's statement — plus the gun — are introduced against him at his trial.
>
> *Held*, even though D was in custody and was under interrogation at the time of his statement, he was not entitled to *Miranda* warnings because the police questioning was motivated by a need to protect the public safety. [*Quarles, supra.*]

1. **Objective standard:** The existence of a threat to the public safety is to be determined by an *objective*, not subjective, standard. That is, the questioning officer's subjective belief that there is or is not a significant threat to the public safety is *irrelevant*, and the test is whether a *reasonable officer* in that position would conclude that there was such a threat.

2. **May still show compulsion:** Despite the "public safety" exception to *Miranda*, the defendant is always allowed to show that his answers were *actually coerced*. If he can make this showing, he will still be entitled to have those answers excluded — this exclusion will be based on lack of voluntariness, not on the police failure to give *Miranda* warnings.

VIII. WAIVER OF *MIRANDA* RIGHTS

A. **Waiver generally:** After being read the *Miranda* warnings, a suspect may *waive* his right to a lawyer and his right to remain silent. Or, the suspect may waive one of these rights without waiving the other. Waivers may be express or implied.

B. **Express waiver:** *Express* waivers raise few problems. Normally, an express waiver will take the form of a writing signed by the suspect, in which she states that she is waiving her right to a lawyer and her right to remain silent. As long as D is induced to sign the waiver without coercion or trickery, no legal problems should be presented.

C. **Implied waiver:** *Miranda* rights may also be subjected to an "*implied* waiver." In an implied waiver, D does not expressly state that he is waiving his rights, but his words or conduct *suggest* that he has decided to relinquish those rights. Courts *scrutinize* an alleged implied waiver far more carefully than an express waiver.

1. **Burden of proof:** The *prosecution* bears the burden of demonstrating that the implied waiver was a *"knowing"* one, at least in the sense that D was aware of his *Miranda* rights and of his right to refuse to waive them.

2. **Silence:** The accused's *silence* after being read his *Miranda* warnings will never by itself be sufficient to demonstrate a waiver.

    Example: D, in custody, is read his *Miranda* warnings. He makes no response. Officer then starts to question D, and D responds, incriminating himself. It is very unlikely that D will be found to have waived his rights, because his only response was silence, followed by his answering of questions. Some more specific indication that D knew of his rights and had voluntarily decided to waive them will be required.

3. **Retained lawyer not consulted:** Where a lawyer has been *retained* by the suspect's family, the suspect's waiver of his *Miranda* rights (and his consequent failure to consult with the lawyer) will be effective even where the police *decline to tell him* that the lawyer has been retained for him, and even where the police *prevent* the lawyer from seeing the suspect. [*Moran v. Burbine*]

4. **Suspect's ignorance of charges:** The police have no obligation to *notify* D accurately of the *charges against him*, or of the matters to which the interrogation will pertain. Even if D believes that he will be interrogated about a minor matter, and is instead questioned about a major crime, the waiver will still be valid. [*Colorado v. Spring*]

5. **Mentally ill defendant:** Where a suspect's waiver is caused in major part by D's *mental illness*, this does not make any difference: as long as the police do not *coerce* D into waiving his rights, D's mental illness will not impair the validity of his waiver. [*Colorado v. Connelly*]

IX. OTHER *MIRANDA* ISSUES

A. **Grand jury witnesses:** A witness who is subpoenaed to appear before a *grand jury* probably does *not* have to be given *Miranda* warnings.

B. **Impeachment:** A confession obtained in violation of *Miranda* may not be introduced as part of the prosecution's case-in-chief. But the prosecution *may* use such statements to *impeach* D's testimony at trial. [*Harris v. New York*]

   Example: D is charged with selling heroin on two occasions. At his trial, he takes the stand and denies making one of these sales. The prosecution then reads a statement, obtained in violation of *Miranda*, in which D admits making both sales. *Held*, even though the statement was made without benefit of *Miranda* warnings, it may be used to impeach D's trial testimony. [*Harris, supra.*]

   1. **Coercion:** Although a statement obtained in violation of *Miranda* may be admissible for impeachment purposes, it may *not* be used even for this limited purpose if it was the product of *coercion*, or was *involuntary* for some other reason. [*Mincey v. Arizona*]

C. **Use of D's silence:**

   1. **Generally not allowed:** The prosecution may *not* introduce in court the fact that D *remained silent* while under police questioning. In other words, the fact that D has asserted his *Miranda* rights may not be used to weaken D's case before the jury. [*Doyle v. Ohio*]

      Example: At trial, D raises an alibi defense, that he was in another city at the time of the crime. The prosecution attempts to impeach this alibi by showing that when D was questioned by the police while under custody, he failed to assert this alibi, as one would expect he would have done if the alibi had been genuine. The prosecution may not impeach D in this manner.

2. Pre-arrest silence: But this rule applies only to D's silence after arrest and *Miranda* warnings — it does not apply to *pre-arrest silence* by the suspect.

> **Example:** D raises a self-defense claim at his murder trial. The prosecution impeaches this claim by pointing out that for two weeks after the murder, D failed to go to the police to surrender himself or to explain that he killed in self-defense. *Held*, this prosecution use of D's silence was proper, because D's silence did not occur while he was in custody. [*Jenkins v. Anderson*]

CHAPTER 6

LINEUPS AND OTHER PRE-TRIAL IDENTIFICATION PROCEDURES

I. I.D. PROCEDURES GENERALLY

A. Various procedures: There are a number of methods by which the police may get an *identification* of a suspect to link him with a crime: *lineups, fingerprints, blood samples, voice prints*, the use of *photographs*, etc.

B. Possible constitutional problems: There are four plausible constitutional objections that D may be able to make to the use of one of these procedures against him: (1) that it violates D's privilege against *self-incrimination*; (2) that it constituted an *unreasonable search or seizure* in violation of the Fourth Amendment; (3) that if D did not have a lawyer present, the use of the procedure violated his *Sixth Amendment right to counsel*; and (4) that the procedure was so suggestive that it violated D's Fifth/Fourteenth Amendment right to *due process*.

C. Right to counsel as main weapon: The objection that is most likely to succeed is that use of one of these procedures (especially a lineup or show-up) without D's lawyer present violated his *right to counsel*; the next most likely to succeed is the argument that the procedure was so *suggestive* that it violated *due process* (most likely to work where the procedure was a lineup, show-up, or photo I.D.). The self-incrimination argument will almost never work, and the search and seizure argument has a chance of working only if the police lacked a warrant and/or probable cause.

II. THE PRIVILEGE AGAINST SELF-INCRIMINATION

A. General rule: *Physical identification procedures* — fingerprints, blood samples, voice prints, etc. — will generally *not* trigger the Fifth Amendment privilege against *self-incrimination*. That privilege protects only against compulsion to give *"testimony or communicative* evidence," and these physical procedures have been found not to be "testimony or communicative." [*Schmerber v. California*]

> **Example:** D is arrested for drunk driving. A blood sample is forcibly taken from him over his objection, by a physician acting under the direction of the police. *Held*, D's privilege against self-incrimination was not violated by the forcible test, because the privilege protects only against being compelled to give testimony or communicative evidence, not being forced to give real or physical evidence. [*Schmerber, supra.*]

1. Other procedures: This principle has been broadly applied, so that D has no self-incrimination privilege against being forced to:

[1] appear in a *lineup*;

[2] *speak* for identification;

[3] give *fingerprints*;

[4] be *photographed*;

[5] be *measured*;

[6] be required to make *physical movements*;

[7] give a *handwriting* sample;

[8] participate in a *courtroom-identification procedure* (e.g., by walking or speaking to aid the jury in determining whether D is the person the witness saw or heard during the course of the crime).

Example 1: A masked man wearing gloves robs the First National Bank, using a handwritten note to the teller demanding the contents of the cash drawer. D is arrested one week later and charged with the crime. At the police station, the police require D, over his protest, to write out the words of the note. They do not inform D that the copy may be used against him at trial. At trial, the prosecution offers the real note and the station-house copy to show that D wrote the real notes. D attempts to suppress the copy on the grounds that its taking violated his rights against self-incrimination and to the *Miranda* warnings.

D will lose. A person has no self-incrimination or *Miranda* rights that are violated when the person is required to give a physical, non-testimonial, sample, such as a handwriting sample.

Example 2: D is arrested and accused of robbing V at gunpoint while wearing a mask that covered only his eyes. He is taken to the police station and placed in a lineup with five other men of similar build. Each is then required to say the sentence spoken by the robber, "I won't hurt you if you give me your wallet right away." V listens to each speaker, and then identifies D by recognizing his voice. At a pre-trial suppression hearing, D argues that use of V's voice identification would violate his right against compulsory self-incrimination.

D will lose. As with the compelled writing sample at issue in the prior example, a person has no self-incrimination (or *Miranda*) right to give a physical sample that does not constitute "testimony." Here, the sentence that D was required to speak was not testimony by him (he wasn't made to assert that something was or was not true) — it was merely a voice sample.

2. **No need for *Miranda* warnings:** Because supplying a non-testimonial physical sample does not trigger Fifth Amendment rights, a suspect is *not entitled to Miranda warnings* before being required to give such a sample. Indeed, not only does the suspect not need to be *told* that he has a right to refuse, the suspect doesn't *have* a right to refuse (see Par. (3) below).

Example: On the facts of Example 2 above, before the police put D in the lineup, they were not required to give him *Miranda* warnings, including the warning that "anything you say may be used against you." *Miranda* is based on the Fifth Amendment freedom from compulsory *testimonial* self-incrimination, so no *Miranda* warnings are needed before someone is asked to (or even forced to) give non-testimonial material.

3. **Non-cooperation:** If the suspect refuses to cooperate with a request to provide one of these sources of physical identification, the court may *order him* to do so. If he still refuses, the court may hold him in contempt and jail him.

   a. **Prosecution's right to comment:** Furthermore, if D refuses to cooperate with such a request, the prosecution may *comment* on that fact at D's later trial.

III. THE RIGHT TO COUNSEL AT PRE-TRIAL CONFRONTATIONS

A. **Rule generally:** A suspect against whom *formal criminal proceedings have been commenced* has an *absolute right* to have *counsel present* at any pre-trial *confrontation* procedure. Such confrontations include both *lineups* (in which a witness picks the suspect out of a group of persons) and *show-ups* (in which the witness is shown only the suspect and asked whether the suspect is the perpetrator). [*U.S. v. Wade*; *Gilbert v. California*]

> **Example:** D is indicted for robbery, arrested, and brought to the police station. He is placed in a lineup with other men of similar appearance. V, the robbery victim, is asked to identify the perpetrator. V picks D out of the lineup. Unless the police offered D the chance to have counsel present at the lineup, the results of the lineup will not be admissible against D at his criminal trial.

1. **Effect on in-court I.D.:** Furthermore, if the confrontation is conducted in violation of the right of counsel, the prosecution will not only be barred from introducing at trial the fact that D was picked out of the lineup, but may even be barred from having the witness who made the identification (V in the above example) *testify in court* that the person sitting in the dock is the person observed by the witness at the scene of the crime. Once the lineup is shown to have been improper, the prosecution will have to come up with *"clear and convincing evidence"* that the in-court identification is not the "fruit of the poisonous tree" (i.e., the product of the improper lineup identification).

B. **Waiver:** The right to have counsel at the pre-trial confrontation proceeding may be *waived*. But the waiver must be an "intelligent" one; probably, the police must inform D of his right to counsel, and D must be capable of understanding that right and must voluntarily choose to give it up.

C. **Exceptions to the right:**

1. **Before formal proceedings against D:** The right to have counsel at the pre-trial confrontation probably applies only to confrontations occurring after the institution of *formal proceedings* against the suspect. [*Kirby v. Illinois*] The right will be triggered by the fact that D has been *formally charged, given a preliminary hearing, indicted, arraigned,* or otherwise subjected to formal judiciary proceedings. But the right is probably *not* triggered if D has merely been *arrested without a warrant* and then put in the lineup or show-up. Certainly the right seems not to be triggered where the police have not even arrested D yet, but have asked him to voluntarily appear in a lineup, and D agrees.

2. **Photo I.D.:** The right to counsel does *not* apply where a witness views *still or moving pictures* of the suspect for identification purposes.

    > **Example:** D is not present when the police bring photos of D, together with photos of innocent people, to V, and ask V to pull the photo of the perpetrator from the group. The fact that D has not been given a chance to have a lawyer present during this procedure makes no difference, because D has no Sixth Amendment right to counsel in this non–face-to-face situation. [*U.S. v. Ash*]

    Note: But the due process right not to be subjected to "unduly suggestive" procedures may be triggered in this photo I.D. situation, as discussed below.

3. **Scientific I.D. procedures:** No Sixth Amendment right to counsel attaches where *scientific methods*, as opposed to eyewitness identification procedures, are used to identify D as the perpetrator. Thus if the police extract or analyze D's fingerprints, blood samples, clothing, hair, voice, handwriting samples, etc., D does not have a right to have counsel present during these extractions or examinations.

IV. DUE PROCESS LIMITS ON I.D. PROCEDURES

A. Suggestive procedures: Even where the right to counsel is never triggered by an identification procedure (or has been triggered but complied with), D may be able to exclude the resulting identification on the grounds that it violated his *due process* rights. To do this, D will have to show that, viewed by the *"totality of the circumstances,"* the identification procedure was so *"unnecessarily suggestive"* and so conducive to mistaken identification, as to be deeply unfair to D.

> **Example:** D is suspected of robbery. D is lined up with men several inches shorter than he. Only D wears a jacket similar to that known to have been used by the robber. After V is unable to positively identify anyone, the police then use a one-man show-up of D. When V is still uncertain, the police put on, several days later, a second lineup, in which D is the only repeater from the previous lineup.
>
> *Held*, the procedures used here were so suggestive that an identification of D as the perpetrator was "all but inevitable." Therefore, the fact that V picked D out of the second lineup must be excluded from D's trial, as a violation of his due process rights. (This is true regardless of whether D had, or used, any right to have counsel present.) [*Foster v. California*]

B. Suggestive procedures allowed if reliable: But an identification procedure is not violative of due process if the court finds that it is *reliable* (i.e., not likely to cause error), even if it is somewhat suggestive.

> **Example:** If V has a long time to view the perpetrator during the crime, under adequate light, up close, these facts will make it more likely that the resulting identification procedures are fair to D, even if there is some suggestiveness during the procedures themselves. Similarly, the fact that V is very certain of the identification, or that V has given an extremely thorough description of the perpetrator before the identification procedure, will make the court more likely to uphold it. [*Neil v. Biggers*]

C. Photo I.D.s: Where a witness identifies the suspect through the use of *photographs*, the "totality of the circumstances" test is used to determine whether D's due process rights have been violated, just as this test is used in the lineup or show-up situation. [*Simmons v. U.S.*; *Manson v. Brathwaite*]

> **Example:** The photo I.D. is more likely to be upheld if the police show V photographs of numerous people — without hinting to V which photo they believe to be of the prime suspect — than if the police show one photo to V, and say, "Is this the guy?"

  1. Must be very likely to be mistaken: As with the lineup and show-up situation, a due process violation will be found only if the photo I.D. session is *very likely* to have produced a misidentification. The fact that the procedure is somewhat "suggestive" will not be enough. Thus if the victim had an unusually good opportunity to view the perpetrator, or was unusually experienced at identifying perpetrators, this will probably overcome some suggestiveness in the procedure (e.g., the use of only a single photo). [See *Manson, supra*.]

Chapter 7
THE EXCLUSIONARY RULE

I. THE RULE GENERALLY

A. Statement of rule: The "exclusionary rule" provides that evidence obtained by violating D's constitutional rights *may not be introduced by the prosecution* at D's criminal trial, at least for purposes of providing direct proof of D's guilt.

- **B. Judge-made rule:** The exclusionary rule is a *judge-made*, not statutory, rule. Over the years, the rule has been shaped by a long series of Supreme Court decisions. The rule is binding on both *state* and *federal* courts.

  1. **Not constitutionally required:** The Supreme Court has held that the exclusionary rule is *not required by the Constitution*. [*U.S. v. Leon*] Instead, the rule has been created by the Supreme Court as a means of *deterring* the police from violating the Fourth, Fifth, and other Amendments.

  2. **State constitutional violation:** By the way, state courts are always free to hold that the *state constitution* forbids police conduct that the federal constitution would not forbid. If so, in a state trial the court is free to apply — and generally *will* apply — the exclusionary rule to this evidence obtained in violation of the state but not federal constitution.

II. STANDING TO ASSERT THE EXCLUSIONARY RULE

- **A. Standing rule generally:** In general, D may assert the exclusionary rule only to bar evidence obtained through violation of *his own* constitutional rights. That is, D may not keep out evidence obtained through police action that was a violation of a third person's rights but not of D's own rights.

  > **Example:** The police illegally wire-tap a conversation between D1 and X (without the knowledge of either). Statements made in this conversation are used at a trial of D2. D2 argues that since the evidence was obtained by a violation of constitutional rights (the rights of D1), the evidence should not be usable against anyone, including D2. *Held*, for the prosecution. Evidence obtained by violation of the Fourth Amendment or any other constitutional provision may only be excluded by a person whose own rights were violated. [*Alderman v. U.S.*]

- **B. Confession cases:** The standing requirement means that in the case of an illegally-obtained confession, only the person who *makes* the confession may have it barred by the exclusionary rule.

  > **Example:** Suspect *A* confesses without being given the required *Miranda* warnings. In his confession, *A* implicates *B*. The confession may still be introduced in evidence against *B* (though not against *A*), because *B*'s constitutional rights were not violated by the obtaining of the confession.) (But *A* will have to be available for cross-examination at *B*'s trial, due to *B*'s rights under the Confrontation Clause; see *infra*, p. 134.)

- **C. Search and seizure cases:** In search and seizure cases, the standing requirement means that D may seek to exclude evidence derived from a search and seizure only if his *own* "legitimate expectation of privacy" was violated by the search. [*Rakas v. Illinois*]

  1. **Possessory interest in items seized:** This means that the mere fact that D has a *possessory interest* in the *items seized* is *not* by itself automatically enough to allow D to challenge the constitutionality of the seizure. Only if D had a *legitimate expectation of privacy* with respect to the items seized, may D exclude those items.

     > **Example:** D and his friend Cox are both searched by the police. In Cox's handbag, the police find 1,800 tablets of LSD and other drugs. D claims ownership of these drugs, and can prove that he owns them. The search and seizure occurred without probable cause. D tries to have the drugs suppressed from his drug possession trial. *Held*, for the prosecution. Even though D owned the drugs, D's own rights were not violated by the search of Cox's

handbag, because once D placed the drugs in Cox's handbag, he had no further legitimate expectation of privacy with respect to those drugs. [*Rawlings v. Kentucky*]

2. **Presence at scene of search:** Similarly, the fact that D is *legitimately on the premises* where a search takes place does *not* mean that D can exclude the fruits of the search if the search was illegal. Again, only if D had a legitimate expectation of privacy with respect to the *areas* where the incriminating materials were found, may D benefit from the exclusionary rule.

   Example: D is riding as a passenger in a car that is illegally searched by the police. The police find a sawed-off rifle under the passenger seat occupied by D. *Held*, the mere fact that D was on the scene during the search did not give him standing to assert the exclusionary rule. Since D did not have a legitimate expectation of privacy as to the area under his seat, he could not assert the exclusionary rule and the rifle could be admitted against him. [*Rakas v. Illinois*]

3. **Occupants of vehicle:** When the police stop a *vehicle*, both the driver and *any passengers* have standing to challenge the constitutionality of the vehicle stop. [*Brendlin v. California*]

   Example: Acting without probable cause, a police officer pulls over a vehicle driven by X in which Y is a passenger. The officer makes Y get out of the car, pats him down, and finds an illegal weapon. Even though Y didn't have any possessory interest in the car, Y has standing to challenge the initial stop of the vehicle, since the stop acted as a seizure of Y's person. Cf. *Brendlin, supra*.

   a. **Ownership of item or car not enough:** But the mere fact that D was the *owner* of an item found in the car — where D was *not physically present* in the car at the time the vehicle was stopped — won't give D a legitimate expectation of privacy in the item, and thus will not give D standing to challenge the seizure.

      Example: D lends his car to X. X is stopped for speeding by Officer. Officer gives X a ticket (without arresting him) and decides to search the passenger compartment. There, she finds an open briefcase with D's name on it, the contents of which reasonably look to Officer like it contains marijuana. She smells the contents, concludes that the contents smell like marijuana, and causes a warrant to be issued for the arrest of D. D moves to suppress the marijuana (which he concedes was owned by him, not X).

      D does not have standing to assert that the police improperly stopped X and/or improperly searched the car's passenger compartment. That's because D was not present, and his ownership of both the car and the brief case did not give him standing. If D had had a reasonable expectation of privacy in the briefcase, D would have had standing. But since the briefcase was open, and since D took the risk that X would look at the briefcase's exposed contents, D had no reasonable expectation of privacy in the briefcase's contents.

III. DERIVATIVE EVIDENCE

A. **Derivative evidence generally:** The exclusionary rule clearly applies to evidence that is the *direct* result of a violation of D's rights (e.g., evidence is seized from D's premises during an illegal search). But the exclusionary rule also applies to some *"derivative evidence,"* that is, evidence that is only *indirectly* obtained by a violation of D's rights. In general, if police wrongdoing leads in a relatively short, unbroken, chain to evidence, that evidence will be barred by the exclusionary rule, even though the evidence was not the direct and immediate fruit of the illegality. The concept is frequently referred to as the *"poisonous tree doctrine"*: once the original evidence (the *"tree"*) is shown to have been unlawfully obtained, *all evidence stemming from it (the "fruit" of the poisonous tree) is equally unusable.*

Example: Federal agents, acting without probable cause, break into Toy's apartment and handcuff him. Toy makes a statement accusing Yee of selling narcotics. The agents go to Yee, from whom they seize heroin.

Held, the drugs seized from Yee are "fruits of the poisonous tree," since they were seized as the direct result of the agents' illegal entry into Toy's apartment. Therefore, the drugs from Yee cannot be introduced against Toy, under the exclusionary rule. [*Wong Sun v. U.S.*]

B. The independent source exception: The "fruits of the poisonous tree" doctrine has a couple of major *exceptions*, one of which is known as the *"independent source"* exception. When the police have *two paths* leading to information, and only one of these paths begins with illegality, the evidence is not deemed fruit of the poisonous tree, and is not barred by the exclusionary rule.

1. **Use for warrantless arrests or seizures:** The main utility of the "independent source" exception arises where the police have probable cause to obtain a search warrant, which would have led them to certain evidence; instead, the police make an illegal search, discover evidence, then go back and get a warrant. Since the police *could have* lawfully obtained a warrant, they are deemed to have had an "independent source" for the evidence, so the evidence will not be barred by the exclusionary rule even though it was illegally obtained.

   Example: The police have probable cause to arrest D for narcotics violations, and probable cause to search his apartment for evidence. The police arrest D outside his apartment. They do not get a search warrant, even though warrantless entry is not allowed without one. They then enter the apartment, where they see narcotics paraphernalia. They post agents to prevent destruction of evidence, and 20 hours later get a warrant; they then conduct a search which turns up narcotics that they had not previously observed.

   Held, the seized narcotics are not the fruit of the poisonous tree, and thus not excludable in D's trial, because the police had an independent source for discovering those narcotics — since the police were already, prior to the illegal entry, entitled to get a search warrant, they could have staked out the apartment from the outside, gotten the warrant and seized the very same evidence. [*Segura v. U.S.*]

2. **Inevitable discovery:** There is a doctrine related to the "independent source" exception, called the *"inevitable discovery"* exception. Evidence may be admitted if it would *"inevitably"* have been discovered by *other police techniques* had it not first been obtained through the illegal discovery.

C. The "purged taint" exception: A second very important exception to the "fruit of the poisonous tree" doctrine is the *"purged taint"* exception. The idea is that if enough additional factors *intervene* between the original illegality and the final discovery of the evidence, the link between the two is so tenuous that the exclusionary rule should not be applied. In this situation, the intervening factors are said to be enough to have "purged the taint" of the original illegal police conduct.

1. **Illegality leads police to focus on particular suspect:** If the illegality (an illegal search, arrest, lineup, etc.) leads the police to *focus on a particular suspect* they were not previously focusing on, usually the final arrest of the suspect will *not* be found to be tainted by the original illegality: the full-scale investigation that the police conduct between the time they first focus on the suspect and the time they arrest him is usually enough to purge this taint.

2. **Confession as tainted fruit:** A *confession* may be found to be tainted fruit. This is especially likely to be the case where the confession stems directly from the *illegal arrest* of the suspect who gives the confession. In general, where the confession comes in the period of *cus-*

tody immediately following the arrest, the court is likely to find that the confession is tainted fruit, and must therefore be excluded from the trial of the confessor.

> **Example:** Acting without probable cause, the police arrest D on suspicion of robbery. While D is in custody, the police give him his *Miranda* warnings, and he waives his rights, then confesses. A court would almost certainly hold that D's confession must be excluded as a fruit of the illegal arrest.

IV. COLLATERAL USE EXCEPTIONS

A. **Collateral use generally:** The exclusionary rule basically applies only to evidence presented by the prosecution as part of its *case in chief* at D's trial. In other contexts, the rule is much less likely to apply, as described below.

B. **Impeachment at trial:** Thus illegally-obtained evidence may be used to *impeach the defendant's trial testimony*, even though it cannot be used in the prosecution's direct case. [*Harris v. N.Y.*]

   1. **Statements made in direct testimony:** Most obviously, illegally-obtained evidence may be used to impeach statements made by D *during his direct testimony*.

      > **Example:** D is arrested on suspicion of burglarizing a particular premises. The police do not give him the required *Miranda* warnings. They ask him where he was on a particular evening, and he replies that he was at his girlfriend's house. At trial, during D's direct testimony after taking the stand, D says that at the time in question, he was at home. The prosecutor may bring out on cross-examination the fact that D told a different story in his non-*Mirandized* confession.

   2. **Impeachment of defense witnesses:** But illegally-obtained evidence may *not* be used to impeach the testimony of *defense witnesses* other than the defendant himself. [*James v. Illinois*]

      > **Example:** While D is under arrest for burglary, and without receiving *Miranda* warnings, D states that he was at home at the time of a burglary under investigation. At trial, D presents as a witness W, D's girlfriend, who says that at the time in question, D was with W at W's house. The prosecution may not impeach W's testimony by introducing D's contrary statement made during the un-*Mirandized* confession.

C. **Impeachment in grand jury proceedings:** A *grand jury witness* cannot prevent illegally-obtained evidence from being introduced against him during the grand jury proceeding. [*U.S. v. Calandra*]

V. THE "GOOD FAITH WARRANT" EXCEPTION

A. **The "good faith warrant" exception:** The exclusionary rule does *not* bar evidence that was obtained by officers acting in *reasonable reliance* on a *search warrant* issued by a proper magistrate but ultimately found to be *unsupported by probable cause*. [*U.S. v. Leon*]

   > **Example:** The police, relying on information from an informant as well as their own investigations, obtain a search warrant that is valid on its face. They search several premises under the warrant, obtaining evidence of narcotics violations. Later, a judge holds that the information presented to the magistrate did not establish probable cause for the search. Now, the issue is whether the illegally-seized evidence may be admitted against D.
   >
   > *Held*, the evidence may be admitted against D, because the exclusionary rule should not be applied where officers have a good-faith, objectively reasonable belief that they have probable cause, and the warrant is issued according to proper procedures. [*Leon, supra.*]

1. **Reliance on non-existent arrest warrant:** The "good faith" exception has been extended to one additional situation: if the police reasonably believe that there is an outstanding *warrant* for the *arrest* of D, and search D while arresting him, the fruits will be admissible even if it turns out that the arrest warrant was not in fact outstanding (at least where the confusion resulted from a court error rather than a police error). [*Ariz. v. Evans*]

2. **Police must behave with objective reasonableness:** The exception applies only where the police behave in *good faith* and in an *objectively reasonable* manner. In particular, the exception does not apply if the police officer who prepares the affidavit for a search warrant *knows* that the information in it is false, or *recklessly disregards* its truth or falsity. Also, the affidavit must on its face seem to be valid, and to be based on probable cause.

   a. **MBE Tip:** So on the MBE, make sure that the officer using the information in the affidavit in support of the warrant request has both a *good faith* and an *objectively-reasonable* belief that the information is correct.

   Example: Officer submits an affidavit to search a house at 481 Main Street, which the affidavit says belongs to and is occupied by D. The affidavit quotes a statement by Informant to Officer that the prior day, Informant purchased narcotics from D at the 481 Main Street address. A magistrate issues the requested warrant. Officer executes the warrant, and during the course of the proper execution of the warrant discovers cocaine. D moves to suppress the cocaine. It develops that Informant was a pathological liar who had an incentive to falsely accuse D to Officer, and that Informant had never been at D's residence or purchased drugs from D.

   If D can show that Officer *knew* that Informant's statement was false in some material respect — or that Officer *recklessly disregarded* the truth or falsity of Informant's statement — the fruits of the search will be excluded, on the theory that Officer did not procure the warrant in good faith. But if all D shows is that Informant lied, this won't be enough for D to win, and the *Leon* good-faith-warrant exception will apply to make the search fruits admissible.

Chapter 8
THE RIGHT TO COUNSEL

I. THE INDIGENT'S RIGHT TO COUNSEL

A. **Introduction:** The Sixth Amendment says that "In all criminal prosecutions, the accused shall enjoy the right . . . to have the Assistance of Counsel for his defense."

   1. **Right to appointed counsel where jail is at stake:** The Sixth Amendment right means that an *indigent* defendant has the right to have counsel *appointed for him by the government* in any prosecution where the accused can be sent to jail. Thus in any felony prosecution, and in any misdemeanor prosecution for which the sentence will be a jail term, the indigent has the right to appointed counsel.

   2. **Right to retained counsel:** The Sixth Amendment also means that the government cannot materially interfere with a non-indigent defendant's right to *retain* (i.e., pay for) his own private lawyer.

B. **The right to appointed counsel, generally:** The most important aspect of the Sixth Amendment is that it guarantees *indigent* defendants the right to have counsel *appointed for them* by the government in felonies and in some misdemeanors.

1. **Applicable to states:** The Sixth Amendment right to counsel applies to the *states*, not just the federal government. [*Gideon v. Wainwright*]

2. **Various stages:** The right to appointed counsel does not mean merely that the accused has the right to have a lawyer *at trial*; other parts of the prosecution that are found to represent a "critical stage" in the proceedings (e.g., the arraignment) also trigger the right to appointed counsel. This is discussed more extensively below.

3. **Right to effective assistance:** The right to counsel includes the right to *effective* assistance — thus if the appointed counsel does not meet a certain minimal standard of competence, the Sixth Amendment has been violated. This aspect, too, is discussed below.

C. **Proceedings where the right applies:** The right to appointed counsel applies *only to proceedings in which the defendant is actually sentenced to imprisonment*. So even if the offense is a *felony* under state law, the state does *not* have to supply an indigent with counsel as long as the judge is willing merely to impose a *fine or probation*. [*Scott v. Illinois*]

D. **Stages at which the right to counsel applies:** In addition to the trial itself, the Sixth Amendment right to counsel applies at various other stages of the proceedings:

1. **The "critical stage" doctrine:** The Sixth Amendment is triggered wherever there is a *"critical stage"* of the proceedings. In brief, a stage will be "critical" if D is compelled to make a decision which may later be formally *used against him*.

    a. **Initial appearance:** Thus the *initial appearance*, the *preliminary hearing*, and the *arraignment* are all likely to be found, in a particular case, to be critical stages. (But if local procedures make it clear that nothing done by D at a particular stage binds him, then presumably counsel does not have to be appointed.)

    b. **Appeals:** A convicted defendant's right to appointed counsel during his *appeals* depends on the nature of the appeal. A defendant has the right to appointed counsel for his *first appeal as of right*, i.e., the appeal made available to all convicted defendants. [*Douglas v. California*]

        i. **Discretionary review:** But D has *no* right to appointed counsel to assist with his applications for *discretionary review*. That is, once D's conviction has been affirmed by the first appellate court, and the government provides a second discretionary review (e.g., discretionary review by the state supreme court, or petition for certiorari to the U.S. Supreme Court), D does not have a right to appointed counsel to help with that appeal. [*Ross v. Moffitt*]

II. WAIVER OF THE RIGHT TO COUNSEL

A. **Appointed vs. retained:** In both the appointed-counsel and retained-counsel situations, the defendant may be found to have *waived* his Sixth Amendment right to counsel. Essentially the same standards apply for both situations.

B. **The "knowingly and intelligently" standard:** D will be found to have waived his right to counsel only if he acted *"knowingly and intelligently."* However, the government must prove merely by a "preponderance of the evidence" that D acted knowingly and intelligently, a relatively easy-to-satisfy standard.

1. *Miranda* **warnings suffice:** If D is given his *Miranda* warnings, and does not ask for counsel, this will be found to be a valid waiver of his Sixth Amendment right to counsel.

C. **Right to defend oneself:** The Sixth Amendment guarantees the right of a defendant to proceed *pro se*, i.e., to *represent himself without counsel*. [*Faretta v. California*] (But by choosing to represent himself, D waives any later claim that he was denied the effective assistance of counsel.)

III. ENTITLEMENTS OF THE RIGHT TO COUNSEL

A. Effectiveness of counsel: The Sixth Amendment entitles D not only to have a lawyer, but to have the *"effective assistance"* of counsel.

  1. **Standard:** Where a lawyer has actually participated in D's trial, D has a hard burden to show that he did not receive "effective assistance." D must show *both* that: (1) counsel's performance was *"deficient,"* in the sense that counsel was not a *"reasonably competent attorney"*; and (2) the deficiencies were *prejudicial* to the defense, in the sense that there is a "reasonable probability that, but for counsel's errors, the result of the proceeding would have been different." [*Strickland v. Washington*]

B. Secret agents: Once a suspect has been *indicted* and has counsel, it is a violation of the right of counsel for a *secret agent* to *deliberately obtain incriminating statements* from D in the absence of counsel, and to pass these on to the prosecution. [*Massiah v. U.S.*]

  > **Example:** D is indicted on charges of stealing jewels from a mansion on Lakeshore Drive, and jailed pending trial. Law enforcement officers assign Art, an undercover police officer, to be D's cellmate. At his bosses' request, Art boasts repeatedly about jewel thefts that he, Art, has committed, and frequently asks D whether D has ever stolen any jewelry. Eventually, D mentions to Art the Lakeshore Drive heist. At trial, D moves to suppress Art's testimony about this statement.
  >
  > D will win. Once D was indicted, he had a Sixth Amendment right not to have a person working on behalf of government deliberately elicit incriminating statements in the absence of counsel for D. That right was violated here, since Art's entire pattern of behavior was intended to elicit, and succeeded in eliciting, an incriminating statement by D about the burglary.

  1. **Must be "deliberately elicited":** But this ban on secret agents applies only where the agent *"deliberately elicits"* the incriminating testimony, not where the agent merely "keeps his ears open." [*Kuhlmann v. Wilson*]

      a. **Does not cover pre-indictment situations:** Even the ban on the deliberate eliciting of confidences by secret agents applies only *after formal proceedings* (e.g., an indictment) have begun against D. So during the pre-indictment investigation stage, the police may use a secret agent to entrap D even if the police or agent know that D has a regular lawyer, and even though the agent passes the confidences on to the police or prosecutors.

CHAPTER 9
FORMAL PROCEEDINGS

I. GRAND JURY PROCEEDINGS

A. Grand jury indictment generally: Defendants accused of federal felonies, and some state-court defendants, are "entitled" to a grand jury indictment.

  1. **Federal practice:** The Fifth Amendment provides that "no person shall be held to answer for a capital, or otherwise infamous crime, unless on a presentment or indictment of a Grand Jury." This provision means that anyone charged with a *federal felony* (i.e., a federal crime punishable by more than one year of imprisonment) may only be tried following issuance of a grand jury indictment.

  2. **State courts:** The Fifth Amendment's right to a grand jury indictment is one of the two Bill of Rights guarantees that is *not* binding on the states by means of the Fourteenth Amendment.

So each individual state decides whether to require a grand jury indictment. Today, about 19 states require indictment for all felonies, with the remaining states dispensing with the requirement in at least some kinds of felonies.

B. Self-incrimination and immunity: The Fifth Amendment privilege against *self-incrimination* will frequently entitle a witness who is subpoenaed by a grand jury to refuse to testify. However, this refusal may be overcome by a grant of *immunity*.

  1. "Use immunity" suffices: To overcome the witness's invocation of the Fifth Amendment, the prosecution needs to confer *only "use immunity,"* not the broader "transaction immunity." Therefore, if the MBE examiners ask you to identify the narrowest means that the prosecution can take to compel a reluctant grand jury witness to testify, the answer will be "use immunity."

    Example: The prosecution calls W to give testimony about a gambling ring of which W seems to have knowledge, and of which he may actually be a member. W pleads the Fifth Amendment. The prosecution can force W to testify merely by giving him "use immunity," i.e., a promise that it will not use either the direct or indirect fruits of W's testimony against him in a later criminal proceeding. The prosecution is *not* required to give W the much broader "transaction immunity," i.e., a promise of immunity from any criminal prosecution — regardless of the evidence on which it is based — for any transaction as to whose details W gives testimony. Therefore, so as long as the prosecution can get evidence against W from means entirely independent of W's grand jury testimony (e.g., testimony against W by X, another suspect whom the police had identified and questioned prior to W's compelled grand jury testimony), the prosecution will be free to prosecute W as to crimes about which he testifies.

C. No right to have attorney present in grand jury room: A witness called before the grand jury does *not* have a constitutional right to *have an attorney present inside the grand jury room*. [*U.S. v. Mandujano* (1976)] That's true even if the lawyer is "retained" rather than court-appointed.

  Example: D is subpoenaed to appear before a grand jury investigating money-laundering. D asks that her privately-retained lawyer, L, be allowed to accompany her into the grand jury room. The prosecutor refuses. The prosecutor then asks D a series of questions. D initially repeatedly leaves the room to consult with L, before returning and each time pleading the Fifth Amendment. Eventually, however, D becomes worn down and answers a question without consulting L or pleading the Fifth; she incriminates herself in her answer. At her trial, D moves to suppress the answer as having been obtained in violation of her asserted right to counsel.

  D's motion will be denied, because a grand jury witness does not have the right to have counsel present with her in the grand jury room. It's not even clear that the prosecutor was required to allow D to leave the room to consult with L from time to time, but it is completely clear that nothing more than this — such as letting L be in the room — was required.

D. Use of illegally obtained evidence: The grand jury may hear and use *illegally obtained evidence*. In other words, there is *no exclusionary rule for grand jury proceedings*. Thus the fruits of a confession obtained in violation of *Miranda*, or of a search conducted in violation of the Fourth Amendment, may be introduced and relied upon by the grand jury. [*U.S. v. Calandra*]. The grand jury may also hear and rely upon inadmissible *hearsay*. [*Costello v. U.S*].

  Example: Acting without either probable cause or a search warrant, the police break into D's house while he is away, ransack his files, and find a handwritten diary in which D admits to having murdered V. The prosecutor presents the diary to a grand jury, and thereby obtains an indictment of D for the murder. At trial, D moves to dismiss the indictment because it was procured through use of evidence obtained in violation of D's Fourth Amendment rights.

  D will lose. It's true that the diary was obtained in gross violation of D's Fourth Amendment rights. And the exclusionary rule would permit D to have the diary excluded from his criminal trial. But there is no exclusionary rule for grand jury proceedings. Therefore, the grand jury was entitled to consider and rely upon illegally-obtained evidence, and the use of such evidence won't be grounds for dismissing the indictment.

1. **MBE Tip:** The MBE examiners may test this principle — that the exclusionary rule doesn't apply to grand jury proceedings — without expressly referring to it (perhaps because they think that referring to the principle might make the question too easy). So in a fact pattern in which the prosecution wants to use illegally-obtained evidence before the grand jury, the question may stipulate that D makes a motion to *bar* the prosecution from even *presenting* the information to the grand jury (as opposed to seeking dismissal of the indictment afterwards because of the use of the illegally-obtained evidence). And in that kind of scenario, the correct choice may be indirect and vague, like "motions to exclude evidence from grand juries are premature."

II. RIGHT TO BAIL

A. **Bail:** The system of *bail* is the way courts have traditionally dealt with the problem of making sure that D shows up for trial. D is required to post an amount of money known as a "bail bond"; if he does not show up for trial, he forfeits this amount.

1. **Right to non-excessive bail:** The Eighth Amendment (applicable in both state and federal proceedings) provides that *"excessive bail shall not be required."* However, the Bail Clause does *not* give D a right to affordable bail in all situations — it merely means that when the court does set bail, it must not do so in an *unduly high* amount, judged on factors such as the seriousness of the offense, the weight of the evidence against D, D's financial abilities and his character.

    Example: If a judge were to set bail of $1 million for an indigent D accused of the non-violent crime of marijuana possession, this might be found to be "excessive" bail, in violation of the Eighth Amendment.

    a. **Individualized consideration:** The guarantee against excessive bail means that the judge must consider D's *individual circumstances* in fixing bail. The court may not consider the seriousness of the offense as the *sole* criterion (so that ability to pay, weight of the evidence, character of D, etc., must all be considered).

    b. **Defendant's ability to pay:** The fact that the defendant *cannot afford* the bail set in the particular case does *not* automatically make the bail "excessive" — D's financial resources are merely one factor to be considered.

B. **Preventive detention:** A jurisdiction may constitutionally decide that bail will simply *not be allowed* at all for certain types of offenses. That is, the state or federal government may set up a *"preventive detention"* scheme, whereby certain types of defendants are automatically held without bail until trial. But a preventive detention scheme will violate the Eighth Amendment if its procedures do not ensure that only those defendants who are genuinely dangerous or likely to flee are denied release.

III. PLEA BARGAINING AND GUILTY PLEAS

A. **Plea bargaining generally:** Most criminal cases are resolved by *plea bargain* rather than by trial. To give D an incentive to "settle" the case (by *pleading guilty*) rather than insist on a trial, the prosecutor normally gives D an inducement of a *lighter sentence* than what he would get if he were convicted at trial.

1. **Common types:** The three common types of plea bargains are:

    [1] D pleads to a *less serious charge*;

    > **Example:** D is allowed to plead guilty to second-degree sexual assault rather than to the rape charge that is supported by the evidence

    [2] D pleads guilty to the crime charged, but the prosecutor agrees to recommend a *lighter sentence* to the judge (but the judge will not necessarily follow the recommendation, though she usually does so); and

    [3] D pleads to one charge in return for the prosecution's promise to *drop other charges* that might also have been brought.

2. **Generally enforceable:** Plea bargains are generally *enforceable*. For instance, if D pleads guilty to a charge, is sentenced, and then has a change of heart, he is almost always stuck with his bargain.

3. **Prosecutor may refuse to bargain:** The prosecutor has *no obligation* to bargain. Even if the prosecutor routinely offers a plea bargain in other, similar, circumstances, she has a right in a particular case to decide to go to trial without offering a plea bargain. [*Weatherford v. Bursey* ("There is no constitutional right to plea bargain…")]

B. **Receipt of plea:** The trial judge may not "receive" (i.e., accept) the plea until she has assured herself that certain requirements, designed to protect D, have been complied with. Thus the judge must be satisfied that:

[1] D is *competent* to enter into the plea, and the plea is truly voluntary;

[2] D *understands the charge*; and

[3] D understands the *consequences* of the plea. For instance, the judge must make sure that D understands that he has a *constitutionally-guaranteed right to a jury trial*, that D has a right against compulsory self-incrimination, and that D has a right to confront his accusers, all of which trial rights D is giving up by pleading guilty.

These requirements are probably constitutionally required. That is, they are probably imposed by the *due process clause* of the federal constitution. [*Boykin v. Alabama*]

1. **Factual basis:** Some states, and the federal system, also require that the judge not take the guilty plea unless the judge is convinced that there is a *factual basis* for the plea.

    a. **Judge may constitutionally reject plea:** So if the trial judge thinks D didn't really do it, it is *constitutional* for the judge to refuse to take the guilty plea — there is no absolute constitutional right to have one's guilty plea accepted by the court. [*North Carolina v. Alford*]

    b. **No right to have judge ascertain actual guilt:** Conversely, D does *not* have a *constitutional right* to have the judge ascertain is that the defendant is in fact guilty. So as a constitutional matter the judge doesn't have to ask the defendant whether he "did it," let alone make an independent attempt to determine whether the defendant indeed really did it.

        Example: At a hearing in state court in which D is about to plead guilty, the judge does not make any attempt to ascertain whether D really committed the crime to which he is pleading guilty. D then pleads guilty. Two months later, D appeals, asserting that D had a constitutional right to have the judge attempt to ascertain D's factual guilty before accepting his guilty plea.

        D will lose. A defendant has no federal constitutional right to have a judge attempt to ascertain the defendant's actual guilt before accepting the guilty plea.

IV. THE RIGHT TO A JURY TRIAL

A. **The right generally:** Criminal defendants have a right to a *jury trial*. This right is conferred by the Sixth Amendment, which says that "The accused shall enjoy the right to a ... public trial, by an *impartial jury* of the State and district wherein the crime shall have been committed[.]"

   1. **Applicable to state trials:** This right applies to both *federal* and *state* trials.

   2. **Serious criminal prosecutions only:** The Sixth Amendment right to jury trial applies only to *criminal prosecutions* for *serious* crimes. That is, the right does not apply where what is charged is a *petty* rather than serious crime.

      a. **Six months as dividing line:** As a general rule, the dividing line between a "serious" crime and a "petty" one is a *potential sentence of greater than six months*. Thus there is automatically a right to jury trial for any crime punish*able* by more than six months in prison, regardless of whether a more-than-six-month sentence is *actually* imposed.

B. **Waiver:** The defendant may *waive* the right to jury trial, provided that the waiver is *voluntary*, *knowing* and *intelligent*.

C. **Issues to which the right applies:** Once the right to jury trial applies to an offense, D has the right to have the jury, rather than the judge, decide *every element* of the offense. Furthermore, the jury must find each element to exist *"beyond a reasonable doubt."*

   1. **No jury right as to sentencing:** On the other hand, the right to a jury trial does not extend to the area of *sentencing*. For instance, the determination of whether particular *"sentencing factors"* specified by the legislature (e.g., existence of a prior conviction) do or do not exist in the particular case can be made by the judge.

   2. **Within range of the maximum sentence:** If the existence of a particular fact *increases the maximum punishment* to which D is subjected, the existence of that fact will be treated as an element of the offense, as to which the jury must make the decision. If, by contrast, the existence of a particular fact merely bears on *where within the range of possible sentences* the defendant's sentence should fall, the existence of that fact will merely be a sentencing factor (on which the judge may constitutionally make the decision). [*Apprendi v. N.J.*]

   3. **Sentencing guidelines:** The principle that punishment-increasing facts must be found by a jury also means that schemes involving mandatory *"sentencing guidelines"* will typically be *invalid*. In such schemes, the legislature establishes both a maximum sentence for a particular offense (say 10 years), and a standard sentence range for that offense (say 3-5 years). The legislature then orders trial judges to add to or subtract time from the standard range according to various aggravating or mitigating factors found to exist by the judge, with the result never exceeding the maximum. The Supreme Court has held that *any increase* in the sentence given to a defendant — beyond the standard range — by virtue of the judge's finding on a guideline-mandated factor *violates* the defendant's right to a jury trial. [*Blakely v. Washington*].

   > **Example:** D is convicted of kidnapping, a Class B felony. The maximum penalty for Class B penalties is 10 years. But state sentencing guidelines prescribe a standard range of 49 to 53 months for kidnapping. However, the guidelines instruct the judge to consider various aggravating (or mitigating) factors that if present can move the sentence out of the standard range. The judge finds that D acted with "deliberate cruelty," an aggravating factor that under the guidelines can add 37 months to the standard range; therefore, the judge sentences D to a term of 90 months (37 months more than the top of the standard range).
   >
   > *Held*, for D: the application of the guidelines to increase D's sentence beyond the maximum that it could otherwise have been (i.e., beyond 53 months), based on a fact (deliber-

ate cruelty) found by a judge, violated D's right to a jury trial on all punishment-increasing elements. See *Blakely v. Washington, supra*, p. 131.

   a. **Federal Guidelines are invalid as written:** This principle means that the *federal Sentencing Guidelines are unconstitutional as written*. The Guidelines *cannot require* (as they purport to) a federal judge to impose a heavier sentence based solely on a fact found by the judge. Instead, the Guidelines are merely *"advisory,"* and it's up to the judge whether to follow them or not in any particular case. [*U.S. v. Booker*]

D. **Size and unanimity of the jury:** The Sixth Amendment places some — but not many — limits on states' ability to restrict the *size* of juries, or states' right to allow *less-than-unanimous* criminal verdicts.

   1. **Size:** Historically, juries have of course been composed of 12 persons. However, the Court has held that *juries of six or more satisfy the Sixth Amendment*. [*Williams v. Florida*] On the other hand, juries of *five or fewer violate* the Sixth Amendment. [*Ballew v. Georgia*]

   2. **Unanimity not required in "big" state jury:** The Sixth Amendment does *not* require that the jury's verdict in a state trial be *unanimous*, at least where the jury has *12 members* and the majority is *"substantial."*

      Example: A state court may constitutionally convict a defendant based on an 11-1 or even 10-2 vote. [*Apodaca v. Oregon*]

      a. **Unanimity required in 6-person jury:** However, when the jury consists of only *six* members, unanimity *is* constitutionally required. [*Burch v. Louisiana*]

      b. **Federal trials:** In all federal criminal trials, unanimity is required, even if the jury has a full 12 members.

V. THE TRIAL

A. **D's right to be present:** The defendant has a constitutional right to be *present* at his trial. This right derives from the Sixth Amendment's right of the accused "to be confronted with the witnesses against him." (However, this right can be lost by D's disruptive behavior which persists after a warning.)

B. **Burden of proof in criminal cases:** The Due Process Clause places limits on the extent to which the *burdens of proof* may be *placed on the defendant:*

   1. **Element distinguished from affirmative defense:** Essentially the state may not require D to bear the burden of proof as to an *"element"* of the offense, but may require D to bear the burden of proof as to an *"affirmative defense."* An element of the crime is an aspect that is part of the basic definition of the crime; an affirmative defense is an aspect that is not part of the basic definition, but which the defendant is allowed to show as a mitigating or exculpating factor.

      Examples: "Intent to kill" is an element of the crime of murder, but "self defense" is generally an affirmative defense.

   2. **General rules of allocation:**

      a. **Elements:** The *state* is constitutionally required to bear *both* the burdens of production and persuasion with respect to *all elements* of the crime.

         i. **"Beyond a reasonable doubt" standard:** For the prosecution to carry its burden of persuasion with respect to an element, it must convince the jury that, *beyond a reasonable doubt,* that element is satisfied. See *Patterson v. New York* (1977): "[T]he Due Process

Clause requires the prosecution to *prove beyond a reasonable doubt all of the elements included in the definition* of the offense of which the defendant is charged."

Example: D is charged with first-degree murder of V. Assume that first-degree murder is defined as "intentionally and maliciously" causing the death of another. Since intentionally causing the death is an element of the crime, the due process clause requires that the prosecution bear two burdens of proof: (1) the burden of initially coming forward with (i.e., "producing") evidence from which a reasonable jury could find, beyond a reasonable doubt, that D intentionally killed V; and (2) the burden of persuading the jury, after all the evidence is in from both sides, that, beyond a reasonable doubt, D intentionally caused V's death.

b. **Affirmative defense:** The *defendant* may constitutionally be required to *bear both burdens* with respect to *affirmative defenses*.

Example: D is charged with murdering V. D claims self-defense. D may be constitutionally required to: (1) come forward with some evidence that D acted in self-defense; and (2) persuade the jury that there is at least some doubt about whether D acted in self-defense.

c. **Allowable affirmative defenses:** At least the following may be established as affirmative defenses on which D bears both burdens: *insanity, self-defense,* and *extreme emotional disturbance*.

d. **MBE Tip:** On the MBE, procedure and substance will overlap when burdens of proof are at issue. You'll have to *know how each crime is defined* (i.e., what its elements are, as opposed to what matters are affirmative defenses), in order to decide whether D may constitutionally be required to bear the burden of production or persuasion as to a particular issue.

Example: D is charged with rape, in a jurisdiction which follows the common-law definition of rape. He asserts that V consented. The prosecution asks the judge to instruct the jury that D has the burden of establishing that V consented. D asserts that this instruction would violate his due process rights, because the prosecution must bear the burden of proving lack of consent.

To know who wins, you'd have to know, as a substantive matter, whether the crime of rape includes lack of consent as an element. The answer is that lack of consent is an element of rape. Therefore, D wins the argument — the prosecution, not D, must bear the burden of both producing evidence of non-consent and persuading the jury, beyond a reasonable doubt, that V did not consent. (But once the prosecution has done that, D can be made to bear the burden of proof as to whether he reasonably made a mistake in believing that V had consented, if the jurisdiction deviates from the common-law rule by allowing the affirmative defense of mistake.)

C. **Motion for directed verdict:** In nearly all states, and in the federal system, the trial judge may *take the case from the jury* on the grounds that the evidence is insufficient for a conviction. Typically, this is done in response to a defense motion for a *directed verdict dismissing the case*. Most states let the defense make this motion at the end of the prosecution's case and/or after both sides have presented their cases.

1. **Standard:** The standard for whether the judge should grant a dismissal motion is whether a *reasonable jury* could find that the prosecution has proved beyond a reasonable doubt all the material elements of the crime. If the judge concludes that there is at least one element of the crime that no jury could find to have been proved beyond a reasonable doubt, the judge can and should direct a verdict for D.

a. **Not enough for dismissal:** On the other hand, if the judge concludes that a reasonable jury could find each element of the case proved beyond a reasonable doubt, the judge should not grant the directed verdict, and should let the case go to the jury. It is not enough that the judge concludes that, if she were sitting on the jury, she would vote to acquit the defendant.

Example: D is charged with stabbing V to death. The case is tried to a jury. D raises an insanity defense. State law provides that once D puts forward some evidence of insanity, proof of sanity becomes an element of the crime. D presents an expert witness, W, who testifies that D has suffered from schizophrenia for the last 10 years, and that in W's opinion D's stabbing of V was the product of D's schizophrenia. The prosecution offers a rebuttal expert who testifies that D does not have schizophrenia or any other mental disease. At the close of the evidence, D moves for a directed verdict dismissing the case.

If the judge believes that no reasonable jury could find that D was sane, the judge should direct a verdict for D. But if the judge believes that a reasonable jury could find D to be sane, the judge should not direct a verdict (i.e., not dismiss). And that's true even if the judge believes that it's more likely than not that D is insane. In other words, the fact that the judge would vote to acquit if she were a juror is not enough to induce the judge to dismiss.

D. **D's Confrontation Clause rights:** The Sixth Amendment gives any criminal defendant "the right . . . to be *confronted with the witnesses against him.*" This is the Confrontation Clause. It applies to the states as well as the federal government. The Confrontation Clause has two main components: (1) the right to compulsory *process*; and (2) the right to *cross-examine* hostile witnesses.

1. **Compulsory process:** The compulsory-process branch of the Confrontation Clause means that D has the right to have the court *issue a subpoena* to compel the testimony of any witness who may have information that would be useful to the defense.

2. **Rule for out-of-court testimonial statements:** The Confrontation Clause also limits the prosecution's right to introduce into evidence an *out-of-court statement* by a third person against D. More particularly, if the out-of-court statement is *"testimonial,"* the statement *may not be admitted against the accused unless the declarant is made available for cross-examination by the accused,* either at the *time of the statement, or at the time of the accused's trial.* [*Crawford v. Washington*]

    a. **Two important scenarios:** For instance, an out-of-court third-party statement by W can't be used against D if the W is not available for cross-examination of D's trial, and the statement was made: (1) *during police interrogation into a past crime;* or (2) in *grand jury testimony.*

    Example 1: D1 and D2 are suspected of robbing a 7/11 together. D1 is interrogated at police headquarters, and implicates D2 in a videotaped statement. D1 and D2 are tried separately. At D2's trial, the prosecution calls D1, but he asserts the Fifth Amendment. The prosecution then offers the videotaped statement by D1, implicating D2, into evidence.

    The judge must exclude the videotape. It contains out-of-court "testimonial" statements, by a person who is not available at the present trial to be cross-examined by the defendant. Therefore, the tape's introduction against D2 would violate D2's Sixth Amendment Confrontation Clause rights.

    Example 2: Same facts as above. This time, D1 is called before a grand jury, and gives testimony implicating D2. At D2's trial, the prosecution calls D1, but he pleads the Fifth Amendment. The prosecution seeks to read a transcript of part of D1's grand jury testimony to the jury.

    Again, the judge must exclude the transcript. It constitutes out-of-court "testimonial" statements, by a person who is not available at the present trial to be cross-examined by the defendant. Therefore, the transcript's introduction against D2 would violate D2's Sixth Amendment Confrontation Clause rights.

- **b. Non-testimonial statements:** But if the out-of-court statement now being sought to be used against D was *"non-testimonial,"* its admission can't violate D's Confrontation Clause rights, even if D is not now available for cross-examination by D and wasn't available for such at the time the statement is made.

    Example: V phones a 911 line, and tells the operator, "My boyfriend is attacking me." The operator, in order to do a records search to find out whether the boyfriend is likely to be dangerous to police officers, asks, "What's your boyfriend's name?" V answers, "His name is John Smith." Because this statement, although made in response to official interrogation, was made under emergency circumstances (rather than as part of an investigation into a completed crime), it is "non-testimonial." It may therefore be admitted against Smith in a criminal trial without Confrontation Clause review. [Cf. *Davis v. Washington*]

3. **Confession implicating someone else, used during joint trial:** Special problems arise when *A* and *B* are *tried together*, and *A*'s confession implicating himself and *B* is sought to be used by the prosecution. If the same jury hears *A*'s confession implicating *B* (and *A* doesn't take the stand), then *B*'s Confrontation Clause rights are violated even if the prosecution only purports to be offering the confession against *A*. That's true even if the judge gives a limiting instruction that the jury must not consider *A*'s confession as evidence against *B*. [*Bruton v. U.S.*]

E. **Defendant's right to remain silent:** The Fifth Amendment provides that no person "shall be *compelled* in any criminal case to be a witness *against himself.*"

1. **Right not to take the stand:** The privilege does not mean merely that D may refuse to answer questions asked of him by the prosecution. Instead, it means that D has the right to *not even take the witness stand.* (Most criminal defendants take advantage of this right.)

    a. **Waiver:** But the privilege may be *waived*. A defendant who *does* take the witness stand has waived his privilege as to *any matters* within the fair scope of cross-examination.

        Example: Once D takes the stand at all, he may be cross-examined about any prior convictions that shed light on his propensity to tell the truth, such as convictions for any crime involving dishonesty or false statement. See FRE 609(a).

2. **Comment by prosecution:** The privilege against self-incrimination means that the prosecution may not *comment* on the fact that the defendant has declined to take the witness stand. [*Griffin v. California*]

VI. DOUBLE JEOPARDY

A. **The guarantee generally:** The Fifth Amendment provides that no person shall "be subject for the same offence to be twice put in jeopardy of life or limb." This is the guarantee against "*double jeopardy.*" The most classic application of the doctrine is to prevent D from being retried after he has been *acquitted* by a jury. But it occasionally applies in other contexts as well (e.g., if D's conviction is reversed on appeal on the grounds that the evidence at trial was insufficient to support a conviction, no reprosecution is allowed).

1. **Applicable to states:** The double jeopardy guarantee applies to *state* as well as federal trials. [*Benton v. Maryland*]

B. **When jeopardy attaches:** The protection against double jeopardy does not apply until jeopardy has *"attached."*

1. **Jury trial:** In a case to be tried by a jury, jeopardy is deemed to "attach" when the jury has been *impaneled and sworn*, i.e., when the whole jury has been selected and taken the oath. [*Crist v. Bretz*]

2. **Bench trial:** If the case is to be tried by a judge sitting without a jury, jeopardy attaches when the *first witness has been sworn.*

3. **Consequence:** So until either the entire jury has been sworn in (if it's going to be a jury trial) or the first witness has been sworn (if it's going to be a bench trial), nothing the prosecution, a grand jury, a magistrate or a judge, does — and no matter how many times they do it — can be a violation of D's double-jeopardy rights.

    a. **Preliminary hearing:** So, for instance, the fact that a *preliminary hearing* has been held does not constitute the attachment of jeopardy. This means that if the magistrate or judge at the preliminary hearing dismisses the case for lack of probable cause, the prosecution can try again.

    b. **Multiple indictments:** Similarly, no actions by the *grand jury* — issuing multiple superseding indictments, for example — can violate double jeopardy.

        Example: The prosecution seeks an indictment of D for murdering V. The grand jury denies the indictment. The prosecution comes back, seeking the murder indictment again. This time, the grand jury issues it. The prosecution then decides that the indictment is flawed because the counts have some of the underlying facts wrong; the prosecution therefore gets a judge to dismiss the indictment, and goes back to the grand jury for yet another indictment of D for the same murder.

        Nothing that has happened here has violated D's double-jeopardy rights, because jeopardy never "attached." Jeopardy could not have attached until either an entire jury was sworn in or the judge in a bench trial swore in the first witness, and neither of those things ever happened here.

C. **Reprosecution after mistrial:** If the trial begins and is then terminated by a *mistrial*, the prosecution is usually *not barred* from retrying the defendant.

   1. **With D's consent:** If the mistrial has been brought about by the request of, or the acquiescence of, the defendant, reprosecution is *always allowed*. This is true even though D's motion for a mistrial is required because of the prosecution's intentional misconduct.

   2. **Without D's consent:** Even where D has *not* consented, the mistrial usually does not bar reprosecution.

      a. **Manifest necessity:** For instance, if the court finds that the mistrial is required by *"manifest necessity,"* reprosecution will be allowed. Most courts are quick to find the requisite necessity.

         Example: If there has been a *hung jury*, or sickness results in there being too few jurors left on the panel, retrial is almost always allowed.

D. **Reprosecution after acquittal:** The classic application of the Double Jeopardy Clause is to prevent reprosecution after the defendant has been *acquitted.*

   1. **Acquittal by jury:** Where the case has been tried to a *jury* and the jury has come in with a verdict of *not guilty*, the clause always prevents D from being retried. This is true even though the acquittal was brought about by the admission of what should have been inadmissible evidence, and even if it was brought about by what can later be proved to have been *perjured testimony* offered by the defense. For this reason, the prosecution is *never* permitted to *appeal* a jury acquittal.

2. **Acquittal by judge:** Similarly, an acquittal by the judge sitting alone is final, and cannot be appealed.

E. **Reprosecution after conviction:** Occasionally, the fact that D has been *convicted* may bar a later prosecution.

1. **Verdict set aside on appeal:** If D is convicted at trial, and then gets the verdict *set aside on appeal*, the double jeopardy rule usually does *not* bar a retrial.

    Example: D is convicted based on the fruits of a search and seizure which, D contends, violated the Fourth Amendment. The appellate court agrees. The Double Jeopardy Clause does not prevent the state from retrying D on the same charge.

    a. **Insufficiency of evidence:** But there is one big exception: if the appellate court reverses because the evidence at trial was *insufficient* to support a conviction (i.e., no reasonable jury could have found D guilty on the evidence presented), a reprosecution is *not* allowed.

2. **Resentencing:** Where D is convicted, then appeals and receives a new trial, the Double Jeopardy Clause places some limits on the *length of imprisonment* that may be imposed on the new conviction.

    a. **Credit for time served:** The Constitution requires that D be given *credit* for the time he served under the first charge before it was overturned. [*North Carolina v. Pearce*]

    b. **Longer sentence:** On the other hand, the judge hearing the second trial is *not* prevented from giving D a *longer sentence* than was imposed following the first conviction. [*North Carolina v. Pearce, supra.*] (But if D in a death penalty case is sentenced to something less than death in the first trial, he may not be sentenced to death upon retrial.)

F. **Reprosecution by a different sovereign:** A conviction or acquittal by *one jurisdiction* does *not* bar a reprosecution by *another jurisdiction*, even on a charge involving exactly the same underlying transaction. This is the so-called *"dual sovereignty"* doctrine.

    Example: D, a police officer, is charged in a state trial with aggravated assault upon X, a suspect in custody. D is acquitted. D is then charged with the federal crime of violating X's civil rights; all of the alleged facts making up this offense are the same as the facts alleged in the earlier, state, trial. The federal prosecution does not violate D's double jeopardy rights, because it is being brought by a different jurisdiction than brought the first case. The same would be true if the federal case came before the state case.

G. **Overlapping offenses:** Occasionally, two different offenses involve the same set of facts to such an extent that the two offenses are deemed the "same" for double jeopardy purposes. You probably need to worry about this "overlapping offenses" problem only where one charge is a *lesser included offense* of the other.

1. **Lesser included offense tried first:** Suppose the lesser included offense is *tried first*. Here, whether the first trial results in an acquittal or a conviction, the prosecution *cannot bring a later prosecution for the greater offense.* [*Brown v. Ohio*]

    a. **Felony-murder scenario on MBE:** On the MBE, be especially on the lookout for the lesser-included-offense-tried-first scenario where the first offense to be tried is a dangerous felony, and the second is *felony-murder* based on the first offense — double jeopardy prevents this.

        Example: V, unconscious from smoke inhalation, is rescued from a burning building. While she remains in a coma, D is charged with arson of the building. He is acquitted after a trial. Two months later, V dies. D is now tried for felony-murder, with arson as the felony.

The felony-murder prosecution constitutes double jeopardy. The arson was a lesser included offense with the felony-murder. Therefore, once D was acquitted of the arson, he could no longer be prosecuted for felony-murder. And that's true even though V had not yet died so that a felony-murder prosecution was not yet possible at the time D's arson trial began.

2. **Lesser included offense tried second:** Conversely, the Double Jeopardy Clause also bars prosecution for the lesser included crime *after* conviction of the greater one.

3. **Unable to try both at once:** But the rule barring serial prosecutions on the greater and lesser included offenses probably does *not apply* where the prosecution is *unable* to try both cases at once for reasons that are not the government's fault, *and* the defendant is convicted in the first trial.

   Example: D, a driver, strikes V, a pedestrian on Jan. 1, 2006. V is hospitalized until Dec. 25, 2006, at which point V dies of her injuries. On March 1, 2006, D pleads guilty to felony reckless driving. On Feb. 1, 2007, D is indicted for involuntary manslaughter of V. D moves to dismiss the indictment on double jeopardy grounds, on the theory that the reckless-driving offense was a lesser-included offense.

   D will probably lose with this argument. Conviction on a lesser-included offense will probably not bar a later prosecution for the greater offense if the facts needed for prosecution of the greater offense either did not exist at the time of the earlier conviction, or had not yet been discovered (through no fault of the prosecution). The former situation applies here — since V was still alive on March 1, 2006, no involuntary-manslaughter prosecution could have been brought on that date. (But if D had been acquitted of the reckless driving felony, this *would* block the later manslaughter charge, even though V hadn't died as of the time of the reckless-driving acquittal.)

MBE-STYLE QUESTIONS ON CRIMINAL LAW AND PROCEDURE

CRIMINAL LAW AND PROCEDURE QUESTIONS

These questions are the Criminal Law and Procedure questions from the Self-Assessment Test. They are presented here in approximately the order in which the main topic or theme of the question is treated in the substantive outline earlier in this book. Thus questions focusing on substantive Criminal Law come first (starting with *Actus Reus* and *Mens Rea*), followed by questions on Criminal Procedure.

As on the MBE itself, you should answer the substantive-law questions on the assumption that common-law concepts and definitions apply, unless the question indicates otherwise.

1. A husband and wife took their 12-year-old son to a political rally to hear a controversial United States senator speak. The speaker was late, and the wife stepped outside to smoke a cigarette. While there, she saw a man placing what she believed to be a bomb against a wall at the back of the building. She went back inside and told her husband what she had seen. Without alerting anyone, they took their son and left. Some 20 minutes later, the bomb exploded, killing eight persons and injuring 50. In the jurisdiction, murder in the first degree is defined as an intentional homicide committed with premeditation and deliberation; murder in the second degree is defined as all other murder at common law; and manslaughter is defined as either a homicide in the heat of passion arising from adequate provocation or a homicide caused by gross negligence or reckless indifference to consequence.

    As to the deaths of the eight persons, what crime, if any, did the wife commit?

    (A) Manslaughter.

    (B) Murder in the first degree.

    (C) Murder in the second degree.

    (D) No crime.

    [Q7026]

2. During an altercation between two men at a company picnic, the victim suffered a knife wound in his abdomen and the defendant was charged with assault and attempted murder. At his trial, the defendant seeks to offer evidence that he had been drinking at the picnic and was highly intoxicated at the time of the altercation.

    In a jurisdiction that follows the common-law rules concerning admissibility of evidence of intoxication, the evidence of the defendant's intoxication should be

    (A) admitted without limitation.

    (B) admitted subject to an instruction that it pertains only to the attempted murder charge.

    (C) admitted subject to an instruction that it pertains only to the assault charge.

    (D) excluded altogether.

    [Q3076]

GO ON TO THE NEXT PAGE

3. The defendant suffered a severe head injury in an accident which occurred three years ago. As a result, she experienced eight incidents of sudden unconsciousness, each lasting approximately two minutes. All the incidents occurred within a three month period immediately following the accident, and all occurred while the defendant was at home. Last week she was driving her automobile in a lawful manner when she suddenly lost consciousness as a result of the head injury which occurred three years ago. Her car swerved out of control onto the sidewalk, striking and permanently injuring a pedestrian. Drake was charged with violating a state statute which defines the crime of "reckless maiming" as "causing permanent injury to another person by acting in knowing disregard of the plain and strong likelihood that death or serious personal injury will result."

Which of the following is the defendant's most effective argument in defense against the charge of reckless maiming?

(A) The pedestrian head injury was not the result of any culpable conduct by the defendant.

(B) After losing consciousness while driving, the defendant was no longer capable of exercising control over the operation of her vehicle.

(C) The defendant reasonably believed that she would not have any further incidents of unconsciousness.

(D) The defendant did not know that her driving would lead to death or serious injury.

[Q5050]

4. Which of the following is most likely to be found to be a strict liability offense?

(A) A city ordinance providing for a fine of not more than $200 for shoplifting

(B) A federal statute making it a felony to possess heroin

(C) A state statute making it a felony to fail to register a firearm

(D) A state statute making the sale of adulterated milk a misdemeanor

[Q4036]

5. The defendant decided to kill his boss, the CEO of the company, after she told the defendant that he would be fired if his work did not improve. The defendant knew the CEO was scheduled to go on a business trip on Monday morning. On Sunday morning, the defendant went to the company parking garage and put a bomb in the company car that the CEO usually drove. The bomb was wired to go off when the car engine started. The defendant then left town. At 5 a.m. Monday, the defendant, after driving all night, was overcome with remorse and had a change of heart. He called the security officer on duty at the company and told him about the bomb. The security officer said he would take care of the matter. An hour later, the officer put a note on the CEO's desk telling her of the message. He then looked at the car but could not see any signs of a bomb. He printed a sign saying "DO NOT USE THIS CAR," put it on the windshield, and went to call the police. Before the police arrived, a vice president of the same company, got into the car and started the engine. The bomb went off, killing her.

The jurisdiction defines murder in the first degree as any homicide committed with premeditation and deliberation or any murder in the commission of a common-law felony. Second-degree murder is defined as all other murder at common law. Manslaughter is defined by the common law.

The defendant is guilty of

(A) murder in the first degree, because, with premeditation and deliberation, he killed whoever would start the car.

(B) murder in the second degree, because he

had no intention of killing the vice president.

(C) manslaughter, because at the time of the explosion, he had no intent to kill, and the death of the vice president was in part the fault of the security officer.

(D) only attempted murder of the CEO, because the death of the vice president was the result of the security officer's negligence.

[Q3133]

6. A professional basketball player was scheduled to play in an important basketball game on Sunday. On Friday, after wagering heavily on the game, a gambler attacked the player with a baseball bat. The gambler's intent was to inflict injuries severe enough to require hospitalization and thus keep the player from playing as planned. As a result of the beating, the player was taken to a hospital, where he was treated by a doctor. The following day, the doctor injected the player with a medicine to relieve his pain. Because of an allergic reaction to the drug, the player died within minutes.

If the gambler is charged with the murder of the player, he should be found

(A) not guilty, because the player's allergic reaction to the drug was an intervening cause of death.

(B) not guilty, if the player's death was proximately caused by the doctor's negligence.

(C) guilty, only if the player's death was proximately caused by the gambler's attack.

(D) guilty, unless the doctor's conduct is found to be reckless or grossly negligent.

[Q5099]

7. The defendant was an alcoholic who frequently experienced auditory hallucinations that commanded him to engage in bizarre and sometimes violent behavior. He generally obeyed their commands. The hallucinations appeared more frequently when he was intoxicated, but he sometimes experienced them when he had not been drinking. After the defendant had been drinking continuously for a three day period, an elderly woman began to reproach him about his drunken condition, slapping him on the face and shoulders as she did so. The defendant believed that he was being unmercifully attacked and heard the hallucinatory voice telling him to strangle his assailant. He did so, and she died.

If the defendant is charged with second degree murder, his best chance of acquittal would be to rely on a defense of

(A) intoxication.

(B) lack of malice aforethought.

(C) self-defense.

(D) insanity.

[Q4040]

8. In a criminal trial, the evidence showed that the defendant's neighbor tried to kill the defendant by stabbing him. The defendant ran to his room, picked up a gun, and told his neighbor to back off. The neighbor did not, but continued her attack and stabbed him in the arm. The defendant then shot the neighbor twice. The neighbor fell to the floor and lay quietly moaning. After a few seconds, the defendant fired a third shot into the neighbor. The jury found that the neighbor died instantly from the third shot and that the defendant was no longer in fear of being attacked by her.

The defendant could properly be convicted of which of the following degrees of criminal homicide, if any?

(A) Attempted murder only.

(B) Manslaughter only.

(C) Murder or manslaughter.

(D) No degree of criminal homicide.

[Q7069]

9. A defendant was charged with assault and battery in a jurisdiction that followed the "retreat" doctrine, and he pleaded self-defense. At his trial, the evidence established the following: A man and his wife were enjoying a drink at a tavern when the defendant entered and stood near the door. The wife whispered to her husband that the defendant was the man who had insulted her on the street the day before. The husband approached the defendant and said, "Get out of here, or I'll break your nose." The defendant said, "Don't come any closer, or I'll hurt you." When the husband raised his fists menacingly, the defendant pulled a can of pepper spray from his pocket, aimed it at the husband's face, and sprayed. The husband fell to the floor, writhing in pain.

Should the defendant be convicted?

(A) No, because he had no obligation to retreat before resorting to nondeadly force.

(B) No, because there is no obligation to retreat when one is in an occupied structure.

(C) Yes, because he failed to retreat even though there was an opportunity available.

(D) Yes, because the husband did not threaten to use deadly force against him.

[Q7096]

10. A woman wanted to make some money, so she decided to sell cocaine. She asked a man, who was reputed to have access to illegal drugs, to supply her with cocaine so she could resell it. The man agreed and sold the woman a bag of white powder. The woman then repackaged the white powder into smaller containers and sold one to an undercover police officer, who promptly arrested the woman. The woman immediately confessed and said that the man was her supplier. Upon examination, the white powder was found not to be cocaine or any type of illegal substance.

If the man knew the white powder was not cocaine but the woman believed it was, which of the following is correct?

(A) Both the man and the woman are guilty of attempting to sell cocaine.

(B) Neither the man nor the woman is guilty of attempting to sell cocaine.

(C) The man is guilty of attempting to sell cocaine, but the woman is not.

(D) The man is not guilty of attempting to sell cocaine, but the woman is.

[Q3002]

11. A student broke into a professor's office in order to look at examination questions. The questions were locked in a drawer, and the student could not find them. The student believed that looking at examination questions was a crime, but in this belief he was mistaken.

Charged with burglary, the student should be

(A) acquitted, because he did not complete the crime and he has not been charged with attempt.

(B) acquitted, because what he intended to do when he broke in was not a crime.

(C) convicted, because he had the necessary mental state and committed the act of breaking and entering.

(D) convicted, because factual impossibility is not a defense.

[Q4037]

12. A young man and an older man planned to break into a federal government office to steal food stamps. The young man telephoned a woman one night and asked whether the woman wanted to buy some "hot" food stamps. The woman, who understood that "hot" meant stolen, said, "Sure, bring them right over." The young man and the older man then successfully executed their scheme. That same night they delivered the food stamps to the woman, who bought them for $500. The woman did not ask when or by whom the stamps were stolen. All three were arrested. The woman was brought to trial on a charge of conspiracy to steal food stamps.

On the evidence stated, the woman should be found

(A) guilty, because when a new confederate enters a conspiracy already in progress, she becomes a party to it.

(B) guilty, because she knowingly and willingly aided and abetted the conspiracy and is chargeable as a principal.

(C) not guilty, because although the woman knew the stamps were stolen, she neither helped to plan nor participated or assisted in the theft.

(D) not guilty, because young man and the older man had not been convicted of or charged with conspiracy, and the woman cannot be guilty of conspiracy by herself.

[Q4002]

13. Bill and Chuck hated Vic and agreed to start a fight with Vic and, if the opportunity arose, to kill him. Bill and Chuck met Vic in the street outside a bar and began to push him around. Ray and Sam, who also hated Vic, stopped to watch. Ray threw Bill a knife. Sam told Bill, "Kill him." Chuck held Vic while Bill stabbed and killed him.

On a charge of murdering Vic, Sam is

(A) not guilty, because his words did not create a "clear and present danger" not already existing.

(B) not guilty, because mere presence and oral encouragement, whether or not he has the requisite intent, will not make him guilty as an accomplice.

(C) guilty, because, with the intent to have Bill kill Vic, he shouted encouragement to Bill.

(D) guilty, because he aided and abetted the murder through his mere presence plus his intent to see Vic killed.

[Q4013]

14. A young man and two of his friends were members of a teenage street gang. While they were returning from a dance late one evening, their car collided with a car driven by an elderly woman. After an argument, the young man attacked the elderly woman with his fists and beat her to death. The two friends watched, and when they saw the woman fall to the ground they urged the young man to flee. The young man was eventually apprehended and tried for manslaughter, but the jury could not decide on a verdict.

If the friends are subsequently tried as accomplices to manslaughter, they should be

(A) acquitted, because the young man was not convicted of the offense.

(B) acquitted, because they did not assist or encourage the young man to commit the crime.

(C) convicted, because they urged the young man to flee.

(D) convicted, because they made no effort to intervene.

[Q3070]

15. The defendant, while intoxicated, drove his car through a playground crowded with children just to watch the children run to get out of his way. His car struck one of the children, killing her instantly.

Which of the following is the best theory for finding the defendant guilty of murder?

(A) Transferred intent.

(B) Felony-murder, with assault with a deadly weapon as the underlying felony.

(C) Intentional killing, since he knew that the children were there and he deliberately drove his car at them.

(D) Commission of an act highly dangerous to life, without an intent to kill but with disregard of the consequences.

[Q4035]

16. Angry because her co-worker had insulted her, the defendant decided to get revenge. Because she worked for an exterminator, the defendant had access to cans of a poison gas called Terminate which was often used to kill termites and other insects. The defendant did not want to kill the co-worker, so she carefully read the use manual supplied by the manufacturer. The manual said that Terminate was not fatal to human beings, but that exposure to it could cause serious ailments including blindness and permanent respiratory irritation. When she was sure that no one would see her, the defendant brought a can of Terminate to the parking lot and released the poison gas into the co-worker's car, hoping to blind her but not kill her. At lunchtime, the co-worker and her friend sat together in the co-worker's car. As a result of their exposure to the Terminate in the car, the friend died and the co-worker became so ill that she was hospitalized for over a month.

If the defendant is charged with the murder of the friend, she should be found

(A) guilty, because the friend's death resulted from an act which the defendant performed with the intent to cause great bodily harm to a human being.

(B) guilty, because the use of poison gas is an inherently dangerous activity.

(C) not guilty, because she did not know that the friend would be exposed to the poison gas.

(D) not guilty, because she did not intend to cause the death of any person.

[Q5017]

17. At 11:00 p.m., a husband and wife were accosted in the entrance to their apartment building by the defendant, who was armed as well as masked. The defendant ordered the couple to take him into their apartment. After they entered the apartment, the defendant forced the wife to bind and gag her husband and then to open a safe which contained a diamond necklace. The defendant then tied the wife up and fled with the necklace. He was apprehended by apartment building security guards. Before the guards could return to the apartment, but after the defendant was arrested, the husband, straining to free himself, suffered a massive heart attack and died.

The defendant is guilty of

(A) burglary, robbery, and murder.

(B) robbery and murder only.

(C) burglary and robbery only.

(D) robbery only.

[Q3101]

18. The defendant, while eating in a restaurant, noticed that a departing customer at the next table had left a five-dollar bill as a tip for the waitress. The defendant reached over, picked up the five-dollar bill, and put it in his pocket. As he stood up to leave, another customer who had seen him take the money ran over to him and hit him in the face with her umbrella. Enraged, the defendant choked the customer to death.

The defendant is charged with murder. He requests the court to charge the jury that they can find him guilty of voluntary manslaughter rather than murder. The defendant's request should be

(A) granted, because the jury could find that the defendant acted recklessly and not with the intent to cause death or serious bodily harm.

(B) granted, because the jury could find that being hit in the face with an umbrella constitutes adequate provocation.

(C) denied, because the evidence shows that the defendant intended to kill or to cause serious bodily harm.

(D) denied, because the evidence shows that the defendant provoked the assault on himself by his criminal misconduct.

[Q4038]

19. A wife was extremely hot tempered and very possessive of her husband. She frequently flew into a hysterical rage if he even looked at another woman. One evening the husband and wife were in a bar when they began arguing. Wanting to hurt the wife, and knowing that it would infuriate her, the husband asked a young woman, who was sitting at the next table, to dance with him. The young woman accepted, but as she and the husband began to dance, the wife became enraged and ran at them, striking the husband over the head with a wine bottle. Later that night, the husband died of a head injury resulting from the blow. The wife was charged with murder, but her lawyer argued that the jury should be given a charge of voluntary manslaughter. Should the wife's lawyer's request be granted?

(A) Yes, on the theory of deliberate provocation.

(B) Yes, because of the wife's extreme feelings of possessiveness regarding the husband.

(C) No, if the ordinary person in the wife's situation would not have become enraged by the husband's dancing with the young woman.

(D) No, on the theory of mistaken justification.

[Q5048]

20. While browsing in a clothing store, the defendant decided to take a purse without paying for it. She placed the purse under her coat and took a couple of steps toward the exit. She then realized that a sensor tag on the purse would set off an alarm. She placed the purse near the counter from which she had removed it.

The defendant has committed

(A) no crime, because the purse was never removed from the store.

(B) no crime, because she withdrew from her criminal enterprise.

(C) only attempted larceny, because she intended to take the purse out of the store.

(D) larceny, because she took the purse from its original location and concealed it with the intent to steal.

[Q3098]

21. A woman decided to steal a necklace that belonged to her neighbor. She knew where the neighbor kept the necklace because she had been in the neighbor's house on many occasions when the neighbor had taken off the necklace and put it away in a jewelry box in the bathroom. One night, the woman went to the neighbor's house. The neighbor was away and the house was dark. The woman opened the bathroom window, saw the jewelry box on the counter, and started to climb inside. As her leg cleared the window sill, the neighbor's cat let out a loud screech. Terrified, the woman bolted back outside and fled.

The crimes below are listed in descending order of seriousness. What is the most serious crime committed by the woman?

(A) Burglary.

(B) Attempted burglary.

(C) Attempted larceny.

(D) No crime.

[Q7027]

GO ON TO THE NEXT PAGE

22. After being fired from his job, the defendant drank almost a quart of vodka and decided to ride the bus home. While on the bus, he saw a briefcase he mistakenly thought was his own, and began struggling with the passenger carrying the briefcase. The defendant knocked the passenger to the floor, took the briefcase, and fled. The defendant was arrested and charged with robbery.

    The defendant should be

    (A) acquitted, because he used no threats and was intoxicated.

    (B) acquitted, because his mistake negated the required specific intent.

    (C) convicted, because his intoxication was voluntary.

    (D) convicted, because mistake is no defense to robbery.

    [Q3007]

    [Start of Criminal Procedure Questions]

23. State troopers lawfully stopped a driver on the turnpike for exceeding the speed limit by four miles per hour. One trooper approached the car to warn the driver to drive within the speed limit. The other trooper remained in the patrol car and ran a computer check of the license number of the driver's car. The computer check indicated that there was an outstanding warrant for the driver's arrest for unpaid traffic tickets. The troopers then arrested the driver. After handcuffing her, the troopers searched her and the car, and discovered 10 glassine bags of heroin in a paper bag on the back seat of the car. Later it was learned that the driver had paid the outstanding traffic tickets 10 days earlier and the warrant had been quashed, but the clerk of the court had failed to update the computer, which continued to list the warrant as outstanding. The driver was charged with unlawful possession of heroin. Her attorney filed a motion to suppress the use as evidence of the heroin found in the car.

    Should the motion be granted?

    (A) No, because the troopers could reasonably rely on the computer report and the search was incident to arrest.

    (B) No, because troopers may lawfully search the passenger compartment of a car incident to a valid traffic stop.

    (C) Yes, because there was no arrest for the traffic violation and no lawful arrest could be made on the basis of the warrant.

    (D) Yes, because there was no probable cause or reasonable suspicion to believe drugs were in the car.

    [Q7042]

24. The police had, over time, accumulated reliable information that a rock singer operated a large cocaine-distribution network, that he and his accomplices often resorted to violence, and that they kept a small arsenal of weapons in his home.

    One day, the police received reliable information that a large brown suitcase with leather straps containing a supply of cocaine had been delivered to the singer's home and that it would be moved to a distribution point the next morning. The police obtained a valid search warrant to search for and seize the brown suitcase and the cocaine and went to the singer's house.

    The police knocked on the singer's door and called out, "Police. Open up. We have a search warrant." After a few seconds with no response, the police forced the door open and entered. Hearing noises in the basement, the police ran down there and found the singer with a large brown suitcase with leather straps. They seized the suitcase and put handcuffs on the singer. A search of his person revealed a switchblade knife and a .45-caliber pistol.

    The police then fanned out through the house, looking in every room and closet. They found no one else, but one officer found an Uzi automatic weapon in a box on a closet shelf in the singer's bedroom.

In addition to charges relating to the cocaine in the suitcase, the singer is charged with unlawful possession of weapons.

The singer moves pre-trial to suppress the use as evidence of the Uzi automatic weapon. The singer's motion to suppress should be

(A) granted, because the search exceeded the scope needed to find out if other persons were present.

(B) granted, because once the object of the warrant—the brown suitcase—had been found and seized, no further search of the house is permitted.

(C) denied, because the police were lawfully in the bedroom and the weapon was immediately identifiable as being subject to seizure.

(D) denied, because the police were lawfully in the house and had probable cause to believe that weapons were in the house.

[Q3068]

25. The defendant belonged to a sorority at a college. Members of the sorority who paid a rent of one hundred dollars per semester were entitled to a double-occupancy bedroom in the sorority house. Although house residents shared kitchen and dining room facilities, the bedrooms were not communal and were normally kept locked by their occupants. With the knowledge of its members, the sorority kept duplicates of all keys so that copies could be made in the event that a resident lost her key.

A cheerleader who was a member of the sorority suspected, based on the stream of visitors to the defendant's room at all hours of the day and night, that the defendant was selling marijuana. One weekend, when she knew that the defendant had gone home to visit her parents, the cheerleader called the police and told them of her suspicions and the facts that had given rise to them. In response to her call, two officers immediately came to the sorority house to interview the cheerleader. During the course of their conversation, the cheerleader stated that she was the defendant's roommate, and offered to let them into the defendant's room. In fact, someone else, not the cheerleader, was the defendant's roommate. The key which the cheerleader used to open the door was actually one of the duplicates kept by the sorority. Upon entering, the police officers saw a tobacco pipe containing traces of marijuana residue on a coffee table in the middle of the room. The defendant was subsequently prosecuted for possession of marijuana. Prior to trial, she made an appropriate motion to suppress the use of the pipe and its contents as evidence.

(A) Overruled, because the cheerleader had apparent authority to permit the entry into the room.

(B) Overruled, because the police had probable cause to believe that they would find marijuana in the room.

(C) Sustained, because the police did not have a warrant to search the room and the cheerleader did not have authority to let them search it.

(D) Sustained, because the police did not have probable cause to believe that they would find marijuana in the room.

[Q5073]

GO ON TO THE NEXT PAGE

26. Police officers received a tip that drug dealing was occurring at a certain ground-floor duplex apartment. They decided to stake out the apartment. The stakeout revealed that a significant number of people visited the apartment for short periods of time and then left. A man exited the apartment and started to walk briskly away. The officers grabbed the man and, when he struggled, wrestled him to the ground. They searched him and found a bag of heroin in one of his pockets. After discovering the heroin on the man, the police decided to enter the apartment. They knocked on the door, which was opened by the woman who lived there. The police asked if they could come inside, and the woman gave them permission to do so. Once inside, the officers observed several bags of heroin on the living room table. The woman is charged with possession of the heroin found on the living room table. She moves pre-trial to suppress the heroin on the ground that it was obtained by virtue of an illegal search and seizure.

Should the woman's motion be granted?

(A) No, because the tip together with the heroin found in the man's pocket provided probable cause for the search.

(B) No, because the woman consented to the officers' entry.

(C) Yes, because the officers' decision to enter the house was the fruit of an illegal search of the man.

(D) Yes, because the officers did not inform the woman that she could refuse consent.

[Q7022]

27. The defendant sold heroin to a football player. The football player was later stopped by police for speeding. The police searched the football player's car and found the heroin concealed under the rear seat. The defendant is charged with illegally selling heroin.

The defendant's motion to prevent introduction of the heroin into evidence will most probably be

(A) granted, because the heroin was not in plain view.

(B) granted, because the scope of the search was excessive.

(C) denied, because the defendant has no standing to object to the search.

(D) denied, because the search was proper as incident to a valid full custodial arrest.

[Q4049]

28. "The Heights" was a poor neighborhood in a city. Because many of the residents of The Heights had been complaining about the exploitation of tenants by absentee landlords, and about the lack of law enforcement in their neighborhood, the City Attorney instituted a campaign of neighborhood reform in The Heights. The City Attorney obtained a series of warrants for inspection of buildings in The Heights. He accomplished this by presenting an affidavit which stated that many health and safety violations had been observed in buildings located in The Heights by police and building inspectors traveling through the neighborhood. Pursuant to the warrants, police officers and building inspectors were ordered to inspect certain buildings. As a result, an apartment building owned by a landlord was found to have more than twenty violations of the city's building code. The landlord was prosecuted under a state law which made it a felony for any landlord to willfully fail to correct health and safety violations in a building which he or she owned.

If the landlord moves to suppress the evidence against him which was obtained as a result of the inspection of his building, his motion should be

(A) granted, unless the affidavit which was submitted in support of the request for a warrant specifically stated that violations had been observed in the landlord's building.

(B) granted, because the inspections were part of a general scheme to enforce the law in a particular neighborhood only.

(C) denied, because no warrant is needed to inspect buildings for health or safety violations.

(D) denied, because the inspection was part of a reasonable administrative scheme to enforce generally-applicable health and safety codes in The Heights.

[Q5022]

29. Acting with a warrant and with probable cause, police arrested the defendant on charges of marijuana cultivation. They advised him of his *Miranda* rights. The defendant asked to have his attorney present and was permitted to telephone her office. He left a message that he had been arrested. When the attorney received the message, she telephoned the county sheriff, asking where the defendant was being held. The sheriff said that he did not know. As a result, it took the attorney several hours to find the defendant. While waiting for the attorney, one of the officers said to the defendant, "Why don't you tell us about it?" whereupon the defendant admitted growing the marijuana. The defendant was subsequently charged with violating a state law which prohibits growing marijuana.

The defendant's attorney made an appropriate motion to prevent the use of the defendant's statement as evidence against him. The motion should be

(A) granted, because the defendant asserted his right to have an attorney present.

(B) granted, only if the sheriff actually knew the defendant's whereabouts when he said that he did not.

(C) denied, if the sheriff actually did not know the defendant's whereabouts when he said that he did not.

(D) denied, because the defendant waived his right to remain silent when he admitted growing the marijuana.

[Q5136]

30. After a liquor store was robbed, the police received an anonymous telephone call naming a store employee as the perpetrator of the robbery. Honestly believing that their actions were permitted by the U.S. Constitution, the police talked one of the employee's neighbors into going to the employee's home with a hidden tape recorder to engage him in a conversation about the crime. During the conversation, the employee admitted committing the robbery. The employee was charged in state court with the robbery. He moved to suppress the recording on the grounds that the method of obtaining it violated his constitutional rights under both the state and federal constitutions. Assume that a clear precedent from the state supreme court holds that the conduct of the police in making the recording violated the employee's rights under the state constitution, and that the exclusionary rule is the proper remedy for this violation.

Should the court grant the employee's motion?

(A) No, because the employee's federal constitutional rights were not violated, and this circumstance overrides any state constitutional provisions.

(B) No, because the police were acting in the good-faith belief that their actions were permitted by the federal Constitution.

(C) Yes, because the making of the recording violated the state constitution.

(D) Yes, because use of the recording would violate the neighbor's federal constitutional rights.

[Q7086]

GO ON TO THE NEXT PAGE

31. A landlord was the owner of a three dwelling unit residential building. She lived in an apartment on the third floor, her son lived with his wife in an apartment on the second floor, and the ground floor apartment was rented to a police officer and his family. One day, while the son and his wife were out of town, the landlord and the officer were having coffee together in the landlord's apartment. During the course of their conversation, the landlord said that she was worried about her son because once, while visiting him, she saw a substance in his apartment which she believed to be cocaine. Since she really did not know what cocaine looked like, however, she was not sure. The officer said, "If you'd like, I'll have a look and let you know whether or not there is anything for you to worry about."

Using her key to open the door to the son's apartment, the landlord brought the officer inside. The officer did not see any coke, but he noticed a television in the living room which looked like one stolen from an appliance store in the neighborhood. Without saying anything about the television to the landlord, the officer obtained a search warrant by submitting an affidavit indicating that he had seen certain items in the son's apartment which he had probable cause to believe were stolen. Later, he returned, entered, and thoroughly searched the apartment pursuant to the warrant. The television which he had seen on his first visit was not stolen, but during the course of his search, he found several items which were stolen. The son was charged with burglary.

If the son makes an appropriate motion to suppress the use of stolen items found in his apartment, his motion should be

(A) denied, since the stolen items were obtained as the result of a lawful search.

(B) denied, since it would not serve the interests of justice to require a police officer to ignore a discovery which he has probable cause to believe is contraband.

(C) granted, if the search warrant was issued as the result of information obtained in an unlawful search.

(D) granted, since his possession of stolen items is not necessarily proof that he stole those items.

[Q5080]

32. The defendant had been arraigned on a charge of burglarizing a home. He was assigned a public defender and pleaded not guilty, but because he was unable to post bail, was in jail awaiting trial. An undercover police officer was ordered by his commanding officer to pose as a prisoner and was placed in the same cell as the defendant. The undercover officer was instructed not to question the defendant about the charge against him. While they were in the cell together, the defendant told the undercover officer that he had committed the burglary with which he was charged.

If the defendant's attorney objects to the testimony of the undercover officer regarding the statement which the defendant made to him in the cell, the objection should be

(A) sustained, because the statement was made to a police officer in the absence of and without the consent of the defendant's attorney.

(B) sustained, because the undercover officer entrapped the defendant into making the statement.

(C) overruled if the undercover officer was placed in the defendant's cell pursuant to a warrant.

(D) overruled, because the defendant made the statement voluntarily.

[Q5021]

33. A state legislature passed a statute providing that juries in criminal trials were to consist of 6 rather than 12 jurors, and providing that jury verdicts did not have to be unanimous but could be based on 5 votes out of 6 jurors. A

defendant was tried for murder. Over his objection, he was tried by a jury composed of 6 jurors. The jurors found him guilty by a vote of 5 to 1 and, over the defendant's objection, the court entered a judgment of conviction, which was affirmed on appeal by the state supreme court. The defendant seeks to overturn his conviction in a habeas corpus action in federal court, claiming his constitutional rights were violated by allowing a jury verdict that was not unanimous and by allowing a jury composed of fewer than 12 members.

How is the federal court likely to rule in this action?

(A) It will set aside the conviction, because the jury was composed of fewer than 12 members.

(B) It will set aside the conviction, because the 6-person jury verdict was not unanimous.

(C) It will set aside the conviction for both reasons.

(D) It will uphold the conviction.

[Q7017]

ANSWERS TO
CRIMINAL LAW AND PROCEDURE QUESTIONS

References to "LaFave" are to Wayne LaFave,
Principles of Criminal Law (Thomson / West, 2003). References to "LaFave Criminal Law"
are to Wayne LaFave, *Criminal Law* Hornbook (3d. Ed., West, 2000).

1. **D** It is a core principle of Anglo-American criminal law that a person (let's call her the "defendant") does not have a duty to warn others of a peril or to assist them to avoid a peril. There are some exceptions to this rule — situations in which there is an affirmative duty to act (e.g., where the defendant brought about the peril) — but none of those exceptions applies here. Therefore, the wife did not have a legal duty, enforceable by the criminal laws, to warn the others about the bomb. See M.P.C., §2.01, Comm. 3; LaFave, §5.2, at 213-17.

    Since (A), (B) and (C) would all make the woman guilty of some crime, these choices are wrong for the reason discussed in the analysis of Choice (D) above.

    [Q7026]

2. **A** This choice is correct because evidence of intoxication might negate the requisite intent for both crimes. Voluntary intoxication evidence may be offered, when the defendant is charged with a crime that requires purpose or intent, to establish that the intoxication may have prevented the defendant from formulating the requisite intent. Each of the crimes charged here requires a particular intent. Assault requires an intent to cause bodily harm. Attempted murder requires an intent to kill. If the defendant was intoxicated, this fact might (would not necessarily, but might) indicate that he could not or did not form the required intent. Therefore, the evidence is relevant to both crimes, and must be admitted.

    (B), (C) and (D) are all wrong because they are inconsistent with the above analysis.

    [Q3076]

3. **C** Since all the incidents of unconsciousness occurred within three months after the accident and nearly three years ago, it was probably reasonable for the defendant to believe that they would not occur again. If she entertained that belief, and if it was reasonable, she cannot be said to have knowingly disregarded the plain and strong likelihood of harm as required by the statute. Although it is not certain that a court would come to that conclusion, (C) contains the only argument listed which could possibly support the defendant's defense.

    (A) is incorrect because if the defendant did knowingly disregard the plain and strong likelihood of further blackouts, it would not matter what caused them.

    (B) is incorrect because the crime, if any, took place when the defendant drove in knowing disregard (etc.), and so would have already been committed by the time the defendant passed out.

    (D) is incorrect because the statute does not require knowledge that death or serious injury will result, but only knowledge that there is strong likelihood that it will.

    [Q5050]

4. **D** Strict liability crimes generally have the following attributes: (1) They are regulatory in nature; (2) They do not involve serious penalties (i.e., they are usually limited to a fine, not imprisonment or even probation); (3) They involve serious harm to the public; and (4) It was easy for the defendant to find out the true facts before he acted. Cf. LaFave, §4.5, p. 188. In fact, statutes regulating food, drugs and misbranded articles, as well as hunting license requirements and the like, are all common forms of valid strict liability statutes. So this choice, involving the sale of adulterated milk, satisfies these tests fairly well: (1) the crime is essentially regulatory; (2) it's a misdemeanor rather than a felony; (3) it involves serious harm to the public; and (4) the defendant ought to be able readily to determine whether milk he's selling was adulterated (though admittedly this is the weak-

est of the four factors as to this choice).

(A) is wrong because it's highly unlikely shoplifting would be regarded a strict liability crime, even if the statute did not specify which *mens rea* it would require. Here, the main thing that would make this statute a less-than-perfect candidate for strict liability is that it is not regulatory in nature (like firearms registration rules, hunting license requirements, and the like). Also, shoplifting is a type of larceny, and thus a court would likely infer a *mens rea* requirement – that is, the intent to steal. So the fact that in this case, the most severe penalty is a $200 fine, would not be dispositive, in view of the moral opprobrium, relation to larceny, and non-regulatory nature of the offense.

(B) is wrong because it's unlikely possessing heroin, defined as a felony, would be a strict liability crime, even if the statute did not mention a *mens rea*. The more serious the potential punishment, the less likely a crime is to be a strict liability one. So the fact that it's a felony here is enough to make it not the best choice.

(C) is wrong because a statute making failure to register a gun a felony is unlikely to be a strict liability crime. What makes this option tempting is that firearms registration statutes are classic strict liability offenses, because they have a regulatory flavor. However, the wrinkle here is that the crime is defined as a *felony* – thus, in view of the stiff potential penalty (more than one year's imprisonment, under common law), the court is likely to infer that the legislature intended to require some sort of mens rea, at least negligence.

[Q4036]

5. A This is basically a problem involving "concurrence" — the examiners are thinking (maybe hoping) you'll reason, "The requisite intent no longer existed at the time of the explosion, therefore the requirement of concurrence between act and mental state has not been satisfied." It's true that "concurrence" is required. But in the case of a crime defined in terms of a particular result (like murder), the requisite concurrence is between *mental state and act*, *not* between *mental state and result*. In other words, at the moment D takes the act that brings about the result, D must be actuated by the appropriate intent; it doesn't matter whether D still has that intent when the result finally occurs. Here, the "act" was the setting of the bomb. When the defendant planted the bomb, he was actuated by an intent to kill the CEO. The fact that before the bomb went off (producing death as a result) he had changed his mind is irrelevant.

There's a further element to worry about: the fact that an unintended victim (the vice president), not the intended victim (the CEO) was killed. But this makes no difference either, under the familiar doctrine of transferred intent, by which, if the type of harm intended is the type that results, the fact that a different victim ended up suffering that harm is irrelevant. Lastly, the fact that the security guard had the opportunity to avoid the harm but failed to do so is irrelevant — the defendant intended to bring about a death by bomb, and his act was the but-for cause of that death by bomb, so the fact that some other actor failed in a chance to avoid the harm makes no difference. And that's true even if the failure by the other person amounted to negligence.

(B) is wrong because under the analysis in Choice (A), two things prevent this choice from being correct: (1) the defendant's intent is measured as of the moment he planted the bomb (and the fact that by the time of death he no longer intended to kill anyone is irrelevant); and (2) the defendant's intent to kill the CEO is deemed "transferred" to the vice president.

(C) is wrong because, under the analysis in Choice (A), two things prevent this choice from being correct: (1) the defendant's intent is measured as of the moment he planted the bomb (and the fact that by the time of death he no longer intended to kill anyone is irrelevant); and (2) the fact that the security officer had a good opportunity to avoid the harm does not prevent the defendant's act from being the legal cause of the harm.

(D) is wrong because the defendant is guilty of murder, not just attempted murder. Under the analysis in Choice (A), the fact that the security officer had a good opportunity to avoid the harm does not prevent the defendant's act from being the legal cause of the harm. And that's true even if the security guard's failure amounted to negligence. The defendant's act of planting the bomb was clearly a "but-for" cause of the death, and was so closely connected with the death that it was certainly a "legal" or "proximate" cause of that death. (The fact that the guard's negligence may have *also* been a proximate cause [and a but-for cause] won't save the defendant from guilt for the death.) Since the defendant caused the death by an act that was intended to cause the death, he's guilty of murder, not just attempted murder.

[Q3133]

6. **C** One mental state that suffices for murder is an intent to commit serious bodily injury. Since it was the defendant's intention to severely injure the player, the intent element is satisfied. The only remaining issue is whether the defendant's act was a proximate cause of the player's death. If it was, then the defendant is guilty of murder.

An intervening cause will not be superseding (i.e., will not prevent the earlier cause from being a proximate cause) only if the intervening cause was not reasonably foreseeable. Although the player's allergic reaction to the drug was an intervening cause of harm to him, the drug was given to relieve pain which resulted from the beating, so the giving of the drug was certainly not unforeseeable. The fatal allergic reaction itself was unusual, but not so uncommon or bizarre as to be fairly called unforeseeable. Indeed, one of the standard risks from conduct that puts a person in need of medical attention is that medical negligence, hospital infections, allergies, and the like, will then ensue, so even if the particular intervening harmful medical event is unusual, the overall class of harmful medical events will be viewed as foreseeable and thus not superseding. And that is true even if the intervening medical event was the product of negligent medical treatment. So the allergy here will not be found to be a supervening event whether the use of the drug was negligent or not, and the defendant's attack will therefore be a proximate cause of the death.

(A) is wrong because, under the analysis in Choice (C) above, although the drug reaction was an intervening cause, it was not a superseding cause, and will therefore not prevent the defendant's attack from being deemed to be a proximate cause.

(B) is wrong because the player's death may have had several proximate causes. The fact that the doctor's conduct was one of them does not mean that the defendant's conduct was not also one of them. Since the doctor's conduct occurred after the defendant's, the doctor's conduct was an *intervening* cause of that death. But an intervening cause does not break the chain of proximate causation, unless that intervention was unforeseeable. As explained in Choice (C) above, the giving of the drug here, and the victim's fatal allergic reaction to it, would not be deemed unforeseeable. Therefore, the defendant will be criminally responsible for the death even if the death was also proximately caused by the doctor's negligence.

(D) is wrong as a statement of law. An intervening cause will be superseding only if that cause was not reasonably foreseeable. The fact that the intervening cause was the product of reckless or gross negligence will not by itself make that cause unforeseeable and thus superseding. Therefore, to the extent that this choice turns solely on whether the doctor's conduct was reckless or grossly negligent, it cannot be the best explanation of the fact that the defendant will be guilty.

[Q5099]

7. **D** The most common test for insanity is the *M'Naghten* Rule, which requires that defendant have a diseased mind which caused a defect of reason, such that when Defendant acted he *either* didn't know his act was wrong *or* he didn't understand the nature and quality of his actions (e.g., mistaking someone's head for a baseball and hitting it with a bat). The *M'Naghten* Rule is also the toughest test for the defendant to meet, so if the defendant can meet it here, he can satisfy virtually any test the jurisdiction is at all likely to use. Here, the defendant satisfies the *M'Naghten* Rule, because he did not know his act was wrong — he thought he was being mercilessly attacked, and

he therefore believed that his act was self-defense and thus not either legally or morally wrong.

(A) is wrong because an intoxication defense would not exonerate the defendant under a murder charge. Murder requires an unlawful killing with malice aforethought. Malice can take the form of intent to kill or inflict great bodily injury, felony-murder, or "depraved heart" (acting in spite of an unjustifiably high risk to human life). Voluntary intoxication, which is involved here, is only a defense to prove a lack of capacity for so-called "specific intent" crimes. Murder, because of the variety of mental states that will suffice for it, is classified as a "general intent" crime, meaning precisely that voluntary intoxication will not furnish a defense as long as the defendant meets any of the possible mental states for the crime. Since the defendant's intoxication did not prevent him from having the desire to kill, the intoxication will not furnish him with a valid defense.

(B) is wrong because it mischaracterizes the facts. It's true that murder requires an unlawful killing with malice aforethought. But "malice aforethought" refers to a variety of mental states any of which can suffice: intent to kill, intent to do great bodily harm, felony-murder, or acting with reckless indifference to the value of human life ("depraved heart"). Since the defendant intended to strangle the woman, he intended either to kill her or at least to do her great bodily injury, so he meets the malice aforethought requirement.

(C) is wrong because self-defense would not be a valid defense to murder on these facts. Self-defense has both an objective and a subjective element: The defendant must *in fact* believe the danger exists (the subjective part), and the defendant must be *reasonable* in this belief (the objective part). Here, the defendant misapprehended the danger – the old woman was only slapping him, and thus deadly force was not required. Since the defendant's perception of danger was not reasonable, self-defense will not be available as a defense.

[Q4040]

8. **C** On these facts, we cannot rule out either a conviction for murder or one for manslaughter. If the defendant fired the third shot while still in the heat of passion from the prior attack by the neighbor, the defendant will qualify for manslaughter of the "imperfect self-defense" variety. If the defendant was *not* still in the heat of passion at the time of the fatal shot, then the defendant will meet all the requirements for murder, since he will have intentionally killed another with no mitigating circumstances or defenses. Because of this absence of information about heat of passion, we do not know which of these two crimes will be applicable, but we know that neither can be excluded.

(A) is wrong because of the word "only." States disagree whether a defendant who succeeded can be convicted of attempt (with the modern view being that he can; see LaFave, §10.5, p. 449); so if the defendant fired in cold blood rather than in heat of passion, the fact that the defendant committed murder might or might not preclude a conviction of attempted murder. But because the defendant is guilty of at least the completed crime of manslaughter, if not murder, for the reasons described in Choice (C) above), it cannot be the case that attempted murder is the "only" crime for which there can be a conviction.

(B) is wrong because we cannot be certain that manslaughter is the only crime for which there could be a conviction. As further described in the discussion of Choice (C) above, there will have to be a conviction of either manslaughter or murder, depending on whether the defendant was still in the heat of passion at the time he fired the last shot. So it's not accurate to say, as a matter of law, that there could be a conviction "only" for manslaughter.

(D) is wrong because we can be certain that at the least, there will be a conviction for manslaughter. Taking the facts most favorable to the defendant, at the time he fired the final and fatal shot he was no longer in fear of being attacked by the neighbor. Therefore, a prerequisite for the defense of self-defense — fear of attack — was not met at the critical moment. If the defendant was still in the heat of passion at the time of the third shot, he will qualify for "imperfect self-defense," entitling him to be convicted only of voluntary manslaughter, not murder. If he was not still in the heat of passion, this will be murder. But the one thing we know is that it will not be "no degree of homicide."

[Q7069]

9. **A** Courts disagree about whether and when a person who wishes to use deadly force in self-defense must instead retreat if this could be done safely. But all courts agree that there is never a requirement to retreat if the defender does not intend to use deadly force. LaFave, §9.4(f) at 411. Since the defense here consisted of pepper spray, and since pepper spray is not a defense method that is likely to cause death or serious bodily injury, it did not constitute the use of deadly force. Therefore, the defendant had no duty to retreat instead of using that non-deadly force.

(B) is wrong because, while this answer correctly states that the defendant should not be convicted, it misstates the legal basis for this conclusion. While states disagree about whether or when a defendant may have to retreat before using deadly force, no jurisdiction requires a person who wishes to use non-deadly force to retreat, regardless of whether the structure is occupied. If this choice looked attractive to you, perhaps you were thinking of the fact that in states that require retreat before the use of deadly force, nearly all make an exception where the defender is in his own dwelling that is not also the dwelling of the person being defended against. But the fact that the force here was non-deadly means that this "dwelling" exception to the requirement of retreat could not matter.

(C) is wrong because even in those states requiring retreat in certain circumstances, retreat is not required if the defender is proposing to use only non-deadly force.

(D) is wrong because the defendant acted within his rights even though the husband did not threaten to use deadly force. A response of nondeadly force is justified where the defender reasonably believes the other is about to inflict unlawful bodily harm, and the threatened harm need not be deadly (i.e., need not consist of death or serious harm).

[Q7096]

10. **D** The man did not have the intent to sell cocaine, while the woman did. The prosecution of the woman poses the classic question of whether "factual impossibility" can be a defense. Factual impossibility is not a defense. That is, impossibility is no defense to an attempt prosecution in those cases where, had the facts been as D believed them to be, D would have had the mental state required for the substantive crime. Here, had the facts been as the woman believed (that the vials contained cocaine), the woman would have had the mental state required for sale of cocaine. Therefore, she had the mental state for attempt. And, since she carried out the physical act of selling the substance, she meets the *actus reus* requirement for attempted drug sale as well.

On the other hand, the man does not have the mental state required for attempted sale of cocaine. The mens rea for an attempt to commit substantive crime X is the desire to commit acts which, if they were committed, would constitute the commission of crime X. Therefore, the mens rea for an attempt to sell drugs is the intent to sell drugs. Since the man didn't intend to sell drugs, he can't be liable for attempted sale of drugs.

(A), (B) and (C) are wrong because each is inconsistent with the analysis in Choice (D) above.

[Q3002]

11. **B** This choice correctly identifies the key factor which will exonerate the student: His mistake negates the necessary *mens rea* for burglary. The key here is to remember the elements of burglary, the defenses that apply, and apply them strictly. Common-law burglary requires the breaking and entering of the dwelling house of another, at night, with the intent to commit a felony therein. Most states broaden this to include entry at all times in all kinds of structures (thus eliminating the breaking, dwelling house, and nighttime requirements). Here, what the student's mistake – believ-

ing looking at the exam questions is criminal when, in fact, it isn't – does is to negate his *mens rea*. There's no burglary when a defendant breaks and enters to commit a non-felony. The defense that covers these facts is legal impossibility – that is, what he intended to do was not criminal. Since this negates the required intent for burglary, he'll be acquitted.

(A) is wrong because it does not correctly apply the burglary definition to these facts. At common law, burglary requires breaking and entering the dwelling house of another, at night, with intent to commit a felony therein. Under most modern statutes, entry at all times in all kinds of structures are covered (thus eliminating the breaking, dwelling house, and nighttime requirements). Thus, the crime is *complete* once the breaking and entering with the appropriate intent has taken place. It's not necessary that the person actually *commit* the felony therein – he need only *intend* to do so. Thus, Choice (A)'s language about the student not completing the crime *cannot* be correct, since if he avoids liability for burglary, it cannot be on that basis. For the same reason, the statement about attempted burglary does not apply to these facts. Attempted burglary would apply under these facts, for instance, to the student being caught *just before* he broke into the professor's office (since attempt requires, at common law, proximity to the actual crime). In fact, what will exonerate the student is his mistaken belief that what he intended to do – look at exam questions – was a crime, as discussed in Choice (B) above.

(C) is wrong because it does not apply to these facts, and arrives at the wrong result. If the student *had* the correct mental state, his breaking and entering would make him liable for burglary. At common law, burglary requires breaking and entering the dwelling house of another, at night, with the intent to commit a felony therein (most modern statutes broaden this to include entry at all times in all kinds of structures, thus eliminating the breaking, dwelling house, and nighttime requirements). Thus, the "mental state" to which (C) refers is *intent.* So the student had to have the intent to do act X inside the dwelling where, if he actually did act X, this would have been a felony. But since act X here (looking at exam papers) would not have been a felony, the student did not have the requisite "intent to commit a felony therein."

(D) is wrong because it misstates the facts – what's involved here is *legal* impossibility, not *factual* impossibility. Factual impossibility occurs when completion of the crime is impossible due to physical facts not known to the defendant, e.g., a pickpocket picking an empty pocket. As (D) correctly states, factual impossibility is no defense. However, what's involved here is *legal* impossibility, which arises when what defendant intends to do is an act that the defendant believes constitutes a crime but that is not in fact defined as a crime. Legal impossibility is a valid defense, and applies to these facts, as further discussed in Choice (B) above.

[Q4037]

12. **C** A conspiracy requires an agreement between at least two people, the intent to enter into such an agreement, and the intent to achieve the agreement's unlawful objective. Here, the woman didn't have the intent to enter into an agreement to steal food stamps, or the intent to steal food stamps; she only had the intent to buy stolen food stamps. As a result, she was not part of a conspiracy to actually steal the food stamps. Had she actually helped to plan or participated in or assisted the theft, these acts would be evidence of her agreement to take part in the conspiracy; but she didn't.

(A) is wrong because although it states a correct rule of law, the rule does not apply to these facts, and the choice arrives at an incorrect result. (A) states as a given that the woman has entered "the conspiracy." This statement overlooks the central issue under these facts: Whether or not the woman actually entered the conspiracy *to steal* the stamps. A conspiracy requires an agreement, an intent to enter into such an agreement, and the intent to achieve the agreement's objectives. Here, the woman did not conspire to actually steal the food stamps, because she didn't intend to steal the food stamps and didn't agree to enter into a plan to effect the stealing of the food stamps.

(B) is wrong because it mischaracterizes the facts, and arrives at an incorrect result. The woman did not knowingly and willingly aid and abet the *theft;* she had no agreement regarding the theft, no intent to enter into such an agreement, and no intent to steal the food stamps. She merely agreed to buy stolen goods, and that wasn't aiding and abetting the theft. More specifically, there's no indication that the woman intended to aid and abet a theft that she believed had not yet occurred — her command to bring the goods over "right now" indicates, on the contrary, that she thought they had already been stolen.

(D) is wrong because it misstates the law. A conspiracy requires that there be an agreement between at least two people, but it doesn't require that they all be charged with conspiracy. Beyond the agreement requirement, conspiracy requires that the defendant have intended to enter such an agreement, and have the intent to achieve the agreement's unlawful objective (at common law, a conspiracy could alternatively involve a lawful ultimate act, to be done unlawfully). If you chose this response, you may have mistaken these facts for a situation where there are two parties to a conspiracy who are both charged with conspiracy, and one is acquitted. The rule under those circumstances is that the other could not be convicted, because it takes at least two guilty parties to have a conspiracy (likewise, with a conspiracy of three persons, and all three are charged with conspiracy, if two are acquitted, the third would have to be also). However, the facts here state that *only the woman has been charged.* Thus, the acquittal-based rule would not apply.
[Q4002]

13. **C** One is liable for a crime, as an accomplice, if he procures, counsels, or commands the commission of that crime. Naturally, this would require that he intend that the crime be committed. Here, Sam's liability would rest on his statement "Kill him." Intent could be established by presumption, since a person of sufficient intelligence to understand the nature of his actions is presumed to intend the natural and probable consequences of his actions. Here, Sam encouraged Bill to kill Vic, so it could be said that Sam intended that Bill kill Vic. Furthermore, his statement would be considered counselling or commanding the commission of the crime of murder. As a result, Sam will be liable as an accomplice for murder.

(A) is wrong because it arrives at the wrong result, and it applies the wrong rule to these facts. The "clear and present danger" test is the test used to determine the validity, for First Amendment purposes, of a law designed to forbid advocacy of unlawful conduct. It provides that advocacy can only be forbidden if its aim is to produce or incite imminent illegal action, and it is likely to produce or incite such action. Whether Sam's speech is protected by the First Amendment is not the issue here; instead, the issue is whether Sam can be held liable for murder for encouraging Bill to kill Vic. Since A does not apply the correct rule, and, beyond that, arrives at the wrong result, it's wrong.

(B) is wrong because it's too broad. Given the requisite intent, "mere presence and oral encouragement" *are* sufficient to make Sam guilty as an accomplice. An accomplice is one who procures, counsels, or commands the commission of a crime. Choice (B) asserts that "mere presence and oral encouragement" are insufficient to make one liable as an accomplice; however, under the definition of accomplice, encouragement would constitute "counseling" or "commanding," and so, if accompanied by an intent that the person being encouraged commit the underlying crime, *would* create accomplice liability.

(D) is wrong because although it arrives at the correct result, the reasoning it gives would not be sufficient to hold Sam liable for murder. It's not Sam's presence and his intent which make him liable, as D suggests – rather, it's his act of *encouraging* the killing that makes him liable. Mere presence wouldn't make him liable, since, in general, one is not obligated to act affirmatively for the benefit of others; furthermore, his intent is not sufficient to create liability, since intent is merely a state of mind and, with nothing more, it's not criminal (until it produces action to bring about the desired results). It's Sam's active encouragement – "kill him" – which makes him liable.
[Q4013]

14. **B** An accomplice is one who, with the intent that the crime be committed, aids, counsels, or encourages the principal before or during the commission of the crime. The young man's friends should be acquitted as accomplices to manslaughter because the facts make clear they did not intend that the young man murder the woman, nor did they do anything during the young man's attack to aid, counsel or encourage him. Only after the crime was complete, when the elderly woman fell to the ground, did they urge the young man to flee. Nor does the fact that the friends did nothing to help the woman — when assistance to her during the beating could conceivably have prevented the death — make any difference. Except in special circumstances (none of which applies here) a witness to a crime has no affirmative duty to intervene to prevent the crime or aid the victim, even if this could be easily done. Therefore, failing to render such assistance cannot give rise to criminal liability.

(A) is wrong because the young man's friends could be found guilty of being accomplices even if the young man was not convicted. An accomplice is one who, with the intent that the crime be committed, aids, counsels, or encourages the principal before or during the commission of the crime. Under the modern view of accomplice liability, the fact that the principal has not yet been convicted of the substantive crime does not bar trial and conviction of the accomplices. If the principal were actually *acquitted*, this might bar prosecution, but that's not what happened here — a mistrial would not in most jurisdictions bar the prosecution of the alleged accomplices.

(C) is wrong because urging the young man to flee was not a form of aid or counsel before or during the crime. An accomplice is one who, with the intent that the crime be committed, aids, counsels, or encourages the principal *before or during* the commission of the crime. The young man's friends should be acquitted because to be accomplices they would have to have, before or during the assault on the victim, aided, counseled or encouraged the young man in the attack, with the intent that the attack be committed. By definition, they could not be accomplices merely by urging the young man to flee after the crime was completed.

(D) is wrong because as a general matter no legal duty is imposed on any person to affirmatively act for the benefit of others. Absent one of several types of legal relationships between two parties (e.g., one put the other in peril), no legal duty is imposed on one person to affirmatively act for the benefit of the other. None of those legal relationships existed here. Therefore, the young man's friends had no duty to intervene to prevent the young man's attack. Consequently, they cannot be made criminally liable for that failure to intervene, whether on an accomplice theory or any other.

[Q3070]

15. **D** The key here is that the defendant had no *intent* to kill or cause a serious injury. Murder is an unlawful killing with malice aforethought. "Malice aforethought" is a term of art, and can be satisfied by various mental states: (1) intent to kill; (2) intent to do serious bodily injury; (3) intent to commit one of various dangerous felonies (producing felony-murder); or (4) acting with reckless disregard of the value of human life (producing "depraved-heart" murder). Depraved heart murder occurs where Defendant engages in conduct which, at the least, a reasonable man would realize creates an extremely high degree of risk to human life, and which results in death. Choice (D), with its language "without an intent to kill but with disregard of the consequences" coupled with an act highly dangerous to life, essentially reflects this rule.

(A) is wrong because it misapplies the doctrine of transferred intent. Under transferred intent, a person intending to commit a crime against one person, accidentally commits a crime against another. His intent will be "transferred" from the person he intended to harm to the person he *actually* harmed (e.g., D tries to shoot A to death and instead kills B). What's missing under these facts is the defendant's intent to kill in the first place – he doesn't intend to kill or even injure *anyone*. If anything, he intends for the children to run out of the way and *not* be injured. Since he has no criminal intent, it can't be transferred.

(B) is wrong because the felony is not sufficiently "independent" from homicide to be covered by the felony-murder rule. The felony-murder rule is as follows: Where a killing is committed during the course of certain "dangerous" felonies (or an attempt at such), the homicide is considered first degree murder, even though there is no intent to kill or cause great bodily harm. Such "dangerous" felonies typically include rape, kidnapping, mayhem, arson, robbery and burglary. The dangerous felony must be reasonably "independent" of the killing. Assault with a deadly weapon would itself require an intent to do serious bodily harm or to kill, so the "independence" required by the felony-murder rule would be lacking.

(C) is wrong because the reasoning it states is insufficient to convict the defendant of intentional killing. While intentional killing is sufficient for murder, intent must be one of two types: Either the actor must consciously desire a result, regardless of the likelihood his conduct will cause it; or, alternatively, he must know the result is practically certain to result from his conduct, regardless of whether he wants it to happen. Thus, under the facts in this question, the defendant would have to want to kill the children, or know he was practically certain to kill one if he drove toward them. Thus, Choice (C) is incorrect in stating that knowing they were there and deliberately driving at them would be sufficient to convict the defendant – in addition, he'd have to know that driving at them would result in one being killed. In fact, the defendant believes they will run to get out of the way – he doesn't know he's practically certain to kill one.

[Q4035]

16. **A** Murder is the unjustified killing of a human being with malice aforethought. "Malice aforethought" is a term of art that covers a number of possible mental states, including an intent to cause great bodily harm to a human being. A defendant "intends" a particular consequence if she desires it or knows to a substantial degree of certainty that it will occur. Since the defendant desired that the exposure to Terminate would cause great bodily harm (blindness) to the co-worker, she will be deemed to have intended to cause great bodily harm to a human being. Since the friend died, the defendant is guilty of his murder. (The doctrine of transferred intent applies — since the defendant had the requisite intent regarding the co-worker, her intent will be "transferred" to the person who actually died, the friend.)

(B) is wrong because engaging in an inherently dangerous activity, even intentionally, does not constitute one of the mental states that will suffice for murder. Engaging in an inherently dangerous activity is a tort concept (producing strict liability), but not a criminal-law concept.

(C) is wrong because the defendant's intent to cause great bodily harm to *any* human being is sufficient to make her guilty of murder in causing the death of the friend, by use of the doctrine of transferred intent (further described in Choice (A) above).

(D) is wrong because, although the intent to kill is one of the mental states that will suffice for murder, it's not the only one. An intent to cause serious bodily harm will also suffice.

[Q5017]

17. **A** The defendant can be found guilty of all three crimes. Let's take the crimes one at a time.

First, let's look at burglary. Common-law burglary is: (1) the breaking, (2) and entering, (3) of the dwelling, (4) of another, (5) at night time, (6) with the intent to commit a felony within. The defendant's actions satisfy all the requirements for burglary. Requirements (1) and (6) are the only ones that are even worth discussing here. As to (1) (breaking), courts recognize "constructive breaking" — if D uses fraud or threat of force to induce the occupants to let him in, that counts as breaking. That's what happened here. As to (6) (intent to commit a felony within), where D commits a felony once inside the premises, courts will in the absence of other evidence presume that D had the intent to commit that felony at the time of entry. So here, the defendant would readily be found to have intended, at the time he entered, to commit the felony of robbery once he was inside. Thus the requisite intent-to-commit-a-felony-within is satisfied.

Next, let's examine robbery. Robbery is: (1) a taking, (2) of the personal property of another, (3) from the other's person or presence, (4) by force or intimidation, (5) with the intent to permanently deprive. Here, the only interesting question is whether taking the property from the safe (rather than directly from the person) of the victim meets requirement (3). But the taking will suffice if it's from the "person or presence" of the owner, and the safe would be found to have been within the husband and wife's presence at the time the defendant took the necklace.

Finally, let's look at murder. There are of course multiple types — ways of committing — murder. Here, the relevant type of murder is felony-murder. Felony-murder is a killing, even an accidental one, committed during the commission of certain dangerous felonies. The defendant's actions satisfy the requirements of felony-murder. The defendant was committing robbery, and robbery is one of the "dangerous" felonies recognized at common law as a predicate-crime for felony-murder. The interesting question is whether the fact that the defendant was arrested before the husband had his heart attack prevents the husband's death from being "during the commission of" the robbery. Notice that the husband's death was very closely causally related to the robbery — the husband had his heart attack because he was trying to free himself from his bonds and gag, and he was bound and gagged because, and solely because, the defendant wanted to commit, and escape from, the robbery. Where there is a close causal relationship between the underlying felony (or the attempt to escape from it) and the death, the requirement of a death "during the commission of" the felony is generally deemed satisfied, even if the death doesn't come until after the felony-and-escape period is in some sense over.

(B), (C) and (D) are not the best response, because each fails to cover at least one of the three crimes that in fact was committed, as described in Choice (A).

[Q3101]

18. **B** This is a somewhat tricky question because it's a hybrid – you need to know the relevant procedural rule as well as the substantive rule. First, procedure: As a general rule, if the evidence would justify a reasonable jury in convicting the defendant of a lesser offense (here, manslaughter), the issue should be submitted to the jury. By stating that whether the issue of manslaughter should go to the jury based on what the jury could find, instead of what the judge believes the evidence shows, (B) correctly states this rule. Next, substance: the reasoning in (B) correctly identifies a basis on which the jury could find the defendant guilty only of manslaughter. Voluntary manslaughter is an unlawful killing committed under adequate provocation. Murder is an unlawful killing committed with malice aforethought. Thus, if the jury finds that an act by the other customer sufficiently provoked the defendant, it will find him guilty of voluntary manslaughter instead of murder. Being hit in the face with an umbrella is just the sort of thing that *could* be considered provocation sufficient to reduce the defendant's liability to manslaughter. A wrinkle in this problem is that the defendant, in a way, provoked the provocation by stealing the tip. But that's not relevant for the defendant's liability in *this* question (whereas it would be relevant to the customer's liability in attacking the defendant, since she would have a crime-prevention argument); see the analysis of Choice (D) for why.

(A) is wrong because it does not apply the correct rule for voluntary manslaughter. In order to be found liable for only voluntary manslaughter instead of murder, the jury would have to find that the defendant acted under provocation; that is, that he committed an unlawful killing with malice aforethought, but was provoked. If you chose (A), you probably did so because you confused the rule for voluntary manslaughter with that for depraved-heart murder, which is what (A) more-or-less states. Thus, if the jury found that the defendant acted with reckless indifference to the value of human life, but not with the intent to kill or seriously injure, it would *still* find him guilty of depraved-heart murder.

(C) is wrong because it arrives at an incorrect result, and does not allow the jury to find voluntary manslaughter, which is possible from these facts. In the jury's role as the finder of *facts,* the jury should be given the option to find any result which is plausible (i.e., that a reasonable jury could find beyond a reasonable doubt) on these facts. And voluntary manslaughter is such a result, because a reasonable jury could find that the defendant was sufficiently provoked to reduce murder to manslaughter. Thus, Choice (C)'s statement that the defendant intended to kill or cause serious harm doesn't go far enough, because even if he *did* act with intent, if he did so under adequate provocation he'll only be liable for voluntary manslaughter.

(D) is wrong because it arrives at the wrong result, based on incorrect legal reasoning. The defendant's provoking the assault on himself would not prevent him from being found guilty of manslaughter. When a defendant would otherwise have the defense of self-defense (leading to outright acquittal), most states make available the doctrine of "imperfect self-defense." Under that doctrine, when the defendant intentionally kills another, he'll be liable for voluntary manslaughter if either he was the initial aggressor in a fight (and therefore not entitled to a self-defense claim), *or* he honestly but unreasonably believed deadly force was necessary. So the fact that the defendant arguably provoked the encounter — assuming that what the defendant did was indeed viewed as "being the aggressor" (which it probably wouldn't be, since the defendant merely stole, rather than being the first to use force) — wouldn't deprive him of the right to be convicted of voluntary manslaughter rather than murder.
[Q4038]

19. **C** Although killing with the intent to cause great bodily harm is ordinarily classified as murder, it may be reduced to voluntary manslaughter if the defendant was acting in the heat of passion. This is only so, however, if the provocation which produced the passion would have caused a person of ordinary temperament to become enraged. (The reasonable person would not become so enraged as to kill; but the test is whether the provocation is such that a reasonable person might have become enraged so as to lose complete control.) So if the judge believes that no reasonable jury could conclude that an ordinary person in the wife's situation would have become enraged by the dancing, the judge must deny the instruction.

(A) is wrong because it is a misstatement of law: there is no "theory of deliberate provocation," and a person who kills will not be entitled to a voluntary manslaughter instruction merely because the victim deliberately provoked the defendant.

(B) is wrong because the objective standard described in the discussion of Choice (C) above (i.e., the likely reaction of a person of ordinary temperament) makes the wife's emotional peculiarities irrelevant.

(D) is wrong because it reflects a misstatement of law. An intentional killing may be reduced from murder to voluntary manslaughter if the defendant was acting under the mistaken belief that the killing was justified (e.g., D mistakenly thought he was being attacked with deadly force). This is known as the theory of mistaken justification. But Choice (D) is wrong because the wife did not act in the mistaken belief that she was justified. Also, this choice suggests that the theory of mistaken justification would apply to prevent a manslaughter instruction, whereas if the theory applied it would require such an instruction.
[Q5048]

20. **D** Larceny is defined at common law as: (1) the trespassory (2) taking and (3) carrying away of the (4) personal property (5) of another (6) with the intent to steal it. LaFave, §16.2, at 671. The defendant committed larceny: (1) She picked up the purse, a taking. (2) She moved it from its original position when she placed it under her coat and took a few steps toward the exit, a carrying away. (3) & (4) The purse is a tangible item owned by another, the clothing store. (5) the defendant took it without the clothing store's consent. (6) When she picked up the purse (exerted control over it) the facts state that she did so with the intent to take it without paying for it. The defendant's actions therefore satisfy all the requirements of larceny. The fact that the defendant did not exit

from the store with the property is irrelevant — the crime was complete once she exerted dominion and carried the item a small distance, while intending to keep it. Nor does the fact that the defendant took only couple of steps with the purse prevent the "carrying away" element from being satisfied — even the smallest movement of the item will suffice.

(A) is wrong because the defendant completed the crime once she exerted dominion over the purse and carried it a small distance, while intending to keep it. See the analysis of Choice (D) above.

(B) is wrong because the defendant completed the crime as soon as her actions matched her intent. The crime was complete once the defendant exerted dominion over the purse and carried it a small distance, while intending to keep it. Nothing she did thereafter — including "withdrawing" from the "criminal enterprise" — could undo the completed crime.

(C) is not wrong because the crime of larceny was complete once the defendant moved the item with intent to take it. Since this choice says that only attempted, not completed, larceny has occurred, it's wrong.

[Q3098]

21. **A** Common-law burglary is defined as the breaking and entering of the dwelling house of another in the night time with the intent to commit a felony. LaFave, Criminal Law, §8.13, at p. 883. The woman satisfies this definition because she unlawfully entered the neighbor's house at night with intent to commit a felony therein (larceny). The "breaking" element is satisfied because the woman opened a window — there is no requirement that the breaking occur by means of force, or that the premises have been secured such as by a lock. *Id.* at 884. The "entering" element is more questionable on these facts, but the woman's actions satisfy this element as well. See LaFave, Criminal Law, §8.13(b), at p. 886 (to constitute burglary it is "sufficient if any part of the actor's person intruded, even momentarily, into the structure. Thus it has been held that the intrusion of a part of a hand in opening a window, or the momentary intrusion of part of a foot in kicking out a window, constituted the requisite entry.").

(B) is wrong, because the woman's action proceeded beyond the point of attempted burglary to the completed crime of burglary, as discussed in the analysis of Choice (A) above.

(C) is wrong, because while the woman may have been guilty of attempted larceny, that crime arguably would merge into, and in any event was less serious than, the burglary crime.

(D) is wrong because the woman is guilty of burglary, since she unlawfully entered the neighbor's house at night with intent to commit a felony (larceny), as more fully discussed in the analysis of Choice (A) above.

[Q7027]

22. **B** The defendant's mistaken belief that the briefcase was his own prevented him from having the required mental state for robbery. Robbery is the: (1) taking, (2) of personal property of another, (3) from the other's person or presence, (4) by force or intimidation, (5) with the intent to permanently deprive him of it. The intent required for robbery is the intent to use force to take "the property of another." Therefore, if D mistakenly (even unreasonably) believes that the property in question is his own, the required "intent to take the property of another" is lacking. The fact that that mistake was brought about by voluntary intoxication — and the fact that the mistake may have been "unreasonable" — makes no difference.

(A) is wrong because (1) the absence of threats would not prevent this from being robbery; and (2) the intoxication would not necessarily prevent this from being robbery. Robbery is the taking of personal property of another from the latter's person or presence, "by force or intimidation." A taking can involve force without involving threats. Here, the defendant struggled with the owner, and knocked him to the floor, so the requisite force was present even though the defendant made no threats. Also, the fact that the defendant was drunk would not necessarily prevent him from being guilty — it was only the defendant's mistaken belief that the briefcase was his that caused him to avoid guilt. (It's true that the intoxication may have been what caused the defendant to have the mistaken belief — but no matter why the mistaken belief occurred, the defendant would have avoided guilt.)

(C) is wrong because voluntary intoxication can still prevent the required specific intent from existing. Robbery requires an intent to take "the property of another." If D fails to have the requisite intent, whatever the reason, the crime has not been committed. Here, the defendant thought the briefcase was his, so he lacked the requisite intent to take "property of another." The fact that the intoxication was "voluntary" would not make a difference, if for any reason (including intoxication) he lacked the requisite intent.

(D) is wrong because mistake *can* be a defense to specific intent crimes. If a mistake of fact prevents the defendant from having the requisite intent for a "specific intent" crime, that mistake is indeed a defense. Here, robbery requires an intent to take "the property of another." If a mistake causes D to believe (whether reasonably or not) that the property is his own rather than another's, that mistake causes D not to meet the intent element for the crime.

[Q3007]

23. **A** There are two issues here: (1) was the stop of the car constitutional? and (2) if the answer to (1) is yes, was the search of the car a permissible adjunct to that arrest? As to (1), under the "good faith reliance" exception to the exclusionary rule, evidence that derives from an initial arrest, stop or search generally will not be suppressed where police reasonably held a good faith but erroneous belief that the arrest, stop or search was authorized by a valid warrant. So, for instance, in facts much like these, the Supreme Court held in *Arizona v. Evans* (1995) that a good-faith-reliance exception to exclusionary rule applied where an arrest and resulting incidental search were based on an outstanding arrest warrant that should have been removed from the computer but still showed up as the result of a court employee's clerical error. In this case, the computer check on the license number of the driver's car revealed that there was an outstanding warrant for the driver's arrest based on unpaid parking tickets; the police had no reason to believe that the warrant was invalid, so the stop of the car and the arrest of the driver were justified on the good-faith-reliance exception of *Evans*.

As to (2), once the stop of the car and the arrest of the driver were established to be valid because of the police's good-faith reliance on the warrant, long-established law says that the police may, incident to the arrest, make a search of the car's entire passenger compartment, and the contents of any containers found in that compartment. *N.Y. v. Belton* (1981). So the police's search of the passenger compartment incident to the arrest, and their consequent discovery of the glassine bags, was valid.

(B) is wrong because, while this answer correctly states that the motion to suppress should not be granted, it misstates the legal basis for that conclusion. Absent a custodial arrest or probable cause, a traffic stop does not authorize a full-blown search of the passenger compartment. See *Knowles v. Iowa* (1998).

(C) is wrong because, as is further described in connection with Choice (A) above, when the police make an arrest in reasonable reliance on erroneous information that an arrest warrant is outstanding, they may make a search incident to that arrest, the fruits of which will not be inadmissible on account of the exclusionary rule. So while it is technically true that "no lawful arrest" could be made on the basis of the warrant here, it does not follow that the evidence from the search was inadmissible.

(D) is wrong because neither probable cause nor reasonable suspicion was required, since the search was incident to an arrest. It is true that the arrest warrant turned out to be invalid, but evidence generally will not be suppressed where, as in this case, police reasonably held a good faith belief that their actions leading to its discovery were authorized by a valid warrant. See the more extensive discussion of this issue in Choice (A) above.

[Q7042]

24. **A** Incident to a lawful arrest in an arrestee's home, the officers executing the warrant may conduct a "protective sweep" of all or part of the premises, if they have a "reasonable belief" that another person who might be dangerous to the officers may be present *in the areas swept. Maryland v. Buie* (1990). So here, the police had the right to search the house for accomplices. The Uzi, however, was found in a box on a closet shelf. Clearly the weapon was neither in plain sight nor in a place where a person could be found. Therefore, the protective-sweep exception doesn't apply. Since the search warrant covered only the brown suitcase (which the police had already seized), their search of the closet could not be justified on the grounds that they were executing the search warrant, either.

    (B) is wrong because the answer misstates the applicable law — the police had the right to search the house for accomplices. As is described in the analysis of Choice (A) above, the police had the right to check protectively for other persons. Therefore, this choice — since it says that no further search of the house was permitted once the suitcase was seized — is inconsistent with the police's right to make the protective search (which may be made at any time when the police are still on the premises and are thus vulnerable to a sudden attack from someone who might be hiding).

    (C) is wrong because the weapon was not in an area that could be searched. It's true that the police were lawfully in the bedroom (under their right to make a protective sweep — see Choice (A)). But while they were in the bedroom, the police were only permitted to look in places where a person might be hiding. They therefore weren't allowed to look in small boxes, as they did here.

    (D) is wrong because, while the police knew that there might well be weapons in the house, they would have needed a warrant in order to look for such weapons at the top of the closet. There are two requirements that must be satisfied before a house may be searched for a particular item, unless there is some applicable exception: (1) probable cause to believe that the item will be found; and (2) a warrant to search for it. Here, since the facts tell us that the police had gotten reliable information that the singer and his accomplices "kept a small arsenal of weapons in [the singer's] home," requirement (1) was satisfied as to the weapons. But although the police procured a search warrant, that warrant did not cover the weapons, only the brown suitcase. Therefore, the fact that the police were already in the home, and the further fact that they had probable cause to believe that the weapons would or might be found, were not enough to permit them to look not either in the bedroom or in the closet. And while their need to make a "protective sweep" justified them in looking in the bedroom, this need did not, as described in the discussion of Choice (A), authorize them to search in a small box on a shelf, since no one could have been hiding there.

[Q3068]

25. **A** A search will be valid if consent to it is given by a person who the police reasonably but mistakenly believe has joint authority over the premises. *Ill. v. Rodriguez* (1990). Here, if the cheerleader actually had been the defendant's roommate, she would have had authority to consent to a search of the common areas of their shared room. Since she told the police that she was, and since she had a key to the room, it was reasonable for them to believe her. When the police went inside and saw the marijuana on a coffee table, it was reasonable for them to believe that this was a portion of the room shared by the defendant and her roommate (reasonably assumed by them to be the cheerleader). the cheerleader's apparent authority therefore justified the search, and would makes the search legal even though it was not supported by a warrant. And this is true even though the police were (reasonably) mistaken in believing that the cheerleader actually had authority.

    (B) is wrong because, even if the police did have probable cause to believe that they would find marijuana in the room (and they probably did), they would still need a search warrant, unless some exception to the warrant requirement applied. Since this answer does not give any hint of the need for a warrant or an exception to the warrant requirement, it cannot be the best answer, even though it correctly predicts the result.

(C) is wrong because, while it is true both that the police did not have a warrant and that the cheerleader did not have authority, neither of these facts matters. That's because, as further described in the analysis of Choice (A) above, the cheerleader had apparent authority, so the police's mistake was a reasonable one and the case is treated as if the cheerleader had had actual authority.

(D) is wrong because: (1) the police probably *did* have probable cause, based upon the cheerleader's suspicions and her explanation of how she came to have those suspicions, to believe that they would find marijuana in the room; and (2) in any event, whether the police had probable cause or not, the cheerleader's apparent authority to consent to a search of what the police thought was the area shared by the cheerleader and the defendant overcame both the need for a warrant and the need for probable cause.

[Q5073]

26. **B** The woman's consent justified the officers' entry. When a person consents to the entry of law enforcement officers into an area as to which the person would otherwise have a justifiable expectation of privacy, that consent validates the police entry, and nullifies any need for either probable cause or a search warrant that may have existed prior to the consent. Once the police then make their consented-to entry, the "plain view" doctrine entitles them to seize any item whose contraband or evidentiary nature is obvious, as long as when they have the view the police are standing in a place where they have a right to be. *Harris v. U.S.* (1968). Since the woman consented to the officers' entry into her house, and since the officers spotted the heroin while standing in a place to which the consent applied, there could not have been either an illegal search or an illegal seizure.

(A) is wrong because, while this answer correctly states that the woman's motion to suppress the heroin should not be granted, it misstates the legal basis for this conclusion. Even assuming there was probable cause to search the home, a warrant would have been required for entry had the woman not consented. See, e.g., *Payton v. New York* (1980).

(C) is wrong because the search of the man, even assuming it was improper, did not violate the woman's rights and therefore provides no basis for suppressing evidence found in her house. That is, the woman did not have "standing" to assert a violation of the constitutional rights of a third party. Cf. *Minnesota v. Carter* (1998) (discussing standing requirements for third-party constitutional claims).

(D) is wrong because there is no requirement that officers inform individuals of their right to refuse consent. See *Schneckloth v. Bustamonte* (1973). Therefore, the consent was valid.

[Q7022]

27. **C** A person only has standing to claim a search or seizure violated the Fourth Amendment when the evidence was obtained from a search or seizure which violated the person's "legitimate expectation of privacy." *Rakas v. Illinois* (1978). This means that even if the defendant owns the property, or is present when the search takes place, he will have no standing to challenge the search *unless* the search violated his legitimate expectation of privacy. Under the facts here, Defendant clearly had no legitimate expectation of privacy as to the back seat of the football player's car, or as to the heroin (which in any event was no longer his property). Thus, he cannot object to the validity of the search, even if it violated the constitutional rights of the football player.

(A) is wrong because the "plain view" doctrine would not be determinative under these facts. The plain view doctrine provides one means by which the police can conduct a warrantless search; it states that police can make a warrantless seizure when they are on the premises for lawful purposes, and they inadvertently discover evidence in plain view. (A) correctly states that since the heroin was under the rear seat, it was not in plain view. However, this choice ignores the central reason why the motion to suppress will be denied: the defendant has no standing to object to the search, since it was the football player's car that was searched, and the defendant had no privacy interest in it.

(B) is wrong because it ignores the central issue in the case: the defendant does not have standing to object to the search. If you chose this response, it's because you overlooked the fact that *the defendant* is objecting to a search of *the football player's* car, in which the defendant has no privacy interest. For some extra credit, let's look at how the case would come out if it was the football player who was on trial, and who was objecting that the search was excessive. In that event, the statement in Choice (B) may or may not be correct — it turns on whether the football player was subjected to a full custodial arrest (as opposed to being given a plain traffic ticket without being taken to the police station). If he *was* arrested, the police would be entitled to then conduct a search of the entire passenger compartment (since the compartment is considered "within the suspect's control," even if he was away from the car when the search took place). That would make the search here valid. If, however, the police *didn't* intend to take the football player into custody, they could only "frisk" his person – making the search *invalid*.

(D) is wrong, because there's no evidence that the football player was subject to a full custodial arrest – the facts only say that the football player was stopped for speeding. Without a full custodial arrest, the police would have no right to perform a search incident to arrest. Furthermore, Choice (D) ignores the central issue, which is that the defendant has no standing to object to the search.

[Q4049]

28. **D** The ownership and operation of ordinary buildings is not subject to the type of intense regulation that would permit inspections that were supported by neither a search warrant nor probable cause. *Camara v. Municipal Court* (1967). So this case does not fall within the special rule allowing warrantless and probable-causeless searches of heavily-regulated businesses like weapons dealers. But even a garden-variety regulatory scheme will allow regulators to conduct a search of the building to look for health and safety violations without probable cause to suspect that there are violations in any particular building, as long as the regulators first get a series of warrants covering each building to be inspected, and as long as the regulators seeking the warrants demonstrate merely that their inspections will be done pursuant to reasonable administrative standards. *Camara, supra*. So here, the fact that there was a warrant covering the defendant's building, when coupled with the fact that the inspections were being done pursuant to an organized attempt to enforce health and safety codes applicable to the neighborhood, sufficed to meet the requirements of the Fourth Amendment even though there was no probable cause to believe that the defendant's building had violations.

(A) is wrong because, even in the absence of probable cause to believe that health and safety violations exist in a particular building, a warrant to search it for such violations may be issued as part of reasonable standards-based efforts to enforce a generally-applicable regulatory scheme.

(B) is wrong because the existence of such a neighborhood-inspection scheme justifies the issuance of warrants like those issued here, rather than invalidating it.

(C) is wrong because it is a misstatement of law. The ownership and operation of ordinary buildings is not subject to the type of intense regulation that would permit inspections that were not supported by a search warrant (as would, for instance, operation of a weapons dealership). *Camara v. Municipal Court* (1967). So a warrant was required by the Fourth Amendment. However, as detailed in Choice (D), the warrant did not need to be supported by probable cause to believe that violations would be found in any particular building.

[Q5022]

29. **A** Once a criminal defendant has asserted his right to have an attorney present, further interrogation

in the absence of the attorney makes any incriminating statements by the defendant inadmissible. Since the defendant was questioned after asserting his right to counsel, the statement which he made in response to that questioning must be excluded.

(B) is wrong because even if the sheriff knew the defendant's whereabouts and lied to the lawyer, this would not affect the outcome. For example, in a roughly analogous case in which the police falsely told the defendant's lawyer that the defendant was not a suspect, and then did not tell the defendant that his lawyer was trying to contact him, the Court held that the defendant's waiver of his right to a lawyer after receiving the *Miranda* warnings was valid. *Moran v. Burbine* (1986). So here, if the defendant had not insisted on the right to a lawyer, the fact that the sheriff blocked the lawyer's access by lying about not knowing the defendant's whereabouts would not have made the defendant's waiver of his *Miranda* rights invalid.

(C) is wrong for the same reason that Choice (B) is wrong: it was solely the defendant's decision to insist on a lawyer that made the subsequent interrogation unlawful. Once the defendant so insisted, his motion would win even if the sheriff lied to the lawyer about not knowing the defendant's whereabouts.

(D) is wrong because, once a defendant has requested counsel, the courts will be extremely reluctant to conclude that the defendant's later conduct constituted a waiver of his already-asserted right to consult a lawyer. As the Supreme Court has put it, "An accused ... having expressed his desire to deal with the police only through counsel, is not subject to further interrogation by the authorities until counsel has been made available to him, unless the *accused himself initiates* further communication, exchanges or conversations with the police." *Edwards v. Ariz.* (1981). Here, after the defendant requested counsel, his admission about growing marijuana came about in response to interrogation initiated by the police, not by the defendant. Therefore the bright-line no-waiver rule of *Edwards* applies, and the confession must be excluded as a violation of *Miranda*.

[Q5136]

30. **C** A state may grant broader rights under its own constitution than are granted by the federal Constitution. See *Michigan v. Long* (1983). Here, the state has a clear precedent that the recording violated the employee's state constitutional rights, and that the recording should be excluded as a remedy. The state court should apply this precedent to grant the employee's motion. In other words, where evidence is obtained in violation of a state constitutional provision and would be inadmissible under the state's policy of excluding evidence obtained in violation of the state constitution, the fact that there has been no federal constitutional violation should not prevent the state court from applying the state exclusionary policy.

(A) is wrong because a state may grant broader rights under its own constitution than are granted by the federal constitution. As further discussed in Choice (C) above, when the state gives broader rights than would be granted by the federal Constitution, a court of that state should apply any state-law exclusionary principle.

(B) is wrong, because it is irrelevant what the police thought about the propriety of their actions under the federal Constitution where the state has granted broader rights under its own constitution. Furthermore, this choice mischaracterizes the federal Constitution on this point: the police's actions *were* allowed by the federal Constitution, so the fact that the police had a "good faith" belief in the correctness of their action under the federal Constitution does not add anything to the analysis.

(D) is wrong because the secret recording of a conversation with a defendant by a government informant, like the recording in this case, does not violate the Fourth Amendment. See *United States v. White* (1971). (Instead, the evidence should be kept out because the state court can and should uphold the policy reflected in the state constitution's ban on the collection of such evidence, as buttressed by the state's exclusionary rule.)

[Q7086]

31. **C** First, we need to consider whether the officer's initial entry into the apartment was a violation of the son's Fourth Amendment rights. An examination of a defendant's effects is a search if it is conducted under circumstances which violate the defendant's reasonable expectation of privacy. Ordinarily, a person has a reasonable expectation that an apartment which s/he has the exclusive right to occupy will remain private. And that's true even if the invasion of privacy is done by, or authorized by, the person's mother — the landlord may have lived in the building, and may have owned the unit, but her son was the exclusive occupant of the second-floor apartment. Therefore, the landlord did not have either apparent or actual authority to consent to a police search of that unit. Since the officer was a police officer, his entry into the space would probably be deemed to be governmental action, even though he was arguably on "private time" when he entered (since he acted as a police employee in noticing the stolen goods and seeking the warrant).

Given that the officer was conducting an illegal search of the son's apartment in the first instance, his reliance on illegally-obtained knowledge as the basis for receiving the warrant would taint the warrant — that is, the warrant would be viewed as poisonous fruit of the poisonous tree (the illegal entry). Since the warrant was invalid, any evidence obtained as a result of the execution of the warrant would also be excludable as poisonous fruit.

(A) is factually and legally wrong: since the warrant was obtained as a result of improperly-obtained initial information, the search done pursuant to that warrant was not legal as this choice asserts, and the fruits of that search must be excluded.

(B) is wrong as a matter of law: where the police officer who makes the discovery is in a position to make that discovery as the result of illegal conduct (here, the officer's initial entry into the apartment), the officer is indeed required to ignore the discovery, rather than using it as the basis for obtaining a warrant.

(D) is wrong because, although possession of stolen items is not by itself sufficient to permit the conclusion that the possessor was the thief, the evidence of that possession is certainly admissible as circumstantial evidence to be considered by the jury (assuming that the method of obtaining the evidence is not itself objectionable, as it is here).

[Q5080]

32. **A** As the result of *Massiah v. U.S.* (1964), once a suspect has been charged and has counsel, it is a violation of his Sixth Amendment right to counsel for a secret agent to "deliberately elicit" imcriminating statements from him in the absence of counsel, and to pass these on to the prosecution. The post-*Massiah* case of *U.S. v. Henry* (1980) establishes that even if the secret agent does not engage in actual questioning, if the agent is motivated to obtain confidences and succeeds in doing so, the agent will be deemed to have "elicited" the statement, and the *Massiah* rule will still be deemed violated. Therefore, since the cellmate was a police officer and was placed in a cell for the purpose of obtaining incriminating remarks outside the presence of the defendant's counsel, use of those remarks would violate the defendant's Sixth Amendment right to counsel as interpreted by *Massiah*.

(B) is wrong because "entrapment" refers only to conduct by a police officer which induces the defendant to commit a crime which he was not otherwise inclined to commit, not conduct that induces the defendant to confess.

(C) is wrong because even a warrant does not justify a police interrogation in violation of the *Massiah* rule described in the discussion of Choice (A) above.

(D) is wrong because even the eliciting of a voluntary statement violates the *Massiah* rule if done as a result of police operation conducted without the presence or consent of the defendant's attorney.

[Q5021]